Christmas 2000

THE TOWER OF LONDON

Love,
Dave

THE TOWER
OF LONDON

A THOUSAND YEARS

DEREK WILSON

a&b

This edition published in Great Britain in 1998 by
Allison & Busby Ltd
114 New Cavendish Street
London W1M 7FD

First published in Great Britain in 1978
by Hamish Hamilton Ltd

A catalogue record for this book is available from the
British Library

ISBN 0 74900 332 4

Printed and bound in Great Britain by
WBC Book Manufacturers
Bridgend, Mid Glamorgan

ILLUSTRATIONS

Between pages 56 and 57

Between pages 152 and 153

Drawings in the text

Illustration 1a is reproduced by kind permission of Mrs Alan Sorrell; illustrations 1b, 2b, 4b, 5b, 7a, 8a and the plan of the Tower of London today are Crown Copyright reproduced with permission of the Controller of Her Majesty's Stationery Office; 2a, 3, 4a by kind permission of the British Library Board; 8b, 12, 14a, 14b, 15a by kind permission of the Trustees of the British Museum; 5a by kind permission of Mary Evans Picture Library; 6 by kind permission of the Society of Antiquaries; 7b, 10, 11a by kind permission of the Mansell Collection; 9, 11b by kind permission of the Museum of London; 13a by kind permission of the Guildhall Library, City of London; 13b, 15b, 16b by kind permission of the Radio Times Hulton Picture Library; and 16a by kind permission of Fox Photos Ltd.

The first five plans were drawn by Graham Carthew and are based largely on information provided by the Department of the Environment and Professor Allen Brown of King's College, London. The interpretation of that information is the author's. Graham Carthew also drew the family tree.

PREFACE TO THE NEW EDITION

The title says it all: The Tower of London has stood guard over the eastern approach to the city ever since William the Conqueror set his masons to work on the keep which later ages would call the White Tower. Why, then, have a Preface? For two reasons. The first is to answer the comment which may occur to some people; 'Not another book about the Tower of London!' Inevitably the rich history of this building which has stood at the centre of national life for almost a millennium has inspired many books from the large studies by Bayley and Sutherland Gower to the lavishly-illustrated, anecdotal accounts of recent years. The millennium itself would be sufficient justification for the production of a volume relating the story again in a simple, chronological manner. But it is not the only justification. For one thing there is no reliable history of the Tower in print. For another, no previously published book has been able to take advantage of all the latest research.

The Tower never sleeps and nor does research into the minutiae of its past. In the twenty years since this book first appeared the investigations of historians and archaeologists have continued, adding to what was already a richly-detailed saga of human and institutional life. It might be thought that there was little more to be discovered about this most studied of British buildings. That this is not the case is attested by the fascinating details added to our knowledge by today's generation of scholars.

Thus, secondly, I welcome the opportunity to produce a new edition of *The Tower of London*, because it enables me to incorporate the very latest research and provide the reader with as accurate a picture as possible of the development of the buildings and the lives of their inmates. I have been greatly helped in this by Mr Jeremy Ashbee and by Mr Graham Keevill of the Oxford Archaeology Unit and his colleagues. My thanks go to them and to staff of the Tower for their unfailing courtesy and enthusiasm.

I

All over the conquered land they grew – alien cubes of timber or stone, stark, hard-edged and tall above the even earth and the huddled dwellings which sprang mushroom-like from it. They were the nodal points of William of Normandy's governmental system. When the stocky, russet-haired Duke crossed the Channel in September 1066 to make himself King of the English it was only for a brief, six-month campaign and during the remaining twenty years of the reign his continental possessions demanded his presence more than the land of the Saxons. Even in 1087 the 'Norman Conquest' was far from being an irreversible fact of history. Thus the feudal barons to whom control and administration were entrusted, and the fortified strongholds of those barons, were vital to the continued existence of the state. And the most important of those strongholds was the one which from a very early age became known as the Tower of London.

London was the largest town in England, a flourishing port and an age-old centre of finance and commerce. Its stout walls and its street plan were still based on the Roman pattern of seven centuries before. Edward the Confessor's establishment of an abbey and a palace at Westminster had begun to give London a political significance. Its self-confident and well-organized citizenry who claimed a role in the election of kings were a force to be reckoned with. So William realized as he rode northwards with his small army after the battle of Hastings. There was no question of attempting a direct assault, yet its independence could not be tolerated. Among the notables within its walls was Edgar Atheling, last representative of the old West Saxon royal house and regarded by many as the rightful heir to the throne. The attitude of the city leaders was, to say the least, enigmatic. They sallied forth across the bridge when William reached Southwark and engaged the invaders in a brief skirmish which was sufficient to make the Normans turn westwards and cross the Thames at distant Wallingford. At length the Conqueror impressed London by a show of force and a succession of minor triumphs. The town submitted without allowing the dust of its streets to be trampled by exultant victors bent on rapine and plunder.

Such an independent and strategic centre had to be permanently overawed by the Norman presence. Within days of his coronation at Westminster (Christmas 1066) William therefore built 'certain

1

strongholds . . . in the town against the fickleness of the vast and fierce populace'. In the south-west corner Montfichet's Tower and Baynard's Castle appeared and in the south-east what came to be known as the Tower of London. The latter was a wooden fort protected on the south and east by the Roman wall and on its other sides by a new ditch and rampart. The castle, garrisoned and in the hands of a trusted henchman, was the keystone of Norman military strategy. Located at important communications centres or potential trouble spots, these architectural innovations ensured stability once the main army had moved on, for nothing like them had been seen in England for a thousand years. They signified the difference between the extensive Viking raids of previous generations and the territorial conquest for which the Normans (the heirs of the Vikings) had a genius. The Tower of London was no different from the castles already thrown up at Hastings and Pevensea. It was of the type known as 'motte and bailey': a mound of earth (the 'motte'), surrounded with a ditch, formed by the excavations, was surmounted by a palisaded rampart (the 'bailey'), within which was a wooden tower. These fortresses, built largely by the unwilling hands of the vanquished, soon studded the landscape as the new regime extended its authority north-wards and westwards. At length there were some eighty-four of these hastily-erected structures throughout the kingdom.[1] By the end of the century a few of them had been replaced by stone castles.

London's principal fortress was one of the few. 'William the first, surnamed Conqueror, builded the Tower of London, to wit, the great white and square tower there, about the year of Christ 1078, appointing Gundulf then Bishop of Rochester, to be principal surveyor and overseer of that work, who was for that time lodged in the house of Edmere a burgess of London.'[2]

Gundulf who came from the great Norman abbey of Bec was, like most leading ecclesiastics, first and foremost an administrator. He was already in his early fifties and had a considerable reputation as a monastic builder when, in 1077, William brought him to England and appointed him to the important see of Rochester. He immediately set to work rebuilding the cathedral, partly destroyed by the Danes, and establishing there a Benedictine community. Doubtless he would have been surprised could he have known that the King's tower and not this house of God would be his most famous and lasting memorial.

Gundulf was a busy and able man, working simultaneously on the Tower, Rochester Cathedral and Rochester Castle. He was also fortunate enough to live to a ripe old age (he died c. 1108) and thus to see most of his projects either completed or carried to an advanced stage. The first and most urgent task to be accomplished was the construction of a massive stone keep. Gundulf probably sited the new fortress immediately to the north of the temporary wooden tower. Blocks of gleaming Caen stone were imported for the keep which was for many years the largest secular building in England and one which very effectively overawed the natives.

In conception it was much the same as most other Norman keeps on both sides of the Channel. Gundulf's workmen dug deep through rubble and clay and laid a foundation of Kentish rag, chalk and flint, bound with mortar and strong enough to take the ninety-foot high rectangular tower whose walls were fifteen feet thick at their base. The lowest floor of the building consisted of a range of vaults and store rooms (one of which contained a well) partly below the level of the mound created by the excavated earth. The whole interior was divided into three sections by a north-south cross wall and another at right angles splitting the eastern half again. Above the basement there were originally two floors, identical in floor areas and layout but not in height. The lower, entered, then as now, by a wooden staircase set against the south wall, was the accommodation of the officers and soldiers of the garrison. It comprised a hall with a fireplace, where the men ate and relaxed between spells of guard duty, a chamber where they slept, and the crypt of St John's Chapel which probably served as their place of prayer and worship. Above were the grand, lofty rooms used by the Constable, the keeper of the Tower, by honoured guests, noble prisoners, and, occasionally, by the King himself. There was a great hall where a monarch could entertain hugely and in style and where often the sounds of minstrelsy and laughter must have echoed around the rafters. A high gallery ran around this hall in the thickness of the outer wall and also around the great chamber next to it. In the latter room the lord of the castle slept, held private meetings and took counsel from his advisers. In all probability they were also further divided by wooden partitions and curtains as occasion demanded.

Immediately to the south of the White Tower was the bailey. Here there was another well and the sprawl of buildings – stables, forge, animal coops, etc. – vital to the well-being of the garrison. This courtyard was first enclosed by the Roman wall and a series of Norman ramparts and earthworks but a stone curtain wall had been built by the time of Gundulf's death.

By then the first two Norman kings had predeceased him. The Conqueror had died on campaign at Rouen, and his son, William Rufus, had succumbed to a fatal arrow in the New Forest, under circumstances never satisfactorily explained, in 1100. It is doubtful whether either of them ever stayed in the Tower. They probably preferred the amenities of Westminster, where William II erected the magnificent Hall and other buildings. The Tower was entrusted to a

Constable, whose office, like most feudal appointments, was either conceived as, or became in practice, hereditary. The first incumbent was Geoffrey de Mandeville who fought beside the Conqueror in many battles and was now amply rewarded with lands in southern and eastern England. The Constable also had control of the City and held the office of sheriff or portreeve. William had granted London a simple charter, confirming their traditional liberties but much of the citizens' land was confiscated for distribution among the King's followers and people from the City and neighbouring areas had to bend their backs hauling the stone, mortar and timber which went into the symbol of their subservience.

> . . . many shires whose labour was due at London were hard pressed because of the wall they built about the Tower, and because of the bridge that was nearly all carried away by the flood, and because of the work on the king's hall that was built at Westminster, and many a man was oppressed thereby.[3]

The native Londoners complained increasingly bitterly at these burdens. In 1089 some of them joined in an abortive rebellion against William II in the name of his brother. Towards the end of that King's reign even Anselm, Archbishop of Canterbury, a Norman, was urging Rufus to practise some moderation. Yet another source of grievance was the Jews. Hundreds of them had been brought over by the Normans who valued their commercial and financial expertise and settled them in their own quarter of the City. The Englishmen hated them for their usury, their sharp business practices and their immunity from many laws. For the Jews were directly under the protection of the Crown. In London that protection was exercised by the Constable of the Tower and it was to his fortress that the Hebrews fled whenever violence flared up against them. What was the symbol of refuge for the Jews was a symbol of oppression for their neighbours. The people of London focused on the Tower and its garrison all the hatred they felt for their Norman overlords.

But the Tower continued to grow, a sign of Norman self-assurance, a token of the very real accomplishment of the new rulers in unifying and controlling most of the land between Tamar and Tweed. Rufus devoted considerable attention to making the castle even more secure. The 'wall' referred to by the chronicler was a stone curtain wall probably with small towers which now replaced the palisade to the north and west of the White Tower. The keep and bailey were now enclosed on all sides by Norman and Roman stone.

That the King was able to be extravagant in his building works at the Tower and Westminster was due in large measure to Rannulf Flambard, a man destined to occupy a unique place in the annals of the fortress. He was a courtier and administrator who possessed those qualities most prized by the Norman kings: clear-sightedness, ruthlessness, ambition and an unswerving loyalty to those best able to reward his talents. He became the chief agent of William II's rapacious fiscal policy and a merciless scourge of the purses of high and low alike. His name was heartily detested throughout the realm but nowhere more so than in the north where, as Bishop of Durham, his

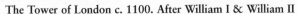

The Tower of London c. 1100. After William I & William II

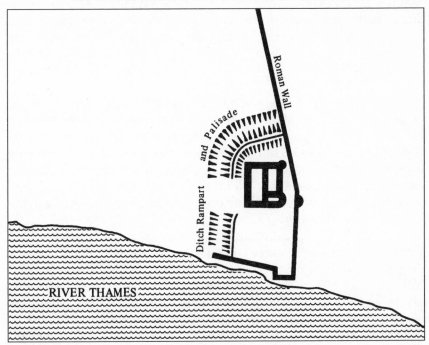

authority was almost unchecked.* The sudden death of his master took Rannulf completely by surprise. The Conqueror's youngest son, Henry, who now seized power, marked the unpopular Bishop for immediate punishment 'for the many injustices which Henry himself and the king's other sons had suffered'. Henry I had Rannulf incarcerated in the Tower of London, thereby, as far as we know from existing records, conferring upon him the distinction of being the first state prisoner to be lodged there.

But the Bishop established for himself another and more remarkable claim to fame: he became the first prisoner ever to escape from the Tower. He spent almost six months in quite congenial confinement, allowed his own servants and permitted to purchase the luxuries

* Among the lasting memorials of his power is the monolithic nave of Durham Cathedral.

which his ill-gotten wealth could command. His money also enabled him to buy collaborators to assist in his bid for freedom. He had a rope smuggled into the fortress inside a butt of wine and a horse ready beneath the walls. On the night of 2 February 1101 the Bishop gave a banquet for his captors. According to the story, he befuddled them with wine, then slipped away to an adjacent chamber where he made fast the rope, eased his gross body through the window and so gained the ground. The story does not tell how Rannulf penetrated the Tower's curtain wall but eventually he reached his horse, the coast and freedom. An early chronicler regarded the feat as so remarkable that it must have been accomplished by witchcraft. He affirmed that the Bishop's mother was a one-eyed sorceress who conveyed him across the Channel by ship but came to grief when her incantations proved powerless against the raging elements.[4] One is tempted to believe that the only magic involved in Rannulf's escape was the magic of gold and that de Mandeville's men were well recompensed for invoking their prince's displeasure. Rannulf Flambard was a born survivor. After years of intrigue, bribery and more than one turn of coat, he made his peace with Henry, was restored to his bishopric and died in 1128, rich and full of years.

Henry I, energetic and sadistically cruel beneath a disarming mask of joviality, reigned until 1135. It was he who really consolidated his father's work of pacification and began to weld Normans and Englishmen into one nation. But he bequeathed to that nation a disputed succession which threatened to ruin all that the new dynasty had achieved. Henry obliged the principal barons to swear fealty to his daughter Matilda but, within days of the old King's death, his nephew Stephen crossed from Boulogne, won the support of London, seized the royal treasury at Winchester and had himself crowned. Most of the barons disliked the idea of having a woman on the throne and those among them who were politically astute saw in Stephen a ruler who would be more pliant than Henry I.

The next nineteen years were to demonstrate the weakness of the feudal system. In the hands of a strong king who could inspire or compel allegiance the system worked. The great landholders, secure in their great castles, made a reality of Norman government. When the king was a man who relied on the barons for his right to rule, those very castles might become centres of autonomous principalities, centres of rebellion. Thus it was in England between 1135 and 1154. Matilda and her husband Geoffrey of Anjou challenged Stephen's position and the greater barons decided in which camp their best interests lay. In the words of the Peterborough chronicle:

. . . every great man built him castles and held them against the king; and they filled the whole land with these castles. They sorely burdened the unhappy people of the country with forced labour on the castles; and when the castles were built they filled them with devils and wicked men . . . Never did a country endure greater misery . . . And men said openly that Christ and his saints slept . . .[5]

It is a one-sided view of the situation, for anarchy was sporadic and never as widespread as the chronicler suggests, but it does make clear an important fact: a new phase in the history of the English castle had arrived. Hitherto Norman fortifications had been erected with the possibility of native rebellion in mind. There was little need for elaborate defence against bands of ill-equipped peasantry. But in the new situation the keepers of private and royal castles faced the threat of attack by trained feudal levies. As a result important political and architectural changes occurred.

Until this time the Tower had been just one of an important chain of royal castles in the south.* No king had used it as a residence for any significant length of time and it was in the hands of trusted and trustworthy guardians. All this now changed. Stephen's first move, as we have seen, was to secure London and that certainly included the Tower. The Constable, Geoffrey de Mandeville, grandson of the Conqueror's companion, did fealty and was well rewarded for his loyalty** which was maintained for five years while the King's support dwindled and he was increasingly involved in campaigns against groups of dissident barons. Stephen rushed about the country, often with de Mandeville at his side, besieging castles, installing men of trust within them and, where necessary, strengthening their defences.

In this situation the Tower assumed an increased significance. The King regarded it as a more secure base than Westminster and at Whitsuntide 1140 he held his court there. It seems certain that the first palace within the Tower had now been built. This was a complex of buildings attached to and running south from the White Tower. There were kitchens, a great hall and chambers for the King, Queen and other members of the household. These early medieval living quarters have long since disappeared so it is impossible to know exactly what they looked like or where they were situated. However, our first general description of the Tower of London dates from only a few years later. William Fitzstephen described it as, 'great and strong with encircling walls rising from a deep foundation and built with

---

* Other examples are Dover, Windsor, Winchester, Hastings and Berkhampstead (originally a private castle which fell into royal hands in Henry II's reign).

** Among other grants of land, de Mandeville was appointed Earl of Essex before 1141. The creation is interesting in that the charter confirming it is the earliest such charter now extant.

mortar tempered with the blood of beasts.'[6] The 'blood of beasts' probably refers to the reddish tinge imparted to the mortar by the large quantity of Roman tiles which were crushed to help make it.

King Stephen was not the only one to appreciate the importance of this well-nigh impregnable fortress. Geoffrey de Mandeville saw that it could be a splendid bargaining counter which he might use to enrich himself and increase his power and prestige. When, within a few months of the Whitsun assembly, the tide of war began to run against the King, the Constable considered transferring his allegiance. His first gesture of defiance was directed against a defenceless French girl. Stephen had betrothed his eleven-year-old son Eustace to Constance, daughter of Louis VI of France. The Princess was brought over for the formal cere-mony and entrusted to de Mandeville's safe keeping. The French alliance was very unpopular with Stephen's opponents because it assured the King a powerful ally and one who would at a later date support the succession of Eustace to the throne. So de Mandeville kept his charge in the Tower and declined to release her until he could be sure which way the wind was blowing.

Matilda had by now landed in England to place herself at the head of her supporters and early in 1141 her armies captured Stephen at the battle of Lincoln. De Mandeville hesitated no longer. He sold his allegiance and the Tower to Matilda in return for confirmation of his earldom, new land grants and important offices and authority in London and the surrounding territory. By the time she entered London in June, the Constable of the Tower had become the richest and most powerful man in England.

Matilda's triumph was short lived. By her imperiousness and inflex-ibility she angered the very people on whose support she still relied. They drove her from London and Geoffrey de Mandeville was in the forefront of the pursuers. He seized and imprisoned in the Tower the Bishop of London, her supporter, then placed his sword once more at the disposal of King Stephen. But he put a price upon it; before yielding the Tower to his liege lord, de Mandeville gained still more estates and jurisdictional powers in Essex, Middlesex and Hertfordshire. Stephen needed the troublesome Earl and could not afford to punish him.

But de Mandeville tried to change sides once too often. 1142 saw him again secretly negotiating with Matilda. Stephen waited his opportunity. When the Earl attended the royal court in September of the following year the King arrested him and, on pain of death, forced him to surrender all his castles, principally the Tower. The Constableship was now vested in one of the King's trusted friends. Clearly the secu-rity of the Tower was too important to permit it to fall into unworthy or jealous hands; its guardianship never again became hereditary.

Thus, after three generations, the name of de Mandeville ceased to have any connection with the Tower but the end of the troublesome Geoffrey is worth relating. Stephen lacked either the courage or wisdom to keep the Earl in custody. De Mandeville left the court 'like a vicious and riderless horse, kicking and biting' in his rage.[7] He established himself in the Fenland where he lived as an outlaw, successfully resisting the royal forces until 1144, when he was fatally wounded in a skirmish. His violent depredations of church property had so enraged the ecclesiastical hierarchy that his body was refused Christian burial. In fact it did not receive decent interment for nearly twenty years.

Henry II was a man who knew about castles. He succeeded peacefully to the throne on the death of Stephen in October 1154 and set about re-establishing an efficient and powerful central government. The country was tired of civil strife and many of the great 'castlemen' were ready to be reconciled with the Crown and each other. Yet they would only relinquish a measure of their new-found independence and local prestige if they were confident that Henry of Anjou was capable of establishing his authority over all the barons. Henry was more than equal to the task. Political acumen and ceaseless energy combined in him to make one of the most remarkable, if enigmatic, rulers in England's history. One aspect of the restoration of royal power was the overhauling of all the important fortresses belonging to the King. Between Easter and Whitsun 1156 an army of masons and carpenters was brought in to carry out the necessary work at the Tower. Their activities were planned and supervised by Henry's able new chancellor. His name was Thomas Becket.

In 1153 Stephen had appointed Richard de Lucy Constable of the Tower and granted him many of the lands and honours forfeited by de Mandeville. Henry confirmed this loyal knight in his office and soon advanced him to fresh honours. De Lucy became Justiciar, the chief political and judicial officer. As such he enjoyed the King's complete trust and acted as his representative when he was out of the country. Henry was not an easy man to follow, yet he inspired considerable devotion among his men, and de Lucy served him tirelessly until shortly before his death in 1179.

Such an important man could obviously not be personally in charge of the Tower at all times, although it is clear that the monarch held the Constable totally responsible for the administration of the castle and the well-being of its staff and prisoners. It is equally clear that permanent quarters were maintained within the Tower for this official and that they were frequently occupied. However from an early date the Constable had the help of a deputy, the Lieutenant of the Tower. The first Lieutenant whose name is preserved is William de

Piuntal who was in office in 1189 but he certainly had predecessors. The job was a highly responsible one and it was rewarded accordingly. In the time of Richard II the Lieutenant was paid twenty pounds a year. This was about a quarter of the income the major household officers derived from their official duties. It was about twice what a very successful master mason might hope to earn. Since the Lieutenant was always a royal servant of some standing he was not totally dependent on his salary; he had income from manors and lands as well as fees for stewardships and other services performed for the Crown. But his position at the Tower brought him not inconsiderable perquisites. Most of them derived from prisoners entrusted to his charge. When a man was arrested his goods were forfeit to the Crown. From them fees were paid to the Lieutenant for the prisoner's keep. The amount varied according to the man's status; in the time of Richard II the scale was fixed as follows:

A duke	5 marks (£3.6s.8d.) per week
A earl	£2 per week
A baron	£1 " "
A knight	10s. " "

Noblemen were allowed a number of servants and the rates for them were also strictly laid down:

A chaplain	6s.8d. per week
A gentleman	6s.8d. " "
A yeoman	3s.4d. " "
Any other servant	3s.4d. per week

There was nothing to prevent the Lieutenant and the gaolers to whom he delegated responsibility from pocketing a proportion of these fees, indeed they were expected to do so. Moreover, wealthy and fastidious prisoners usually paid for extra privileges – food and wine of better quality, furniture, tapestries, mattresses, etc. (We have already noted that Flambard's escape was possible because he was in the habit of having barrels of wine delivered to his quarters in the White Tower.) Whatever his status a prisoner could improve his conditions by paying for extra services or luxuries.

This arrangement suited both parties and it is important to understand that in the medieval period there was nothing improper about it. If a prisoner in Dartmoor or Pentonville today were discovered to be obtaining privileges from a warder by paying for them the public would, very correctly, be scandalized. This is because imprisonment is now considered to be a form of punishment in itself and that punishment involves depersonalizing the prisoner, stripping him of all rank and status, and severing his contact with the outside world in the apparent belief that this will make him a better citizen when his liberty is restored. Medieval society was a system of patronage in which those in the upper layers of the feudal pyramid paid with money, lands or protection for services provided by their social inferiors. A prisoner was not cut off from this society when the doors of the Tower clanged behind him. Therefore, unless a vindictive or outraged king gave orders that a detainee was to be singled out for harsh treatment, he was entitled to whatever services wealth and status could command. He received visits from family and friends. He established his own household within the castle and his servants were able to come and go freely in pursuance of his wants. As the Tower grew it was possible to provide more accommodation for prisoners of quality and it was customary to assign the whole of a tower to a confined dignitary for the use of himself and his suite. There were, of course, less fortunate prisoners; poor men who had to be content with an unfurnished cell and frugal rations but then for many such wretches life outside prison was scarcely less hard.

In the early centuries very few humble men found themselves in the Tower of London. Whatever its later history, it was not designed as a common prison. It was a royal castle where, from time to time, the king confined, usually for short periods, powerful men who had offended him or who were awaiting trial, prisoners of war detained pending payment of ransom, or potential troublemakers whose continued liberty was undesirable for political reasons. For common criminals the City had prisons in plenty and in them conditions were far worse than in the royal Tower. No place of detention is pleasant and no prisoner ever enjoyed going to the Tower, but it was not until the sixteenth century, when large numbers of prisoners were shut in there for treason and religious offences, that the building acquired its reputation as a place of narrow, damp dungeons and torture chambers.

Having, hopefully, dispelled one of the commonest myths about the Tower of London we must acknowledge that from an early period there did exist in the Tower cramped and unwholesome dungeons where prisoners who, in the opinion of the king, had merited harsh treatment could be confined in conditions that were deliberately made as uncomfortable as possible. In the reign of Henry III William Marish, an outlaw accused of piracy, robbery, murder and treason, was captured and delivered with some of his colleagues to the Lieutenant of the Tower with strict instructions 'that they should be safely confined in the direst and most secure prison in that fortress, and so loaded with irons, and in such place be kept that there could be no fear of their escape'.[8]

The murder of Archbishop Becket in December 1170 sent a shock of horror through Christian Europe which was not to be paralleled

11

until the execution of Thomas More three and a half centuries later. The saint's memory was particularly revered in London which was very proud of its great son. Henry II did penance and gradually his reputation recovered. He was not undevout; at the end of his life he was even seriously considering going on crusade; but many church-men never forgave him. His fits of violent rage in which he was heard to utter the most obscene blasphemies were well known and many a cleric or peasant householder would nod sagely when hearing of the King's latest outrage and remind his companions of the old legend that the devil's blood ran in the veins of the Counts of Anjou. It must have been to counter such unpleasant rumours that, in about 1185, Henry ordered certain improvements to the parish church which stood just outside the castle's rampart so that he and his court could hear mass there. The object of this was that the King might be 'seen to worship' in public, instead of within the White Tower. There may have been another reason why Henry thought it advisable to demonstrate his Christian devotion. At the beginning of that same year, 1185, he had been offered the crown of the Kingdom of Jerusalem. For reasons of state he declined the honour, a decision which caused offence in some ecclesiastical quarters and must have set the old rumours in motion once again. Nothing now remains of the Norman building which was ultimately engulfed by the fortress and became the first Chapel of St Peter ad Vincula. We know that it must have been a substantial church with two chancels in which stood the altars of St Mary and St Peter as well as chapels or nave altars dedicated to St Nicholas and St Catherine. A royal pew was maintained in the chapel by Henry's successors (though as early as 1241 it was in need of repair).

Troubled times returned to England with the death of Henry II and the successive reigns of his sons Richard I and John. Richard was more concerned with the struggle of Christian Europe against the Turks than in the well-being of his own patrimony. During the ten years of his sovereignty (1189-1199) he spent five months in England. His younger brother would willingly have made good Richard's deficiency and, against the King's orders, he crossed to England in 1191 to try to establish his mastery. He had a secure power base in the West and Midlands but when he attempted to extend his authority he found himself opposed by Richard's representative, William Longchamp. Longchamp, Bishop of Ely, Justiciar of all England, and Constable of the Tower of London, was ugly, arrogant and unpopular. He did not like the English, did not know their language and travelled everywhere with a pomp and splendour designed to impress peasant and baron alike with his importance. A contemporary chronicler wrote, 'the laity found him more than a king, the clergy more than a pope, and both an intolerable tyrant'.[9] In brief, he was the sort of adversary who made

John's task easy. The barons joined the prince in increasing numbers and gave their support against the hated Justiciar.

This clash of personality and authority led directly to the next major phase of building at the Tower – a phase which was not altogether successful. Longchamp knew that he would have to make his principal fortress impregnable in case it was called upon to face up to the forces of a substantial number of the barons. He, therefore, built a further line of defences and, in doing so, created an outer ward. The line of the Roman wall was continued westwards along the waterfront and the Bell Tower was built. From there a new wall was probably built northwards to roughly where the Beauchamp Tower now stands. Thence it ran east by north-east to link up with Rufus's curtain wall. So far so good, but Longchamp's next innovation was a failure. He had a wide, deep ditch dug around his new wall and, perhaps, beyond the Roman wall also. These were connected to the Thames with the intention of flooding the moat but the experiment failed, perhaps because the Justiciar and his workmen had insufficient understanding of sluices. However, Longchamp probably felt reasonably secure in his enlarged fortress which was complete by the time Prince John arrived in England.

For some months the two rivals moved around the country like wrestlers circling each other in the ring. With their bands of armed

The Tower of London c. 1200 showing Bishop Longchamp's Extension

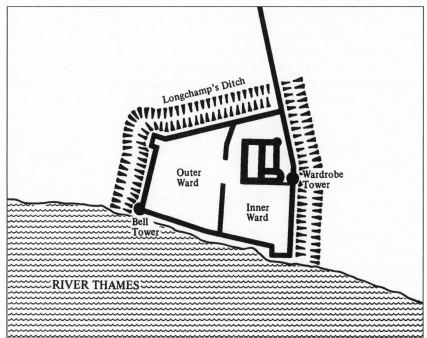

retainers they made a show of strength and confronted each other with haughty messages and verbal taunts. On 6 October 1191 the Bishop was at Windsor when he learned that John's supporters were marching on London. He immediately pursued them, fought his way through them and reached the Tower first, resolved to put his impressive fortifications to the test.

The first siege of the Tower of London lasted only three days. It was Longchamp's nerve and not the fortress walls which broke. The Bishop apparently decided that discretion would gain him more than defiance. He surrendered, yielded up all his offices and the keys of the Tower and cast himself on Prince John's mercy. Subsequently he escaped across the Channel and continued to serve King Richard until he died in 1197. His greatest offence may have been in allowing loyalty to blind him to the need to practise the subtle arts of government. All England rejoiced at his death and his only lasting memorial was a few yards of stone wall and an empty ditch. Even the wall was not an unqualified success: in 1211 part of it, undermined by Longchamp's hasty moat excavations, fell down.

The ambitions of the royal rivals once more divided England into baronial factions. John intrigued with King Philip of France and hired foreign mercenaries. Walter of Coutances, Archbishop of Rouen, whom Richard had appointed in place of Longchamp, led the resistance. On his way back from the Third Crusade, Coeur de Lion was imprisoned by the Holy Roman Emperor and held to ransom. John spread the rumour that his brother was dead, seized Wallingford and Windsor and demanded the surrender of London. But the Tower garrison remained loyal and the gates of the City were closed. Soon Walter of Coutances was organizing resistance to the prince throughout the country and laying siege to his castles. Ultimately, however, the royal brothers were reconciled, Richard named John his heir, and the latter succeeded peacefully to the throne in 1199.

The rivalry of the royal brothers and their noble representatives provided the opportunity for the London burgesses to gain, at long last, a measure of self-government. The activity and prosperity of the City as a port and commercial centre had been increasing steadily and for many generations its businessmen had been trying to obtain a commune, a town parliament, of the type achieved by some continental cities. But the wealth and strategic importance of the capital were too great for the King willingly to relax his grip. Control of the City was habitually vested in some trusted feudal magnate, usually the Constable of the Tower. This lord held the farm of taxes (i.e. he collected all financial levies in return for a fixed payment to the Crown). The Constable was ultimately responsible for the maintenance of law and order within the walls and for special areas of jurisdiction, such as governance of the Jewry, as were reserved to the King. He had to exercise his protection of the Jews in 1189. Traditional hatred of the privileged group was fanned by the preaching of the crusade against enemies of the Christian faith. An incident at King Richard's coronation sparked off a fearful massacre and the Constable opened the gates of the Tower to the screaming men and women who rushed up to them. Afterwards the culprits were severely punished.

The Constable also had complete control of the river and the port and took tolls of all ships landing merchandise on the wharfs between the Tower and the Bridge. Day to day administration and justice were the province of the traditional authorities and courts of the City, the aldermen and folkmoots, but the ground immediately round the castle was from the beginning a sensitive area and the Constable reserved to himself jurisdiction over it. All this began to change in the 1190s and the concessions won by the citizens in those years heralded a very long period of sporadic conflict between the mayors and aldermen of London on the one side and the constables and lieutenants of the Tower of London on the other.

In 1190 the City fathers found themselves in a position to bargain with William Longchamp who was hard pressed to meet his master's increasing demands for money. On payment of a large sum they gained the tax farm of London and Middlesex, together with the right to elect their own sheriffs. A few months later they followed up this success by negotiating their longed-for commune. The first Mayor, Henry Fitz Ailwin, took office in 1191 and was assisted by a council of aldermen. But by no means all the citizens supported the new constitution. It was an oligarchy, representative essentially of the mercantile interest. Many Londoners were suspicious of it and looked to the Constable of the Tower to protect them, in the King's name, from their wealthy neighbours. If that failed they were not averse to appealing directly to the monarch.

Trouble flared up first in 1195–6. The root of the problem was the ransom of £100,000 demanded by the Emperor Henry VI for the release of Richard the Lionheart. The Justiciar and other royal officials set about collecting this incredibly large sum by taxing all land holders and civic authorities. Some citizens claimed, with considerable justification, that the Mayor and corporation of London had assessed themselves and their friends lightly for the tax and passed the greater part of the burden on to their poorer neighbours. The complainers found a champion in the person of William Fitzosbert, a member of a prominent London family. He was something of a trouble-maker – a loudmouth, a mob orator, a self-appointed champion of the oppressed. By all accounts he was about as attractive as an unkempt student demonstrator. And like many student demonstrators he took his stand on principle and attracted a large personal following. Fitzosbert denounced the civic leaders at the folkmoot in St Paul's churchyard on more than one occasion. Craftsmen, shopkeepers and labourers flocked to hear him. Soon the Mayor and aldermen were terrified of an insurrection. The government was no less concerned, for trouble in the City might well spread to the surrounding country. Fitzosbert crossed to France and complained in person to Richard, who had recently been released, about the iniquitous exactions of the city authorities. He received assurances of the King's support but these carried little weight with the Justiciar, Hubert Walter, who was faced with a city about to flame into revolt.

Royal forces moved against the popular hero as soon as he returned to London, but secure in his headquarters and surrounded by followers, Fitzosbert felt safe. However, a body of armed men attacked the potential rebels and in the ensuing fracas Fitzosbert killed one of the King's men. It was one of those psychological moments which puts leadership to the test. If he had brandished his dripping sword he would have been followed through the City by a growing army of cheering rebels. In the event, he recoiled in shock and horror at the enormity of his crime. He rushed from the spot and took refuge in nearby Bow Church, where he and a few friends claimed sanctuary. Hubert Walter judged the situation too serious for niceties of ecclesiastical law to be considered. He sent armed soldiers into the church to lay hands on the offenders. Fitzosbert and his friends shut themselves in the tower. The soldiers smoked them out. Choking and bleeding from wounds, Fitzosbert stumbled into Bow Lane. He was bound, tied to a horse's tail and dragged through the City. Through the mud and filth of Bridge Row, Canwick Street and Eastcheap his lacerated body was towed, and the agony did not stop until he reached the Tower.

There he was cast, his wounds untended, into one of the most loathsome dungeons. Who knows what illegal tortures and indignities he was subjected to by the garrison while awaiting his trial? The sentence of death was a foregone conclusion. On 6 April 1196 he left the Tower in the same way that he had entered it. Once more he was dragged through the City, this time to Smithfield where he was hanged in chains with nine of his companions. Few of the spectators cheered or jeered as was the common practice at public executions. They regarded Fitzosbert as a martyr. His gibbet was carried off and kept as a relic. Men scooped the earth from the spot where it had stood. The chains which had held his decomposing body were claimed to have miraculous powers. There was widespread agreement with the chronicler who recorded that Fitzosbert died 'a shameful death for upholding the cause of truth and of the poor'. It must have seemed to those poor that with City and royal authority against them their plight was desperate indeed. However, the citizens were gradually reconciled to accepting the new constitution, perhaps because their hatred of the Tower was greater than their distrust of the powerful burgesses.

The bad government and anarchy which marked the reign of John 'Lackland' are legendary and, in this instance at least, legend does not exaggerate. The lawlessness of the times moved the citizens of London to strengthen their defences. Between 1211 and 1213 they copied Longchamp's initiative and dug a moat around their own city wall. At its eastern end it terminated close to the Tower and for centuries provided yet another cause for friction between the Mayor and the Lieutenant, the complaint frequently being made that the City ditch was allowed to drain into the Tower moat.

By the autumn of 1214 John's arbitrary and tyrannical rule had driven many of the leading barons into concerted action which would make constitutional history. They met at Bury St Edmunds and there reviewed the ancient liberties of which, they complained, the King had deprived them. They listed them in a document and 'swore on the great altar that if the King refused to grant these liberties and laws, they themselves would withdraw their allegiance to him, and make war upon him till he should, by a charter under his own seal, confirm to them everything they required.'[10]

The demands were presented to John as he lodged at the Temple the following January. He put the barons off with promises and prepared for a trial of strength. But all over the country the great men were levying their powers and at Easter they began to move on London. John withdrew to Windsor and on 17 May the citizens of the capital joyfully threw open their gates to the army led by Robert Fitzwalter, styled by his colleagues, 'Marshal of the army of God and Holy Church'.

Fitzwalter was no stranger to the City for he was the lord of Baynard's Castle. He immediately set about repairing London's walls and laying siege to the Tower. The fortress was under-garrisoned for John needed all the troops he could muster. He had recently, however, installed William, Archdeacon of Huntingdon, as Lieutenant and this loyal official resisted the combined force of baronage and citizenry. Within weeks, however, the King was forced to negotiate and to set his seal to Magna Carta at Runnymede. The threat to the Tower was, therefore averted.

But the barons, quite rightly as events turned out, did not trust John's promises of reform. They kept their men armed and encamped. Fitzwalter retained his hold on London. In the war which soon followed the rebels maintained control of the capital and before long the Tower garrison had made common cause with them. In 1216 Fitzwalter and his colleagues deposed King John and offered the crown to the French Dauphin, Louis. The new 'king' was brought across and held his first court in the Tower of London. All was going well for the rebels until, in October 1216, John died. Fitzwalter was committed to Louis but increasing support was given to young Prince Henry, the legitimate heir. Fitzwalter fought bravely until his defeat and capture at Lincoln, the following summer. Even then London and its Tower did not submit until convinced that the Dauphin's cause was lost. By the treaty of Lambeth the nine-year-old Henry III was universally acclaimed and the liberties for which so many Englishmen had fought were guaranteed. Fitzwalter became one of the legendary heroes of the fight for freedom. He spent a year in prison after the battle of Lincoln and went on to win fresh laurels during the fifth crusade. Henry III was to prove himself the monarch who would make more impression on the Tower of London than any of his predecessors.

The fact that the Mayor of London was among the barons at Runnymede indicates the importance of the City and the rapid acceptance of the new constitution. Nor was he slow in ensuring that the rights of the capital were enshrined in Magna Carta. One of its clauses pinpoints precisely a source of friction between the City and the Tower. Kiddles were the offending objects. A kiddle was a barrier to which fish nets were attached. When set in a stream or tideway it efficiently scooped up fish of every description. Now the Constable of the Tower regarded himself as possessing the right to erect kiddles, not only in the Thames opposite the Tower but in the tributaries of the Lea and Wandle. The citizens claimed that they had ancient rights of free fishing and that, in any case, the charter they had obtained from Richard I gave the Mayor and corporation control of the river. It was not only the activities of the Constable and the Lieutenant to which they objected; those officers had the even more infuriating habit of granting licences to their friends and servants to set up kiddles. Sporadic protests and the occasional cutting of nets on dark nights availed the Londoners nothing. Thus they seized their opportunity in 1215. King John was made to promise, under pain of excommunication, that the abuse would cease.

If the details of Magna Carta ever filtered through to the Lieutenant he ignored them. The kiddling continued even though the Sheriff of London took an armed band out onto the river and seized the Lieutenant's nets. Twenty years later a more resolute effort was made to enforce the charter. The corporation despatched another armed group as far as the mouth of the Medway to arrest a number of men fishing under Tower licence and to confiscate their nets. A case was brought before the King's justices and decision given in favour of the Londoners. The offenders were ordered to pay fines of ten pounds each. There was rejoicing throughout the City and a bonfire of kiddles in Westcheap.

2

In the reign of Henry III the Tower became for the first time a major royal palace. The new king was very different from his bloody and aggressive predecessors. He was a French aesthete occupying a throne traditionally held by warrior kings. He loved beauty and elegance and made a point of surrounding himself with the finest works of art that genius and craftsmanship could devise. He was sincerely religious, a devoted son of the church. His barons did not understand him and he certainly took no trouble to understand them. Revenue was lavished on the adornment of royal homes and the accomplishment of grandiose enterprises such as the building of Westminster Abbey. He showed suspicion and hostility to the great men of the realm and made no concession to the aspirations of power-sharing they had come to cherish during the reigns of Richard and John. This would have been excellent if he had been a king like Henry II whose charisma inspired fear and respect. He was not. Therefore, throughout most of his long reign (1216–1272) he was in conflict with many groups of subjects. All these aspects of Henry's personality and situation have left their mark on the Tower of London.

During Henry's minority the man who held most authority was the experienced soldier and administrator, Hubert de Burgh. As Justiciar he faithfully upheld the interests of the crown and imparted a much-needed strength and rigidity to royal government. Among his offices was that of Constable of the Tower, a fact which imparts a sad irony to the events of 1232. By then Henry III had been his own master for five years since assuming full responsibility for his government in 1227. For a while he was content to rely heavily on Hubert but soon his own expansive and headstrong ideas began to conflict with the cautious wisdom of his aged councillor. The King fell under the influence of a succession of favourites and flatterers, most of whom were bent upon the downfall of the efficient and unyielding Justiciar. In the summer of 1232 Henry struck suddenly and viciously. He deprived Hubert of all his offices and lands, and laid a series of charges against him, some of which were serious allegations of administrative malpractice while others were absurd accusations based on malicious rumour. The disgraced minister, a man in his sixties, fled into Essex and claimed sanctuary at Brentwood. On Henry's order he was starved out, loaded with chains, brought back to London and thrown into one of the Tower dungeons. Fortunately for the old man, the King's moods were as changeable as they were extreme; the conditions of Hubert's imprisonment were soon eased and two years later he was restored to royal favour.

But there was no restoration of peace and harmony. Henry and his court became increasingly estranged from the baronage. The King claimed the right to choose his own officials and advisers; the magnates demanded a permanent share in a government which they supported with military aid and which they helped to finance. Most of Henry's close friends were Poitevins, Frenchmen from Poitou, and foremost among them was his own young half-brother, William de Valence. Upon these despised aliens the King lavished money, lands and titles. They controlled the royal household and exercised a great influence on policy. The court became a glittering, closed, introspective world, a brilliant cultural microcosm set in a hostile environment it did its best to ignore. The homes around which this household toured were beautiful within and strong without.

It was probably in the 1220s when he was still a minor that Henry III began a series of improvements to the Tower buildings and for the rest of the reign scarce a year passed during which masons, carpenters and painters were not employed somewhere on the complex. The main objective of the vast expansion which now took place was to provide the King with a refuge and power base from which he could defy all opposition. The Roman wall was demolished to make way for a new outer curtain which considerably increased the size of the Outer Ward. The southern flank of the castle now extended from the Bell Tower to the Salt Tower and was washed by the Thames along most of its length. The central bastion in this wall was the Wakefield Tower which guarded the main watergate (now part of the Bloody Tower). Immediately east of the Wakefield Tower was a small, private watergate for the use of the King and his intimates. This gave access to the Wakefield Tower and the Royal Lodgings in the Inner Ward. The east and north walls with their towers are essentially the inner ballium as it can still be seen today. Henry completed his defences with a City-facing wall (from the Bell Tower to the Devereux Tower) in the centre of which was situated a new, imposing land gate. He now filled in Longchamp's ditch and had a wide moat dug all around the landward sides of the castle. To ensure that this watercourse should be more successful than its predecessor Henry obtained the services of a ditch-digger from the Low Countries, called Master John, but unfortunately for Henry this foreign expert was unable to cope with the peculiar problems of the site.

The object of all this defensive work was to make the king's stronghold secure against fractious nobles and the no-less-troublesome

London citizenry. The inhabitants of the capital watched with indignation and anger as masons raised the massive walls and gateway, Master John's men excavated the moat and carpenters constructed its timber bridge. It was, therefore, with excited jubilation that on the morning of 24 April 1240 they rushed to the bank opposite the Tower and saw a pile of rubble where Henry's noble gateway had stood. The royal engineers were immediately set to work rebuilding the structure and strengthening the foundations which had been undermined by the moat. Then, exactly a year to the day, an adjacent section of wall collapsed. London preachers claimed that this divine visitation was the direct result of St Thomas Becket's intercession (see Appendix 1).

The holy martyr had good cause to intervene, for Henry's extension had brought within the curtain wall one of the City's churches (thereafter known as St Peter ad Vincula). It may have been partly to pacify parishioners that Henry went to considerable expense to refurbish the church. On 10 December 1241 he directed the chancel of St Mary and the royal stall in the chancel of St Peter to be repaired and redecorated. The King's instructions were specific:

> The little Mary with her tabernacle and the figures of St Peter, St Nicholas and St Catherine to be newly coloured, all with the best colours; the beam beyond the altar of St Peter and the little cross with its images to be refreshed with good colours. Two fair tables [to] be made with the histories of St Nicholas and St Catherine

The Tower of London c. 1270 after Henry III

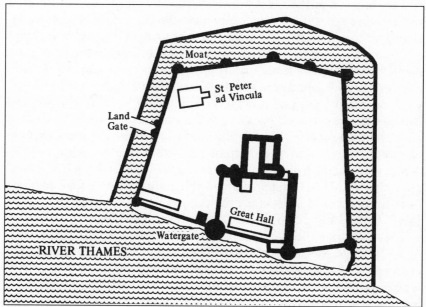

before their altars in the said church; also two fair cherubim with cheerful and pleasant countenances to be placed on either side of the great crucifix; and a marble font with columns to be provided.[1]

Ten years later Henry provided a peal of bells for St Peters'. Each of the chaplains who served the Tower altars received fifty shillings a year, the standard emolument for all royal chaplains. For some years the Tower's neighbours probably continued to worship in their old parish church.

But Henry III was not concerned only with the outer defences of the Tower. If he, his family and his friends were to spend a great deal of time in the fortress it must be a home worthy of them. The King spent considerable sums, therefore, on the Inner Ward and the Palace. To guard the landward approach he built the immensely strong Coldharbour Gate and connected this to the Wakefield Tower with a massive Main Guard wall. He built or rebuilt the Great Hall and vastly improved the facilities available to his household by constructing new lodgings and kitchens. The King's own apartments included and were adjacent to the Wakefield Tower, The upper floor of the Wakefield Tower was Henry's Privy Chamber and had an oratory attached to it. The Royal Lodgings were redecorated within and without. Orders are still extant for such improvements as the wainscoting of the Queen's rooms in the Lanthorn Tower and an adjoining building and the provision of frescos depicting the story of Antiochus the Great for the King's Privy Chamber.

The chapel of St John was much enriched by this pious and cultured King. As we see it now in its simple, unadorned Norman grandeur it is difficult to imagine what it looked like throughout the medieval period – shadowy, candle-lit, glowing with colour and gilt. Henry set up a painted rood-screen surmounted by a crucifix and the figures of St Mary and St John. He ordered stained-glass windows depicting the Virgin with the infant Jesus and 'the Holy Trinity with St John, Apostle and Evangelist', and gave other, unspecified, images. The King must often have attended mass in this sumptuous chapel, looking down upon the chanting priests and their attendants from the triforium which connected with the gallery running around the walls of the original royal apartments. In 1261 Henry granted the annual sum of fifty shillings to St Katharine's Hospital for providing a chaplain to pray daily in St John's Chapel for the soul of his sister-in-law (Senchia).

The most dramatic alteration that Henry III made to the Tower was, in many ways, the simplest. He ordered the palace buildings and the great keep to be limewashed. From that time onward the 'White Tower' would stand out above its encircling wall in sun-catching brilliance, a landmark visible for miles across the river, the Surrey flats and the huddled roofs of the City. What his purpose was we can only conjecture. One guess which is fully in keeping with Henry's character is that he painted the White Tower as a magnificent gesture of defiance. Frequently he took refuge there and, increasingly, he preferred it to Westminster because of its greater security. Perhaps in this symbolic act he was saying to Londoners, the barons and anyone else who needed to be impressed, 'Here is royalty – pure, proud and impregnable'.

The citizens of London certainly grew more apprehensive as the Tower became larger and more massive. They resented every block of stone that contributed to the strength of Henry's fortress. As well as the psychological impact of the Tower and the by now traditional causes of friction between the Mayor and the Lieutenant, the people had fresh grievances. In 1251 the sheriffs were ordered to pay fourpence a day for the upkeep of the King's polar bear and to provide a muzzle and chain. There may have been some slight justification for this seemingly arbitrary impost: the bear was, apparently, a very entertaining Tower inmate and crowds would flock to watch him fishing in the river. Doubtless Henry considered that an animal which gave pleasure to all should be supported by all. Perhaps the same motive inspired him three years later when he sent fresh instructions to the sheriffs. They were to build a house at the Tower forty feet by twenty for the King's elephant and they were to ensure 'that it be strong'.

These are the first references we have to what became the royal menagerie, a source of fascination for visitors to the Tower during the next six hundred years. The dilettante Henry III counted the study of strange beasts among his many interests but he was by no means the first English or European monarch to possess a private zoo. Most of his animals were diplomatic gifts from foreign kings: the bear came from Norway; the Holy Roman Emperor sent him three leopards; the elephant, the prize of the royal collection, was a present from the King of France. Sadly, the creature did not take very kindly to his new surroundings: he died within two years. There is no way of knowing where these animals were kept, but the original site of the menagerie must have been somewhere in the Outer Bailey, to which the public had reasonable access. After the elephant's demise his house was sometimes used as a prison which indicates that it must have been securely within the walls. The Barbican built as a part of Edward I's outer Tower defence was from a very early date known as the Lion Tower so it may well have housed the royal beasts soon after its construction. This was certainly the location of the menagerie in later centuries. By Edward II's reign the Keeper of the King's Lions and Leopards was a regular appointment carrying a fixed wage and specific lodgings within the Tower.

The Jews continued to be a source of friction between City and royal officials. As we have already seen, the Jewry (the area adjacent to Cheapside still commemorated in the street called 'Old Jewry') was the first of the Tower 'liberties'. Within it the Constable of the Tower kept the peace, administered justice between Jew and Jew and between Jew and Christian. It is not difficult to see how resentment might grow and spread as a result of disputed decisions by the Constable's court especially as offenders waiting trial or suffering punishment were usually locked up in the Tower. The protection of the castle still had to be extended to the Jews from time to time. In 1220 during Henry's re-coronation and again in 1236 the entire community was moved into the Tower for its own safety. Just how deep was the feeling against the Jews was shown in 1264 when the King temporarily lost control of the Tower (see below, p. 25). There was an immediate uprising against the King and his Semitic 'friends', hundreds of whom were slaughtered. The majority of Londoners were probably convinced that royal justice was weighted in favour of the Jews. Generally speaking it was not so: they certainly underwent heavy taxation which did not fall upon the rest of the community. In 1240 and again in 1279 large numbers of Jews were imprisoned in the Tower because they could not pay the large imposts levied upon them and while they languished in the cells, their property was seized.

It was not only Londoners who saw the Tower as a symbol of oppression. Henry made sporadic attempts to establish this stronghold as the home of his governmental machine. He frequently held court there and used the fortress on occasions as a refuge for himself and his family when baronial opposition became too strong. At least twice he summoned a parliament to meet there (1236 and 1261) but the magnates' representatives would not allow themselves to be lured within the forbidding walls. As we shall see later some important administrative and judicial offices were established, for a time at least, in the Tower. How daunting it must have been for suitors having financial or legal business with the crown to present themselves at the Tower, where stout doors clanged behind them, armed guards watched from the battlements and haggard prisoners could be glimpsed at barred windows.

The constitutional crisis came to a head in the 1250s. The discontented barons, as well as groups of gentry and burgesses placed themselves under the leadership of the Earl of Leicester, Simon de Montfort. In addition to the ratification of traditional privileges they wanted Henry to agree to the summoning of regular parliaments and a say in the appointment of officers of state. In 1258 the King was forced to agree to most of their demands, which were enshrined in the Provisions of Oxford. One of them, significantly, was the surrender of the Tower which was placed in the hands of Hugh Bigod, a powerful East Anglian magnate. Henry, however, had no intention of allowing his royal power to be limited. As soon as he could do so he defied Simon's supporters and obtained papal dispensation from the oath he had made in 1258. In the spring of 1261 he brought mercenary troops into the country and installed his court once more in the Tower. He obliged all London citizens over the age of twelve to swear fealty to him and summoned the barons to a parliament (as we have seen they refused to come). Those magnates he could trust were commanded to present themselves with their feudal levies. Bigod was dismissed and the London fortress was entrusted to John Mansel. From his new-found security Henry made a clean sweep of all the major offices of state, removing his opponents. Throughout this time of tension there was at least one happy event within the Tower: the young Alexander III of Scotland brought his wife there to visit her father and it was during their stay that she gave birth to their first child, Margaret, later to become Queen of Norway.

Months of fruitless negotiations between parties who did not trust each other ended in the summer of 1263. Henry demanded that the barons should recognize Prince Edward as his heir. Simon's supporters made their agreement dependent on certain guarantees which the King refused to give. He shut himself in the Tower and defied his enemies. But he had chosen his time badly: Edward and the royal army were fighting in Wales, while Simon could count on considerable support from the barons and from London. No army moved against the Tower but the King was, for all practical purposes, besieged there. That became quite clear when he sent his Queen to carry a request for aid to Edward. Eleanor left by water with the intention of heading for Windsor. She got no further than London Bridge. A hostile mob gathered there and pelted the royal barge with stones, mud and bad eggs. So furious was the fusillade that the frightened Queen had to turn back. Henry was forced to agree to a truce, the foremost article of which was that he should surrender the Tower to Hugh le Despenser, the Justiciar.

Simon de Montfort and his allies now controlled the capital but there was a royal faction within the City which nearly brought about the Earl's downfall within months. As soon as Henry could do so he resumed the armed struggle and, in October, he intrigued with friends in London to seize Simon as he lay at Southwark. News of the plot leaked out, however, and the Mayor sent an armed force hurrying across London Bridge to warn the Earl and bring him to safety. The King's friends soon found themselves in the Tower. Simon imposed a heavy fine upon them and used the money to strengthen the City's defences. London now was committed to the side of the rebels. Its gates were firmly closed to the King in December and when Despenser set out to sack the manor of Isleworth, belonging to one of Henry's allies, it was at the head of a combined army of soldiers and citizens.

The Justiciar and Earl Simon may have been gratified to have such an enthusiastic force at their disposal but they were soon to learn the folly of relying upon an ill-disciplined mob. The following spring, while the royal and baronial armies were fighting elsewhere, the citizens took matters into their own hands. What sparked off the holocaust we do not know, but the angry Londoners went on a rampage of murder and looting, largely at the expense of the Jews. They presented Despenser with a list of demands which he had no power whatsoever to grant. To appease them he yielded up the royal treasure lodged within the Tower. It was an expensive way of securing the support of the capital. Yet it is doubtful whether the Justiciar could have taken any other course of action. Henry was acutely inconvenienced by the loss of the City and the Tower. It was a vital factor in his downfall in May at the battle of Lewes where the royal army was routed and the King surrendered to his adversaries.

For fifteen months Simon de Montfort was virtually the ruler of England. He carried out business in the King's name and took Henry with him in his entourage wherever he went. But, significantly, when the court was in London it did not lodge at the Tower. The King was accommodated at Westminster or St Paul's. It was during these months that Simon de Montfort summoned one of the most important assemblies in the history of the English parliament: for the first time two representatives from each free borough were called upon to meet with knights, barons and princes of the church. It was not democracy but it was an important step in that direction.

Unfortunately for this constitutional experiment, Simon de Montfort's faction began to fragment almost as soon as it had achieved its objectives. On 4 August 1265 both the Earl and Hugh le Despenser fell at the battle of Evesham, fighting desperately against an overwhelming royal army. Henry III had won back his kingdom – and his Tower. The rebellious subjects were made to pay for their disloyalty; some of the London leaders made the short journey to the royal dungeons and the whole City was fined in the sum of twenty thousand marks.

A show of magnanimity in his hour of triumph would have won Henry the grudging support if not the love of his people, but he had neither the largeness of spirit nor the political acumen necessary for such a gesture. Not content with punishing the bodies and grasping the wealth of his enemies, he attacked their immortal souls also. Henry had always maintained good relations with the Pope. Now he obtained the services of the papal legate, Cardinal Ottobuono, to pronounce excommunication against those who still resisted their sovereign and to impose spiritual sanctions on rebel bishops and clergy. Moreover, he gave Ottobuono custody of the Tower. The result was inevitable: within months the dispersed forces of discontent were gathering again. Soon they had found a successor to Simon de Montfort in the person of Gilbert de Clare, Earl of Gloucester. 'Gilbert the Red', as he was popularly known, lacked the idealism of the hero of Lewes but he was a suitably martial figure to attract a following. At the beginning of April 1267 he returned swiftly from a Welsh border campaign, entered the capital where he was welcomed enthusiastically, and laid siege to the Tower, proclaiming, with some justification, that the custody of the castle 'was not a post to be trusted in the hands of a foreigner, much less of an ecclesiastic'. Ottobuono conducted a spirited defence with considerable help from the Jews who once again sought refuge there and the Earl discovered that Henry's enlarged fortress was too strong to be taken with siege engines and a sizeable army.

Meanwhile the King rushed back to London from East Anglia at the head of his troops. The City refused to yield but Henry did succeed in rescuing the Cardinal, by water, before withdrawing and pitching camp at West Ham. Shortly afterwards a fleet of royal ships from Gascony anchored in the Thames opposite the Tower. It was obvious that there would have to be a truce and negotiations soon began. Understandably, the Londoners were very anxious about what would happen when their City was once again surrendered to the King. To his credit, Earl Gilbert refused to yield until royal promises and guarantees on this score had been given.

Peace descended on London and its fortress for the few remaining years of the reign. The benevolent Walter Gifford, Archbishop of York, was Constable and it was he who took over the leadership of the government at the death of Henry III in 1272 until Edward I returned from the crusades.

Throughout the troubled reign of Henry the Builder, the Tower of London had played a prominent part in national history, as we have seen. It also continued to fulfil its less dramatic function as a state prison. One of the important 'guests' detained there wrote a unique and unfortunate page in the history of the Tower. This was Gruffydd ap Llewelyn, a tall, heavily-built, truculent Celt. He was by all accounts not a very estimable man. He rose against his own father, Llewelyn the Great, a man who had done more than any of his predecessors to create an extensive and autonomous kingdom. The conflict continued into the reign of Llewelyn's heir, Davydd, and eventually Henry III was obliged to intervene personally in the family feud. Davydd persuaded the English King that Wales would know no peace until his troublesome half-brother were secured under lock and key in some place far from the border. Henry knew just such a place.

Gruffydd was installed in the state apartments of the White Tower in September 1241. His was an honourable confinement. He enjoyed the company of his son, Owain, and a number of his friends and supporters. He received visits from his wife, and the government allotted half a mark a day for his food. But prison is prison and exile is exile and both were galling to the ardent and ambitious Nationalist. For two years and five months Gruffydd endured his confinement, daily hoping to hear that a change in the political situation demanded his return to Wales. No such message came and at last the Prince could stand the inactivity no longer. On the night of 1 March 1244, he made a rope by knotting together all the sheets, bed coverings and hangings he could find. Probably he had heard of Rannulf Flambard's daring escape and believed that he could emulate it. Unlike the Bishop, he did not lower himself from a window; he took his improvised cable to the roof of the White Tower, fastened one end to the parapet and began his descent. Scarcely had he started when the rope gave way and the luckless Welshman plummeted about ninety feet to his death. According to a contemporary chronicler 'His head and neck were crushed between his shoulders, a most horrid spectacle.' Gruffydd's mutilated remains were interred in the Tower graveyard until, in 1248, permission was granted for them to be moved to Aberconway Abbey. So, at last, the patriot returned home, but the Tower had not seen the last of Gruffydd's clan. His three sons, Llewelyn, Owain and Davydd, eventually shared the rule of Wales between them and, inevitably, were soon fighting for absolute power. Their squabbles, just as inevitably, involved the King of England, Edward I. In 1282 and 1283 respectively Llewelyn and Davydd returned to the Tower. Or rather, their heads returned, to be set on poles so that the world could see the just end of traitors.

In Henry III's reign certain important changes were made in the central administration which were to affect the whole later development of the Tower. The government of the Norman and Angevin monarchs was 'household government'. That is to say that the King administered his court, his demesne lands and his realm through his own immediate servants, the household officers. Thus, men such as the Chancellor, Chamberlain and Keeper of the Wardrobe, as well as their obvious day-to-day responsibilities at court, had far wider fields of care and concern. As government became more complex the household 'departments' grew in size and number, each requiring a large staff of clerks and minor officials. For generation after generation the ever-growing entourage moved with the King and it became an increasing problem to find quarters for all the household personnel, their chests of documents and tallies, their waggonloads of supplies and other paraphernalia. From an early date the custom

28

developed of establishing depots of articles which were not immediately required. For example the royal treasure was frequently lodged in the strong room of some great monastic house (commonly Winchester, Westminster or the London Temple). The next step was for departments or sub-departments to establish headquarters where they could keep their records and be available to suitors. The ultimate development was the establishment of state departments and offices in and around Westminster but that was still centuries in the future when Henry III was King of England.

It was probably early in his reign that the royal regalia and some, at least, of the royal treasure began to be stored in the Tower. In 1230, on returning from a visit to France, Henry gave orders to his Treasurer, Walter Mauclerc, to replace his jewels in the Tower of London as they had been before. The royal regalia consisted not only of the crown, sceptre, sword and other symbols of authority, but also personal jewellery and plate which had been obtained by Henry and his predecessors as gifts from subjects and other monarchs, as spoils of war, or which had been purchased from craftsmen. It constituted a considerable part of the King's only portable wealth and it was useful as a means of raising cash. Henry later pawned his jewels to Flemish merchants and he was neither the first nor the last monarch to use them in this way. The royal treasure was particularly important to a king striving to maintain his independence from powerful barons and it is not surprising that we find Henry III making elaborate plans for the security of his gold, silver and jewels. In 1239 he had some of his treasure secretly conveyed to the Tower from its official depository and a few years later he sent the royal regalia to France for safe keeping. However, from this time the Tower of London established itself as the normal storehouse for the personal riches of the sovereign. A special building was provided and a trusted keeper was appointed to have charge of it. This extremely responsible position was well rewarded. In the time of Edward III 12d. per day was paid to the 'keeper of the jewels, armouries and other things'. Gradually this officer took on other functions. By the sixteenth century the Master and Treasurer of the Jewel House was responsible for the care of the regalia, the purchase and custody of gold and silver plate, the appointment of royal goldsmiths and jewellers and the allocation of plate to English ambassadors. He always moved with the court and had to be sure that such precious items as were required were to hand. Everything else was safely stored in the Jewel House at the Tower, except the coronation regalia which was kept at Westminster.

By the thirteenth century the Wardrobe had already developed from what the name suggests – the place where the garments and accoutrements of the King and all his servants were kept – into the main financial department of the household. When the Exchequer became separated from the court and largely concerned with state finance, the King found the Wardrobe organization the most direct and efficient channel through which to organize the equipping of his household and, more important, of his armies. The waging of war was the King's prerogative and it entailed large supplies of armour, bows, swords, bills, glaives, lances and later cannon, powder and shot. Early in Henry III's reign if not before, this unwieldy department had split: the Great Wardrobe had hived off from the Wardrobe. The Great Wardrobe was so called because it handled the larger, bulkier objects. It established its headquarters in the Tower (in the Wardrobe Tower, of course) and was joined there a century later by yet another offshoot, the Privy Wardrobe, concerned more specifically with the day-to-day requirements of the court. In the later medieval period the Wardrobe accommodation in the Tower was considerably extended and its activities included not only the storage but also the manufacture of arms and armour. Even so, the Tower was not the only repository of the Wardrobe: other storehouses in royal manors and in London were also used.

When, in 1253, Henry renewed the City's charter, he did so on certain conditions. One was that every incoming mayor should be presented to him for his approval. If he was not immediately available, the new official was to be brought into the Tower and there examined by the Barons of the Exchequer. By this time the Exchequer had emerged as a department with a twofold function: it dealt with all payments to and disbursements from the crown arising from extra-household activities, and it was a judicial court for hearing pleas of a financial nature. It had not yet acquired a permanent home but it was too cumbersome to move everywhere with the household. It was usually based at Westminster but it could be moved if the King wished. For instance, during Edward I's Scottish wars it was sited at York for several years. It was probably its connection with Jewish pleas that gave its officers a close connection with the Tower. As we have seen judicial cases concerning the London Jews were supervised by the Constable though, of course, adjudicated by the King's justices. Most of these cases involved finance and were of concern to the Exchequer. The Barons of the Exchequer came to hear pleas often in the Tower, as, indeed, did the officials of other royal courts until Westminster became firmly established as the home of the law courts. Even then the Exchequer did not completely sever its connections with the castle: the subsidiary office of the Rolls, where classified records of all writs issued were stored, was established there.

Edward I spent very little time in his capital. He travelled constantly, making royal government a reality in the remoter corners of the realm and subduing the Scots and Welsh. Yet it was Edward I who was responsible for the last and most extensive major construction programme at the Tower. 'Longshanks', the perfect image of chivalry, was the most accomplished patron of castle-building ever to occupy the English throne and arguably the greatest royal expert on defence works in medieval Europe. In the Levant he had seen magnificently designed crusader castles such as the Krak des Chevaliers and he had experienced the devastating effects of siege engines and mining techniques. He was determined that the important fortifications of his realm should be as secure as possible.

The new style, exemplified by such splendid castles as Caernarvon, Conway, Beaumaris and Caerphilly (the latter built during Henry III's reign) relied not on a massive central keep but on concentric circles of walls providing successive lines of defence which ensured that the whole complex of buildings within was uniformly free from attack. Edward's massive remodelling of the Tower was carried out between 1275 and 1285 at an enormous cost of £21,000. First of all a new moat was dug beyond Henry III's, the work being supervised by another Flemish expert, Master Walter. The old moat was filled in and became, in effect, an outer ward between the old wall and the new wall which Edward now constructed. Just what this further encroachment meant for some of the Tower's neighbours is illustrated by the following extract from the close rolls:

> As it is intimated to the King on the part of the Abbot of Lilleshall that a part of his land in the parish of St Olave, near the Tower, has been occupied from the time when the King caused the ditch of the Tower to be made until now by earth raised from the ditch and thrown up upon the said land, and it is now as it is said, cleared thereof; the King orders the Constable to permit the Abbot to enter his said land when it has been cleared of the King's earth and hold it as he held it before the occupation aforesaid.[2]

The most formidable aspects of this most formidable fortress were the entrances. A new watergate was constructed with a massive tower, St Thomas's, which formed part of the royal accommodation and was connected by a bridge with the Wakefield Tower and the palace complex. The landward approach was now guarded by two gatehouses and the Lion Tower Barbican, connected by three bridges spanning the moat. Henry III's western wall was now completely rebuilt and the old land gate was replaced by the Beauchamp Tower. In order to render the garrison as self-sufficient as possible, the King set up two watermills, one at the south-east and the other at the south-west corner of the moat. By the time the work was finished William the Conqueror's Tower had been standing for almost exactly two hundred years. Since then the general layout has remained unchanged. Let us, therefore, try

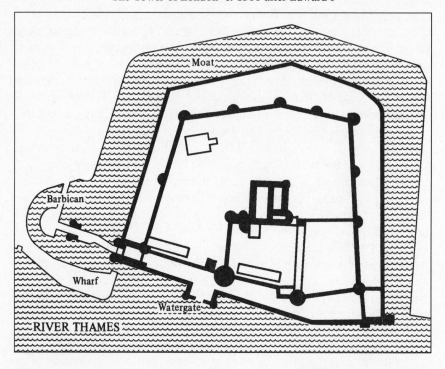

to picture the appearance of the Tower of London and its environs as they must have been in the time of Edward Longshanks.

The first Normans cleared a large area of Tower Hill and the riverside in order to surround the keep with an open space providing no cover for potential attackers. By 1300 the fortress itself had 'spread' and now covered some eighteen acres. To the south it was washed by the river. Westwards towards the City, wharfs, shops and houses had straggled to within a few yards of the Tower's outer gate. On all other sides were wide expanses of grass intersected by rutted tracks. The City wall and ditch divided Tower Hill proper from the area known as Little Tower Hill or East Smithfield. The wall ended at the postern gate immediately opposite the northernmost point of the Tower defences. Most of the encroachment on this greensward had been at the hands of religious foundations. The church of All Hallows Barking-by-the-Tower was of ancient origins. North of it, the conventual buildings and gardens of the Crutched Friars fringed Tower Hill. Beyond the City wall lay the house of the nuns of the Poor Clares. They were also called Minoresses and their name still survives in the street known as the Minories. Another reminder of an old religious building is St Katharine's Dock. This takes its name from St Katharine's Hospital founded on the river bank by King

Stephen's Queen. These were the only major buildings near the Tower, and guards patrolling the walls seven hundred years ago must have enjoyed a pleasant and open aspect across the uncluttered hillside, the monastic orchards and vineyards (still commemorated in the name of Vine Street), and cloisters, the roofs and steeples of London.

Yet, apparently, the air was not as wholesome as the view; pollution is not a legacy of the industrial revolution. In 1307 King Edward ordered all production at the City's brick kilns to cease:

> so long as Queen Margaret shall stay at the Tower, whereby the air may be in any way infected or corrupted as the Queen is going to the Tower shortly to stay there for some time and the King wishes to avoid the danger that may arise to her and other magnates who are coming to be there from the infection and corruption of the air by such burning of kilns.[3]

A visitor approaching the Tower for the first time would quickly discover just how formidably secure its successive walls and gateways were. If he came along Tower Street and past All Hallows Church he would be confronted by the Lion Gate which gave access to the bridge crossing the moat. The first section of this was a drawbridge which was raised every night. Safely across the drawbridge, the visitor would pass the Barbican to the accompaniment of the roars and screeches of the King's beasts caged within. The Middle Tower with its double portcullis rose out of the centre of the moat. On across the bridge, the visitor now came to the Byward Tower, another massive bulwark equipped with a portcullis. Having negotiated these three portals, the newcomer found himself in the Outer Ward, the area between the two walls of the Tower. This is probably as far as he would get, for the Inner Ward was reserved for prisoners, guests, courtiers and those on royal business. The Outer Ward housed stables, storehouses and quarters for soldiers, guards, servants and the less important members of the Tower staff.

The only entrance to the Inner Ward was through the archway of the Bloody Tower which could be instantly blocked by lowering the portcullis. Even if he was admitted by the guard to the Inner Ward our visitor still had not obtained access to the royal sanctum at the heart of the Tower. The Great Hall and Royal Lodgings lay within an enclosed courtyard flanked by the White Tower, the Wakefield Tower and the Lanthorn Tower. These buildings were now more frequently used by the court than the original state apartments in the keep.

The only major change within the walls during Edward's reign was the rebuilding of St Peter ad Vincula. Despite the care lavished on it by the King's father, the chapel seems to have been in a poor state of repair. Towards the end of his reign Edward ordered it to be demolished and a new church built in the prevailing, Decorated, style. It cost forty-six shillings to clear the site and another forty shillings to dig the new foundations. These charges were initially borne by the Constable, Ralph de Sandwich, who was reimbursed by royal warrant on 11 July 1306 – nineteen years after the building's completion!

Most of the towers in Henry III's ballium wall, as well as providing guard posts and vantage points, contained extra accommodation for prisoners. Some, however, had special functions. The Lanthorn Tower, as its name indicates, was surmounted by a round turret in which a light was kept burning at night for the benefit of boats approaching the Tower after dark. The wooden belfry atop the Bell Tower was the centre of the castle's alarm system. The guard positioned on its battlements had an excellent view of the landward approach of the wharf and was thus well placed to give warning of impending danger. The bell was also rung at dusk as a signal that such prisoners and their servants as were allowed limited freedom of movement within the Tower were to be locked in for the night. The Beauchamp Tower was probably used originally as a mess by officers of the garrison. The Bowyer Tower was the dwelling and workshop of the royal bow-maker. Here were manufactured not only hand weapons such as longbows and, later, crossbows, but also siege engines and catapults.

Edward's Tower certainly had the appearance of impregnability but the security of any fortress is only as trustworthy as the men who keep it. Over the centuries many enemies of the crown were to break into and out of the Tower of London. Usually their success was the result of inefficiency or collusion on the part of members of the garrison. As early as 1312 a gang of desperate prisoners overpowered their guards, ran the gauntlet of the elaborate series of towers, drawbridges and portcullises, and escaped into the City. Only when the soldiers rang the bells of All Hallows to raise the hue and cry were the prisoners apprehended with the aid of the citizens. Despite popular legend London's Tower was no Bastille or Château d'If.

Yet it was grim enough for the procession of prisoners who continued to be incarcerated there. In 1278 some six hundred Jews were herded into the Tower's cells on the mass charge of clipping coin. The excuse for this harassment of the Jewish community was the need for a major reform of the currency. But the deliberate reversal of his father's policy was based on Edward's desire to win popularity, a desire he could afford to indulge because, having established relations with Italian bankers, he no longer needed the Jews. The persecution began in 1276 with severe restrictions being placed on their financial activities and culminated in 1290 with the expulsion from England of all Jews who refused Christian baptism. One judge, Henry de Bray, stood up to his master and made a plea for the Jewish community. This immediately roused Edward's fiery temper. He ordered de Bray to be taken to join his 'friends' in the Tower. The King's wrath so distressed de Bray that he broke away from his escort on the way there and tried to drown himself. Thwarted in this attempt, he later committed suicide in his cell.

That was a measure of the dread Edward I inspired in his subjects and particularly in his chief officials. It explains how he was able to restore order swiftly after his father's disastrous reign and how he maintained the stability of his government despite his almost perpetual absence on campaign. In 1289 he held a sudden enquiry into the activities of his law courts. As a result, six of the eight senior justices of King's Bench and Common Pleas found themselves fined, imprisoned or driven into exile. In 1303 Richard Podelicote devised a scheme to steal that part of the royal treasure still housed in Westminster Abbey. He drew into his plan William le Palmere, Custodian of Westminster Palace, and several of the monks. The crime went without a hitch and the culprits, knowing that Edward was away in Scotland, doubtless thought themselves safe. They reckoned without the galvanic effect of the King's anger. Messengers were soon speeding southwards with orders as drastic as they were simple: the Abbot of Westminster and all his monks were to be locked in the Tower. It is not surprising to learn that these tactics were completely successful in bringing the real culprits to book. Even so the Abbot and his brethren remained in prison for almost two years.

Of much shorter duration was the stay of the great Scottish patriot, William Wallace. For eight years Wallace headed the independence movement, a charismatic figure gathering high and low to his standard, defeating Edward's generals and dispossessing his castellans. He was the only man who stood between the English King and final victory north of the border. To the end he remained undefeated. Unable to conquer his foe, Longshanks had to buy him. In August 1305 Wallace was delivered up by treachery. He was despatched immediately to London and put on public trial in Westminster Hall. Standing on a raised platform with a mock-crown of laurel on his head he watched the travesty of a trial and heard the inevitable verdict. The sentence was familiar in its savagery:

You shall be carried from Westminster to the Tower, and from the Tower to Aldgate, and so through the City to the Elms at Smithfield, and for your robberies, homicides and felonies . . . you shall be there hanged and drawn, and as an outlaw beheaded, and afterwards for your burning churches and relics your heart, liver, lungs and entrails from which your wicked thoughts came shall be burned, and finally, because your sedition, depredations, fires, and homicides were not only against the King, but against the people of England and Scotland, your head shall be placed on London Bridge in sight both of land and water travellers, and your quarters hung on gibbets at Newcastle, Berwick, Stirling, and Perth, to the terror of all who pass by.

Many Scottish prisoners made the long journey from blood-stained battlefield to Tower cell during the reign of Edward, the Hammer of the Scots. The weak King John Balliol was honourably lodged there with his son from 1297 to 1299. Sir William Douglas, sire of a bloody and valiant clan, died there, a broken penitent. Sir Simon Fraser, Sir Christopher Seton and the Earl of Athol donated their heads for the decoration of the White Tower's turrets. Perhaps these defeated knights and nobles had the last laugh: King Edward died on the Solway shore, his conquest of Scotland incomplete and destined to remain so.

One more development must be mentioned before we leave the thirteenth century: the establishment of the Royal Mint at the Tower of London. This probably occurred shortly after Edward I had completed the new outer wall, for the Mint was established in the western section of the Outer Ward in the area which has ever since been known as Mint Street. Before that the London coiners occupied premises in Sermon (a corruption of Sheremonier) Lane near St Paul's. The London Mint was only one of several. In 1300 others were situated at Canterbury, Kingston-on-Hull, Newcastle-upon-Tyne, Bristol, Exeter and Dublin. They were not government offices but operated under licence from the crown and were very strictly supervised by the Master of the Money and the Warden of the King's Exchanges. Out of every 10 lbs of coins made one penny or four farthings had to be placed in a box or pyx. Four times a year this had to be taken to the Barons of the Exchequer before whom the coins were tried by the King's Assayer. Probably the Tower Mint was established in time for the new coinage which was first produced in 1280. The London Mint was one of the four which were allowed to make the new silver pennies, farthings, groats and (later) halfpennies. Certainly it was about this time that the inhabitants of the Tower heard for the first time the roar of the furnaces and the hammering of the moneyers which were to become so familiar. All the staff of the Mint considered themselves members of the Tower community, 'belonging to and under the protection of the Constable of the Tower, with sufferance of burial and other ancient church rites', for which the Master paid 13s.4d. annually to the parson of St Peter's and 4d. to the sexton.

3

The first state prisoner to be sent to the Tower by Edward II was Walter Langton, Bishop of Lichfield, the old King's Treasurer, principal adviser and confidant. Once again the hereditary principle had played England false. Longshank's son was a frivolous, emotionally unstable, wilful boy, with little interest in government or war and constantly under the influence of unworthy favourites. His twenty-year reign (1307-1327) was marked by a return to the conflict between crown and barons, the disaster of Bannockburn and the final overthrow of the King by his own Queen and her lover. Edward II was deposed in January 1327 and murdered eight months later at Berkeley Castle.

It seems to have been a misfortune of the medieval Tower to be associated particularly closely with bad or weak kings. Like his grandfather, Edward II relied heavily on the strength and security of his London fortress. He often sheltered there with his family and favourites such as the hated Piers Gaveston. His eldest daughter was, in fact, born there and was always known as 'Joanna of the Tower'.

But that was later in the reign. Edward had hardly accustomed himself to his new regality when he was involved in one of the nastiest pieces of ruthless, cynical manoeuvring ever to stain our political history. To do the King justice, he was neither its instigator nor its enthusiastic supporter. He could, however, have refused to become involved in a series of events which shocked and horrified most Englishmen and many of his advisers, including the Constable of the Tower. In fact the story of the annihilation of the Order of Knights Templars is interesting for the light it throws on the personnel of the Tower and their treatment of prisoners.

The Poor Knights of Christ and of the Temple of Solomon was an order of Christian chivalry founded in 1119 to protect pilgrims travelling to the Holy Land. As the fortunes of the crusaders rose and fell the functions of the Templars changed. By the middle of the thirteenth century they constituted an influential independent force in the secular and religious political life of Europe. More important still, they had grown immensely wealthy on the donations of the pious and on treasure captured from the infidel. They were the principal bankers of Christendom and many sovereigns were in their debt.

One of them was Philip IV of France. Philip was in the midst of terrifying difficulties, not all of them financial, and was forced to contemplate desperate remedies. The cancellation of his debt to the Templars and the confiscation of their French possessions would transform his circumstances. In 1305 the anarchic situation at Rome gave Philip his opportunity. He engineered the election of a Frenchman as Pope Clement V. Clement removed his residence to Avignon where he was completely under the control of King Philip. It was now comparatively easy to enforce an ecclesiastical enquiry into the activities of the knights by laying against them absurdly false charges of heresy, idolatry and sodomy. The full force of the Inquisition was unleashed against members of the Order in France. They were imprisoned, examined, tortured and subjected to every indignity to make them confess their 'crimes'. And, of course, some of them did confess. The Pope now extended the purge to the rest of the community. In October 1307 he wrote to Edward II requesting him to follow the Christian example of his brother monarch in rooting out these weeds from the Lord's vineyard *and confiscating their property*.

Edward did not rise to the bait. He knew William de la More, the Grand Preceptor of the Order in England, to be a devout Christian knight against whom there had never been any suggestion of heresy. He resisted repeated entreaties by the Pope and would do no more than place restrictions on the movements of the Templars. In September 1309 Inquisitors arrived in England bearing fresh orders from Avignon. Now the King submitted. De la More and his brethren were arrested. Some were imprisoned in Lincoln and some in York, but the Grand Preceptor and many other knights were lodged in the Tower of London. The examinations began. Not surprisingly, none of the Templars would admit to being immoral apostates. As a matter of course, the Inquisitors ordered the Lieutenant to apply torture to the prisoners so as to extract the required confessions. He refused.

Magna Carta had established that 'No freeman shall be taken or imprisoned, or disseised, or outlawed or exiled, *or in any way destroyed*, nor will we go upon him, nor will we send upon him, except by the lawful judgment of his peers or by the law of the land.' Later jurists were to affirm that the words I have italicized comprehended torture, which was never sanctioned by common law. Never sanctioned, that is, if we understand by torture the deliberate infliction of pain upon unconvicted prisoners in order to punish or to extract a confession or to obtain information. The freedom from torture, thus defined, was a right of which Englishmen were very jealous. That fact is more remarkable than it might at first sight appear for this was a brutal age in which men were not squeamish. Torture was widely used on the Continent and in England the actual punishment of convicted criminals was both cruel and public. Men and women took a sadistic pleasure in seeing offenders disembowelled, having their ears or hands cut off, branded with hot irons, or burned at the stake. They took part in the ducking of scolds, the floating of witches and the pelting of prisoners in the stocks. But secret torture was something which they resisted. It is, of course, impossible for us to draw the line between torture and deliberately unpleasant prison conditions. The medieval mind took little account of the physical and psychological effects of damp, noisome dungeons, irregular and inadequate meals, chaining with heavy fetters and solitary confinement.

Having said that, it must be confessed that men, and occasionally women, were tortured in castles and gaols throughout the land. Personal vendettas, over-zealous castellans, truculent prisoners, a severe crisis – there were many factors which might lead to the strictly illegal application of torture. In royal castles torture was, officially, only inflicted on warrant from the King or one of his officers. Such warrants were issued rarely. Certainly the Tower never housed a 'torture chamber' of the type beloved by writers of historical romance – a deep dungeon replete with every kind of fearful contrivance the twisted minds of professional sadists could invent, where blood ran freely and the cries of the tormented never penetrated the slimy walls. In later ages the rack was kept in the basement of the White Tower. Most other instruments of torture (of which there was never a great variety) were portable and were applied in the victims' own cells. Kings and ministers were also socially selective in their ordering of torture. The exemptions of Magna Carta had applied only to 'freemen'. At that time most Englishmen were very unfree, for villains had few rights and might receive every kind of cruelty at the hands of their overlords. Yet even when the decline of the feudal system blurred social distinctions there remained strict limits to the type of punishments that might be inflicted on different classes of prisoner. The torturing of anyone above the rank of yeoman was unthinkable and very rarely carried out.

It is, therefore, not difficult to appreciate why the Lieutenant and his men were reluctant to comply with the Inquisitors' wishes. The Tower guards had respect both for the law and for their devout prisoners. The Templars were as comfortably housed and as well fed as was possible and the Lieutenant hoped that this grotesque affair would soon come to an end so that he could release de la More and his men.

But Edward was beginning to weaken. The fear of papal sanctions and the lure of the Templars' treasure were having their effect. He ordered the Constable and his staff to co-operate with the Inquisitors. Their compliance with this order can only have been half-hearted, for by June 1310 the Inquisitors still had not obtained the evidence they wanted. They complained that their examinations were doomed to failure unless the prisoners were released from the control of the King's officers. Edward sent fresh orders to the Constable. The conditions of the knights' imprisonment were to be tightened: they were to be kept in solitary confinement, manacled and allowed only bread and water every alternate day. Whenever he was required to do so, the Lieutenant was to yield them up to the ecclesiastical authorities who would take them to various places in London where they could carry out their examinations in secret.

Under these conditions the Templars' ordeal began again in September. Every morning the members of the Order, young and old, were marched out of the Tower and taken in batches to the City prisons at Newgate, Aldgate, Cripplegate and Ludgate. Every evening they stumbled back, limbs aching and faces distorted with pain through streets lined with Londoners calling out encouragement and shrieking curses at their guards. Strengthened by their innocence and encouraged by this moral support the captives remained obdurate to the fury of their frustrated examiners. Once again Clement was obliged to write to the King complaining that the Inquisitors were encountering severe obstruction in their work, to 'the great injury of the Christian faith, the contempt of the Holy See, and the scandal of many'.

The sordid business entered its fifth year with the Inquisitors using every method inspired by fanaticism and sanctioned by totalitarian authority. Not until June 1311 did they succeed in breaking one of the knights, a young recent recruit to the Order who was terrified into confessing that the Templars denied the divinity of Christ and conducted secret invocations of evil spirits. By the end of the summer, long imprisonment and sporadic torture had induced three Templars out of the several hundred-strong community to admit to doctrinal error and immorality. The steadfastness of the vast majority is a remarkable example of constancy. The opposition of ordinary Englishmen and, in particular, of the Tower staff to the aims and methods of the Inquisition is commendable.

The ecclesiastical authorities had no stomach for the arduous continuation of persecution within a hostile environment. The meagre testimony they had obtained was technically sufficient to justify Pope Clement's condemnation of the entire Order. The English properties of the Knights Templars were confiscated by the crown; the community was disbanded and its surviving members were sent in batches to fourteen English monasteries, there to perform penance. Not so William de la More. He refused to accept absolution and penance for sins he had not committed. Edward was, thus, obliged to keep the old man in the Tower while his case went laboriously through the church courts. But King and Pope were not to be troubled much longer with the stubborn Preceptor; worn out by his sufferings, William de la More died in the Tower in 1312. The conditions of his confinement are not known but they were probably similar to those of a fellow prisoner, Himbert Blanke, Preceptor of the Auvergne Temple who was arrested in England and incarcerated with de la More. The ecclesiastical judges informed King Edward that they had not yet reached a conclusion in Blanke's case. Pending the outcome of their deliberations he is to be 'bound with double fetters of iron and shut up in the vilest dungeon, where he is to remain until further orders, and meanwhile to be visited to see whether he will confess anything more'.[1]

During the years of the Templars' downfall the King's situation had deteriorated rapidly. His closest friend, Gaveston, had been murdered and the crown had been reduced to little more than a cipher by a group of nobles calling themselves the 'Lord's Ordainers' who had taken over all effective executive power. In 1312 Edward broke out of this constitutional straight-jacket. He took the field against his enemies and further strengthened some of his castles including the Tower. Much to the annoyance of the citizens he built a new rampart beyond the Lion Gate. The new wall was both an eyesore and an affront. Possibly it also encroached on the City's land. What is certain is that the structure was so offensive that, on a summer's night in 1315, several of the leading citizens took matters into their own hands. It was a desperate act and they could not expect to escape detection:

> Whereas an earthen wall of the King's opposite the outer gate of the Tower of London was lately thrown down in the night by malefactors of the City of London with a body of armed men on horseback and on foot, by reason whereof the King conceived wrath and indignation against the community of the City, Sir John Gisors, Mayor, Nicholas Farindon, John de Wengrave, Robert de Kellseye and other aldermen and citizens came to the King in his chamber of Westminster before him and his Council and humbly besought on their knees his grace and goodwill. And the King, having deliberated with his Council for a short time restored the Mayor, aldermen, citizens and community to their former state and remitted his indignation against them of his special grace, and for 600 marks, which they promised to pay him at the Exchequer, provided that they cause the wall to be re-erected at their cost with all speed and that they punish the malefactors of the City so that they shall not hereafter forfeit to the King; otherwise this remission shall be annulled and they shall be punished for the said trespass . . .[2]

Another person who affronted the royal dignity did not escape with a fine and warning. This was the high-spirited Lady Baddlesmere who has the dubious distinction of being the first woman recorded to be thrown into the Tower as a prisoner. In 1322 she was temporarily in charge of Leeds Castle, Kent, during the absence of her husband. One evening the Queen approached, on her way from the martyr's shrine at Canterbury, and sent servants ahead to demand a night's lodging. Lord Baddlesmere was one of the leading opponents of the crown, and his wife not only firmly closed the castle gates, she also ordered the royal messengers to be killed. Such defiance could not go unpunished. Edward personally led the siege of Leeds Castle. He had its governor hanged and Lady Baddlesmere lodged in the Tower.

The next name of note in the annals of the royal fortress is that of Roger Mortimer, Earl of March. He was one of the lords of the Welsh border who became involved in rebellion against the King in 1321. In one of his rare bursts of martial enterprise, Edward took the field against them, and was victorious. By January 1322 Mortimer was a captive in the Tower. He was sentenced to death but this was later commuted to life imprisonment – a fateful decision for Edward and England. For two years the Earl remained in quarters, described tartly by the contemporary chronicler as 'less elegant than were seemly', but he had powerful friends, foremost among whom was the Bishop of Hereford, and these planned an elaborate escape. First they won over Gerard de Alspaye, the Sub-Lieutenant. Then they fixed upon the evening of Lammas Day (1 August) for their attempt. This was the day on which the garrison celebrated the feast of St Peter ad Vincula and the conspirators could be certain that all the soldiers would drink heavily. Gerard made sure that their ale or wine was drugged. He could not, however, let the prisoner out of his cell without incriminating himself. Instead he let Mortimer's friends *in* armed with picks and crowbars. They made a hole in the cell wall and this brought them into the King's kitchen. With the aid of ropes Mortimer made his way over roofs and walls to the river where a boat was waiting. The details are scanty and our knowledge of the geography of the Tower at that time is not complete but it seems probable that Mortimer was lodged in the Lanthorn Tower and subsequently made his way over the roofs of the Wakefield and St Thomas's towers, which were connected in those days. His rope would then permit him to reach the water.

Mortimer went to the French court. There he later met Edward's Queen, Isabella, when she arrived on a visit to Charles IV. Within months Edward II was a cuckold and the lovers were planning to deprive him of his kingdom as well as his honour. In 1327 they returned to England where the Bishop of Hereford and a large number of barons joined them. One of Mortimer's first actions was to gain control of the Tower and release the prisoners. He was warmly welcomed by the people of the City who had already risen up against the Bishop of Exeter, deputed by the King to take charge of the capital. Edward was captured and deposed in favour of his young son, Edward III. Through his paramour and his cronies the Earl ruled England for three years, amassing enormous personal wealth, displaying vindictiveness to his enemies, and surrounding himself with supra-regal pomp. Mortimer's power lasted just as long as the boy King remained under his tutelage and no longer. On 19 October 1330 the universally-detested Earl was captured at Nottingham by Edward III and his accomplices. By 27 October Mortimer was back in the Tower. This time there was no escape. He did not attend his own trial, did not hear the condemnation and sentence. He only made one more journey – the familiar route to the Elms.

For most people in medieval England life went on monotonously from year to year, season to season, largely unaffected by what happened in the high councils of the realm. Yet in a very real sense the personality of the man on the throne imparted a flavour to the age. The flavour certainly changed drastically when Edward III took power into his own hands.

> Generous, impulsive, profuse in display, a laggard neither in love nor war, with a boyish charm which won the hearts of warriors and fair women, Edward III was the beau-ideal of chivalry and of the elaborate code of knightly conduct and manners known as courtesy that had grown up in the French-speaking courts of western Christendom. A few months before he and his companions made their coup against Mortimer they had taken part together in a three days' tournament in Cheapside at which, dressed as Tartars and each leading a lady robed in ruby velvet by a silver chain, they had ridden to the lists through the London streets to the sound of trumpets, challenging all comers. In an age when for the great mass of men life was harsh and bleak, and even for the favoured few, perilous and uncertain, princes and great lords who could afford such costly pageantry loved to re-enact in costly habiliments the legends of an imaginary past. Splendid in armour and emblazonry, Edward seemed to the young English nobles the very reincarnation of their hero, King Arthur. It was so that he saw himself – the crowned leader of a brotherhood of Christian knights.[3]

For half a century, despite the grim interlude of the Black Death, it was a fine and proud thing to be an Englishman. Ascendancy over Scotland was restored; at Crécy and Poitiers Edward's armies proved

43

themselves to be the best in Europe; the King carved out a new empire in France; and there was a resurgence of commercial prosperity.

During those triumphant years the Tower welcomed a succession of vanquished kings, lords and knights, lodged there while delicate negotiations over their ransoms were concluded. 1346 was the *annus mirabilis*. In July Edward's army had its first major continental success at the siege of Caen. Back to the Tower went the Count of Tankerville and the Constable of France together with 300 wealthy burghers of the great Norman city, described by Froissart as 'a goodly town, and full of drapery and other merchandise, and rich burgesses, and noble ladies and damsels, and fair churches, and one of the fairest castles in all Normandy'. Later in the year David II of Scotland, son of the Bruce who had decimated the English host at Bannockburn, took advantage of Edward's preoccupation with France to cross the border at the head of an army. He was captured at the battle of Neville's Cross and conveyed southwards accompanied by many of his nobles. The procession through London had the magnitude and magnificence of a Roman triumph. The whole City turned out to savour its revenge and gaze at the prisoners. The guilds were assembled in their liveries and all the civic dignitaries had places of honour and vantage. King David was mounted on a large black charger so that he could be the more easily seen. With him were the lords of Sutherland, Carrick, Fife, Menteith, Wigton, Douglas and fifty other noblemen. They had an escort, according to a contemporary chronicle, of twenty thousand armed men and they were met at the Lion Gate by John Darcy, Constable of the Tower. King David was a prisoner in England for eleven years and was eventually ransomed for 100,000 marks. His confinement in various fortresses was honourable, though he had to pay his own expenses and for many years was deprived of the company of his wife (Joanna of the Tower, Edward III's sister). Of the other Scottish notables all were held for shorter or longer periods depending on the arrangement of ransoms, except for the Earl of Menteith who suffered the hideous death of a traitor in 1347.

When David Bruce arrived in London his brother-in-law was engaged in an eleven-month siege of Calais. Soon after, the town at last fell. The brave Governor, John de Vienne, and twelve leading citizens took their places among the congregation of notable prisoners in the Tower. Shortly afterwards they were joined by Charles, Count of Blois, claimant to the Dukedom of Brittany, who was defeated by English allies of his rival John de Montfort. The Tower had to wait another decade, however, for its most illustrious prisoner. In 1357, Edward the Black Prince won a resounding victory over the French at Poitiers, taking many captives foremost among whom was John II, King of France. The scenes of triumphant rejoicing in the streets of London which welcomed the Prince's return far excelled those which had greeted the Scottish King's arrival. The Frenchman rode a milk-white steed through cheering crowds and thoroughfares hung with tapestries. Church bells rang and the fountains spouted wine.

There was a sound financial basis for all this gaiety. The spoils of war, in the form of booty and ransom, brought unprecedented wealth into the country. The French King's ransom enriched the royal treasury by 300,000 crowns, but by no means all the money raised in this way went to the government. Any valiant knight setting out for the wars had the dream of capturing some great nobleman and re-establishing his family fortunes on a completely new basis. Charles of Blois was arrested by Sir Thomas Dagworth who subsequently became the richer by £4,900. King David II was a royal prisoner but out of the ransom collected for him by the peasants, knights and gentlemen of Scotland £500 a year went to the north-country squire who had captured him. As for the young 'nobody' who seized the person of the Constable of France, he became a medieval 'millionaire', was able to marry a princess and become Earl of Kent. Even the humble bowman came home with rich spoils and it was said that there was scarce a woman in England without some jewel, goblet or piece of fine linen brought from the chateaux and burghers' houses of France.

Yet such gilded tales conceal the often grim reality of what it meant to be a prisoner of repute forced to haggle over the size of a ransom. The story of John, Earl of Murray, is a case in point. Captured at the Scottish siege of Newcastle in 1335, the Earl was lodged successively in the castles of Nottingham, Windsor and Winchester before finally being sent to the Tower, loaded with chains. The conditions of his imprisonment deteriorated in direct proportion to the difficulty of extracting a ransom. Murray's Scottish stewards simply could not find the required sum. Nor had the captive sufficient money to keep himself in reasonable comfort: 26s.8d. per week was allowed out of the Exchequer for Murray's keep. After five years neither royal diplomacy nor Murray's plight had succeeded in calling forth the required money. At length, through the good offices of the Scottish King, he was exchanged for the Earl of Salisbury, currently a prisoner in France.

King John and other notable prisoners were not kept in the Tower all the time, for which they must have been heartily glad. Even those lodged in the better apartments found the Tower uncomfortable and cramped. Other royal fortresses, such as Windsor offered more luxury and the occasional opportunity of hunting or similar outdoor exercise. The only entertainment in the Tower was the conversation of guards and other prisoners, and walks in the Inner Ward or along the battlements. Edward granted his honoured 'guests' as much freedom as possible but when he went campaigning or when there was threat of French invasion security demanded that they be returned to the castle.

Not that the security of the Tower was all that it might always have been. Both disrepair and the slackness of the garrison caused Edward III concern. A commission appointed by the King in 1336 reported considerable decay of the fabric and in the following year Edward ordered the sheriffs of London to provide forty pounds 'to be spent about the tower of the Tower of London, which is in great need of repair'.[4] At the same time the sheriff of Kent was instructed to provide timber for the same purpose.

Dilapidation was not the only problem: the Tower was becoming overcrowded. More and more space was devoted to storage of court records and royal possessions. This was all very well under normal conditions but when a large number of prisoners – and especially noble prisoners requiring spacious quarters – were brought there it was difficult to make room for them. For instance, in order to lodge the French King in the old state apartments of the White Tower a large quantity of judicial records had to be moved out. It is one of the features of the architectural history of the Tower that the functions of the buildings within were always changing. The Wardrobe accommodation had to be extended and it was probably at this time that a long building was erected from the Wardrobe Tower to the Broad Arrow Tower to house the overflow of personal and military supplies. As for the Great Hall, it was used to make and store stone cannon balls.

The early years of the reign were anxious ones and there was a very real fear of French invasion. In 1338 the guard on the City and the Tower was increased. A siege catapult was stationed at the Postern Gate and a new stone and timber palisade was erected in Petty Wales, close by the later Bulwark Gate. A strict curfew was enforced within the Tower. On return from campaign in 1340 Edward resolved to test the new defences for himself. Arriving unannounced one November night he discovered, to his fury, that he and his handful of companions were able to deceive the guards and gain easy access to the castle. The Constable, Sir Nicholas de la Becke, and several of his officers paid dearly for their lack of diligence.

The action was typical of this decisive and imaginative King. So was the purge of most of the high offices of state which occurred the following day. Edward, far from pleased with the way the realm had been governed in his absence, summoned to the Tower the Lord Chancellor, the Lord Treasurer and other ministers and relieved them of their duties. For most of the next two years the King resided in the Tower, personally supervising the repair works, entertaining his more celebrated prisoners and planning his next military foray into Brittany. However, Edward's most important contribution to the fabric of the Tower dates from a few years later. Between 1348 and 1355 John of Leicester, a royal mason, supervised the rebuilding of the outer curtain wall east of St Thomas's Tower and the construction of the Cradle Tower as a private watergate. This was, for the time, a remarkable building. Defended by a double portcullis, it also contained a mechanism, the cradle, for raising a boat from the water to the level of the landing stage. The reason for this elaborate arrangement is not difficult to discern. Traitors' Gate, the only other entrance to the fortress by water must frequently have been cluttered with boats and barges conveying prisoners, Tower officials and supplies. The Cradle Tower enabled the King to come and go freely at all times for, when it was built, the wharf did not extend much beyond St Thomas's Tower and the new entrance could be approached directly from the river. It was the variation in water level due to tides which made the hoisting gear very convenient. A passageway in the inner curtain wall opposite the Cradle Tower completed the new arrangements for access to the palace apartments.

These new works indicate that the royal apartments within the Tower had moved yet again. The palace buildings now enclosed two courtyards. The 'old courtyard' was bounded by the White, Wardrobe, Lanthorn and Wakefield towers. To the east of it there probably now appeared a set of buildings within the space formed by the Wardrobe, Broad Arrow, Salt and Lanthorn towers, to which Edward III's new gate in the inner wall gave access. The King's Privy Chamber now seems to have been located in a building adjoining the Lanthorn Tower and an agglomeration of other royal chambers were adjacent to it. At some stage this tower was joined to another (now disappeared) in the outer curtain wall.

Other buildings were steadily encroaching on the Tower. In 1351 the King founded a Cistercian abbey on the east side of the fortress and there are contemporary records referring to alehouses and other commercial buildings being erected eastwards from the City. Tower Hill remained an open place, however, and a very unsavoury open space at that. The area was not under the jurisdiction of the Mayor and aldermen, and the Constables, for their part, seem to have paid little attention to the open space north of the Tower. As a result it became a communal rubbish dump. People came from considerable distances with cartloads of garbage and unwanted goods and tipped them on Tower Hill. The fourteenth century was an age far less squeamish about hygiene than our own but by 1371 the situation had become intolerable:

> . . . the King has learned by credible witness, that the air upon Tower Hill is so tainted . . . as to strike the men dwelling all about

47

and the passer by with disgust and loathing, and that great danger is acknowledged to arise therefrom, to the nuisance of the said men and others there having their conversation or passing by and to the manifest peril of their life: and the King will no longer endure these grievous and intolerable faults.[5]

As a result of the royal order some, at least, of the offenders were punished, the area was cleared, and the nuisance was not allowed to be repeated.

It seems that the area of the royal demesne surrounding the Tower (later to be known as the Liberty of Tower Hill) had never been properly defined. Though London had won its charter, its exact rights were the subject of frequent dispute and were not altogether secure. The City lost its charter for several years as a result of its support for Simon de Montfort and from 1285 to 1298 Edward I again placed it under direct royal rule. In the later medieval period we find the Constable and Lieutenant of the Tower still claiming a wide range of privileges including: the right to take tolls of wine, oysters, mussels, cockles and rushes brought to London by sea, all swans floating below London Bridge, all cattle falling off the Bridge, all flotsam and jetsam and carts falling into the moat.

Sporadic attempts were made to solve this conflict of interests, the most important occurring in 1382. Then it was agreed that 'The Franchise of the Tower stretcheth from the end of Petty Wales to the end of Tower Street, and so straight north unto a mud wall: and from thence straight east unto the wall of the City, and from thence to the Postern south, and from thence straight to a great elm before the Abbot of Tower Hill's rent: and from thence to another elm standing upon the Tower ditch; and from that elm along by a mud wall straight forth into Thames.' In order to ensure that there should never arise any doubt over these bounds the 'Constable if he be present shall upon every Ascension Day go on procession worshipfully about the Tower and St Katharine, having with him his Lieutenant and all the freemen and inhabitants within the Franchise of the Tower in their best array.'

The Constable was now granted considerable rights over land traffic passing through the Liberty as well as over shipping. All waggons passing over Tower Hill and between St Katharine's Hospital and the Tower moat were subject to a levy while any waggon falling into the moat was immediately forfeit. Similarly the Constable was entitled to extract a fine from the owner of every animal discovered drinking the waters of the moat. The agreed rate was 1d. per animal foot! Another honour enjoyed by the Constable from an early date seems to have been the right of immediate access to his sovereign. For one office holder this proved a fatal privilege. One day in 1399 Thomas Rempston went to Westminster to appeal to the King on behalf of a prisoner. On his way back his boat overturned in the dangerous rapids swirling beneath London Bridge and the unfortunate Constable was drowned.

The inhabitants of the Liberty had other responsibilities besides the annual beating of the bounds. They were to 'wait upon the Lieutenant such time as he shall call upon them as well for fetching of prisoners to the Tower as for carrying of them to Westminster or to any other place.'[6]

About this time we catch our first glimpse of another important officer of the Tower. This was the Porter, who had charge of all the gates. The holder of the office in Edward III's reign was paid 4d. a day and 2d. for a 'varlet' to carry his keys. He also controlled all grazing rights on Tower Hill.

These agreements must have done a great deal to improve the appearance of the Tower's environs. Medieval kings were extremely sensitive to the surroundings of their principal residences, visited as they were by both English and foreign notables. Very early in the reign Edward had ordered the removal of offal shops from High Street and Eastcheap to the side lanes so that 'a clean and decent way may be prepared for magnates and other people going towards the Tower of London on their affairs'.[7]

One wonders why the Tower Hill rubbish dump was allowed to remain so long. Perhaps the answer lies in the Black Death of 1348 and the severe sporadic outbreaks of bubonic plague which occurred in subsequent years. The pestilence accounted for almost fifty per cent of the population before the end of the century and the proportion of deaths was undoubtedly higher in the towns than in the country. Disposal of rubbish – especially tainted clothing and personal effects – must have been an even more acute problem than usual and open spaces such as Tower Hill away from dwellings had obvious attractions. No records have survived concerning the Black Death and the Tower. It is inconceivable that the castle personnel can have escaped contagion; there must have been rats abounding in its damp and unwashed vaults. Yet it was more possible to control any outbreak there than in a populous and open city such as London. The gates could be, and doubtless were, closed to all unnecessary visitors. Any parts of the Tower where infection appeared could be isolated. Such simple precautions were as effective as any known to fourteenth-century science and certainly afforded the inhabitants of the Tower more protection than their unfortunate neighbours.

Edward III had the misfortune to outlive his early popularity and success. Old, ill and besotted with his mistress, Alice Perrers, the King left martial endeavours to his eldest son, the Black Prince, and politics to his fourth son, John of Gaunt. After the former's death in 1371 the French war drifted into a state of inglorious and expensive stalemate while, at home, constitutional demands by the Lords and Commons led to a confrontation between court and parliament. Pestilence, famine and the erosion of feudal organization had created deep social unrest. In 1377 the King died bequeathing his throne and his problems to a minor. The Tower of London was destined to witness most of the tragic scenes in the reign of that minor.

It all began in the Tower. The ten-year-old King spent the days before his coronation there and rode through the City to Westminster for the ceremony, a custom that was to be maintained by his successors for three hundred years, the first of two precedents established during this unhappy reign (for the other see below p. 54). It was a splendid and joyful occasion; Richard, clad all in white, rode out through the Byward Tower and across the moat attended by nobles and gentlemen whose gilded harness and chains of office gleamed in the July sunlight. The Mayor, sheriffs and aldermen met him on Tower Hill and rode with him through a City gay with coloured drapes, triumphal arches and cheering citizenry. The bells rang, the conduits ran wine and at many points the procession stopped to witness loyal pageants.

All the enthusiasm demonstrated the people's hope that a new king meant a new beginning and a fresh approach to old problems. But the problems were too deep, the monarch too young, and expectation soon turned to despair. The hated Gaunt continued in effective control of the government. The war went so badly that, in the early months of the reign, French invaders were able to harry the coast from Rye to Plymouth. To pay for the conflict an additional poll or 'head' tax was levied. Only with the greatest difficulty were the commissioners able to collect this revenue while throughout the country local orators inveighed from town and village cross against the King's evil ministers, especially against the Treasurer, Robert Hales, and Simon of Sudbury who was both Lord Chancellor and Archbishop of Canterbury. But discontent ran deeper than criticism of individual officials and it achieved more eloquent expression. This was the age of Chaucer, of John Wycliffe and of William Langland, author of *The Vision of Piers Plowman*, who in satirical verse, outraged pamphlet and fiery pulpit oratory struck at the very roots of contemporary society, especially the wealth and corruption of leaders in church and state.

In the summer of 1381 words became actions. It was the attempt to extract a third poll tax which drove the men of Kent and Essex into open rebellion but they aspired to more than the redress of unjust financial measures: goaded by Wycliffite or 'Lollard' preachers who told them that they could learn of Christ directly from the Bible and needed no indolent, immoral priests, and by mob orators who insinuated that the existing order was not of divine ordinance – 'When Adam delved and Eve span, who was then the gentleman' – Wat Tyler and his followers looked for a radical re-ordering of society.

In the early days of June the two peasant armies converged on London, knowing that there was considerable sympathy for their cause in the capital and that their brethren in more distant counties were also on the move. The government was caught completely off guard. They were surprised by the outbreak yet, at the same time, they appreciated that popular opinion lay more with the rebels than with themselves. Only this explains the panic and the lack of policy on the part of Richard's advisers. Most of them, with the King, locked themselves in the Tower. Among the company, according to Froissart, were 'the princess his mother, and his two brothers, the earl of Kent and the lord John Holland, the earls of Salisbury, Warwick and Suffolk, the archbishop of Canterbury, the lord of St John's, Sir Robert of Namur, the lord of Vertaigne, the lord of Gomegynes, Sir Henry Sauselles, the Mayor of London, and divers other notable burgesses.'

At Rochester the Kentishmen seized the castle and took prisoner its governor, Sir John Newton. At Canterbury they exhorted the monks to elect a new archbishop for, they claimed, Simon of Sudbury's days were numbered. At Blackheath they camped and sent Sir John Newton up the river with a message for the King, holding his children as hostage for the knight's good behaviour. Their request was a simple one: they wanted Richard to come to Blackheath to hear their grievances. The young King was not lacking in bravery; the following morning (13 June), after mass in St John's Chapel, five barges set out from Traitors' Gate bearing Richard, his councillors and a sizeable armed guard. As the boat drew near to Greenwich its occupants saw with mounting apprehension the enormous crowd which lined both banks, shouting and chanting a confused babel of demands and imprecations. Richard's nerve did not break but that of his companions, Salisbury, Warwick and Suffolk, did. They probably knew that they were in greater danger than the King, for the rebels continually protested their loyalty to the crown and their determination to remove his wicked advisers. Whatever their motives, they persuaded Richard to turn the barge round and return to the safety of the Tower.

The effect of this manoeuvre on the rebels was disastrous. It seemed to confirm their suspicion that those closest to the King were determined to keep him apart from the 'loyal commons' and to prevent him considering their demands. A shout of 'Treason' went up and both hosts immediately marched westwards towards London. They had little difficulty in gaining admittance. Mayor Walworth had done his best to organize the defence of the capital and to deny the rebels access to its vital supplies of victuals but there were too many within the walls who sympathized with the insurgents. When Wat Tyler's party reached London Bridge the drawbridge was lowered for them.

At about the same time Aldgate was opened to the Essex rebels. Once inside the City, the exultant malcontents helped themselves liberally to food and drink, opened the prisons and surged through the streets with lighted torches to vent their anger on the property of those they considered their enemies. Their principal objective was Gaunt's great and luxuriously furnished palace of the Savoy a mile beyond the town. The rebels slashed sheets and tapestries, took axes to furniture and panelling, emptied chests and barrels and finally made a bonfire of the entire mansion. The houses of lawyers and officials suffered a similar fate and that night King Richard watched the beacons of hate from his vantage point on the roof of the White Tower.

But there was little time for gazing at the devastation. Long before darkness fell the combined rebel army had camped on Tower Hill and St Katharine's Hill and throughout the night the air was periodically rent by their drunken singing and their bloodcurdling screams for vengeance. Once, in that long summer evening, the King braved them. From one of the towers facing St Katharine's Hospital he called to them across the moat, promising attention to their complaints and a free pardon if they would disperse. The rebels were not so easily fooled. In the anxious council meeting that followed Richard accepted the judgement of seasoned campaigners such as the Earl of Salisbury that the military situation was hopeless; the royal party was vastly outnumbered and cut off from supplies and succour by an army which had access to enough food to last several weeks. Diplomacy and deceit were their only avenues of escape.

The following morning a proclamation was made from the walls: the King would ride out to Mile End fields to parley with the commons. A cheer went up from the peasant camp and a large part of the crowd moved off along the Brentwood road for the meeting. One objective of the royal strategy was that Sudbury, Hales and other marked men would be able to slip away from the fortress once the rebels' attention was diverted. As soon as the royal party was well clear of the Tower, the Archbishop and his companions left by way of the Cradle Tower watergate. They had ventured but a few oar strokes across the river when a shout went up from St Katharine's Hill. They had been recognized and escape was obviously impossible. They hurried back within the safety of the Tower.

But the Tower was no longer safe. There are conflicting reports about what happened next. Some accounts suggest that it was insurgents returning from the Mile End meeting who entered the castle. According to one contemporary they even had the King's approval for their actions. Others state that the Tower was breached by those who remained behind. One fact is quite clear: sometime on 14 June a party of rebels entered the Tower of London unopposed by any members of the twelve hundred strong garrison. What could the royal soldiers do? Even if they were not secretly in sympathy with the insurgents they were in no position to oppose them. Their master was in the rebels' hands; if the peasants were thwarted of their vengeance now the consequences might be terrible in the extreme. The jubilant yokels rushed through the narrow streets and passageways, making their unfamiliar way to the heart of the fortress. At last they came to St John's Chapel and there they found Sudbury, Hales and other members of the royal entourage. Fearing the worst, the Archbishop had shriven his companions and now waited with them in prayer, hoping that their enemies would respect the sanctuary of the church.

It was a vain hope. The prelate was dragged out with Treasurer Hales, John Legge, one of the Kent tax commissioners, and William Appleton, whose only crime seems to have been that he was John of Gaunt's physician. The four men were hustled out of the fortress and up Tower Hill. There a crowd of rebels and sightseers gathered around a large log which was to serve as a makeshift block. Archbishop Simon was the first to face death. According to the records he did so with courage and calm. He needed all his resources, for the inexperienced executioner, either through nerves or because his sword was blunt, bungled the job most appallingly:

> [The Archbishop] after forgiveness granted to the executioner that should behead him, kneeling down, he offered his neck to him that should smite off his head. Being stricken in the neck but not deadly, he putting his hand to his neck said, 'Aha, it is the hand of God.' He had not removed his hand from the place where the pain was, but that being suddenly stricken again, his finger ends being cut off and parts of the arteries, he fell down, but yet he died not, till being mangled with eight several strokes in the neck and head, he fulfilled most worthy martyrdom. His body lay unburied all that day and the morrow till afternoon, none daring to deliver his body to sepulture. His head those wicked villains took and nailing thereon his hood they fixed it on a pole and set it on London Bridge.[8]

How the other unfortunates faced death after that fearful demonstration is not recorded.

In their rampage through the royal apartments the excited mob ripped the King's bed to pieces and offered such insults to his mother that she fainted and was eventually conveyed away by his servants in a barge. In one respect the peasants were thwarted: search as they might they could not find Henry Bolingbroke, Gaunt's son and heir.

The lad was concealed by one of his father's retainers, who thus inadvertently changed the course of history. We mentioned earlier that two important innovations were established during Richard II's reign. One was the custom of the coronation procession from the Tower to Westminster Abbey. The other was the use of Tower Hill as a site for public executions. The hasty murder of Sudbury and his companions by enemies of the crown established a precedent that kings and queens of England found useful to follow throughout the next three hundred and seventy years.

The triumph of the rebels was short-lived. Richard made such promises on his royal oath that part of the host at Mile End was persuaded to disperse. The King's party then retreated to Baynard's Castle for the night. During the ensuing hours the good order of the insurgents broke down completely. They swept through the City in an orgy of looting, murder and destruction. It was but a disorganized rabble which met the King again at Smithfield the following day. At the very moment when the news from London was inspiring fresh outbreaks throughout the home counties, the movement lost its moral impetus. The Wat Tyler who rode forward to parley with the King at five o'clock on a hot Saturday afternoon was no longer a crusading hero but a swaggering, petty tyrant who stood in clear contrast to Richard's royal dignity. During the long interview he behaved with an unseemly arrogance which at last goaded Mayor Walworth into an argument with him. The two men fell to blows. Others joined in. Swords were drawn. Tyler's horse bore his mortally-wounded rider towards the rebel army. In the open ground between the two groups the leader of the commons toppled from the saddle and lay still upon the grass.

It was a crucial moment. Among the rebel ranks arrows were fitted to bows and strings were drawn taut. Only one man could have saved the day and the crisis did not find him wanting. Richard spurred forward. 'Sirs, will you shoot your king? I am your captain. I will be your leader. Let him who loves me follow me.' Slowly he rode northwards away from the City. And the peasant army followed. The King's followers were able to hurry back into the capital, assemble the Tower garrison and a large contingent of Londoners, who having witnessed the unbridled excesses of the mob had lost their taste for revolution. The King was rescued from his loyal commons most of whom were allowed to return home unmolested. By the end of the month the Peasants' Revolt was over. Wat Tyler's head replaced Archbishop Sudbury's on London Bridge and about a hundred and fifty other rebels were executed, most of them after due process of law had been observed.

It is not surprising that, after the traumatic events of 1381, Richard II had no love for the Tower. Yet, six years later, he found himself once more a virtual prisoner in the royal fortress facing another constitutional crisis. This time it was not the commons who were challenging his authority; the old conflict between majesty and nobility had broken out once more. Richard, a lover of peace and beauty, patron of artists and poets, had little understanding of, or sympathy for, most of the hereditary lords of the realm. He kept his own council, chose his own friends, nominated his own advisers and appointed to high office those whom he approved. Nor would he brook any challenge to his divinely-appointed sovereignty. Shakespeare well understood Richard's attitude when he put the following words into his mouth:

> . . . no hand of blood and bone
> Can gripe the sacred handle of our sceptre,
> Unless he do profane, steal and usurp.
> . . . my master, God omnipotent,
> Is mustering in his clouds on our behalf,
> Armies of pestilence; and they shall strike
> Your children yet unborn and unbegot,
> That lift your vassal hands against my head,
> And threat the glory of my precious crown.

Noblemen whose ancestors had resisted John and deposed Edward II could scarcely share the exalted doctrine of divine right.

By 1386 the leadership of the baronage had devolved upon Thomas, Duke of Gloucester. In parliament in the autumn of that year he succeeded in removing some of Richard's favourites from office and in establishing a council, responsible only to parliament, to rule England for a year. For twelve months the humiliated King toured the country seeking support and looking for ways of shaking off the control of Gloucester's faction. But in November 1387 his enemies accused five of Richard's friends of treason. The King agreed to their trial but then helped four of the accused to escape. He was hoping that his defiance would soon be supported by the Earl of Oxford who was bringing an army from Cheshire but the Earl was defeated at Radcot Bridge, Oxfordshire. When Richard received this news he hurried to the Tower and there celebrated Christmas while his opponents, known as the Lords Appellant, mustered their forces beyond the City. They were now joined by Henry Bolingbroke, the young man who had so narrowly escaped death at the hands of Wat Tyler's thugs.

Most of the citizens made common cause with the Appellants whose soldiers were allowed to pass through London and camp around the Tower. As well as the troops a large crowd gathered on Tower Hill demanding the dismissal of unpopular officials and a return to the custom of rule with the consent of Lords and Commons. Richard received his enemies in the throne room of the Palace and argued with them to the accompaniment of shouts from the mob without. The King's position was hopeless: the choice presented to him was 'agree to the Appellants' demands or be deposed'. He submitted and as a result more of his friends were removed from office and some were executed. The bitterest blow of all was the beheading of his old tutor Sir Simon Burley on Tower Hill. Burley was a close companion and a loyal servant who had proved his valour in Edward III's wars. His death was a serious mistake by the Appellants for Richard refused to forgive or forget it.

The King was prepared to wait for his revenge. During the years which immediately followed he devoted much time and energy to reestablishing the magnificence of the monarchy. He adored fine clothes and sumptuous displays of pomp and chivalry. Nor did he reserve such exhibitions for the closed world of the court. On the contrary, he took every opportunity to impress his people with the grandeur of divinely-ordained royalty. For example, a tournament held over several days in the autumn of 1390 provided the citizens of the capital with a fine spectacle. The royal entourage assembled in the Tower and made its glittering way through the City to Smithfield. To the sound of trumpet, drum and minstrelsy sixty squires on gaily caparisoned chargers preceded sixty gorgeously-robed ladies on palfreys each of whom led her champion knight by a silver chain. Each night, after the day's sport, there was sumptuous feasting, dancing and elaborate entertainment. Everyone enjoyed himself, and the King increased his popularity. In 1396 Richard married for the second time. His bride was the young Isabel, daughter of the King of France. Once again the opportunity was taken for a lavish display. The Princess was royally lodged and entertained in the Tower and emerged for her crowning at the head of a magnificent procession of knights, ecclesiastics, nobles and ladies which wound through the City to Westminster.

In 1397 Richard felt strong enough to act. He invited Gloucester, Arundel and Warwick, the leading Lords Appellant, to a banquet at the Lord Chancellor's house in the Strand. Two of the royal guests were suspicious but Thomas Beauchamp, Earl of Warwick arrived. After the meal he was arrested, hustled through the garden to a waiting barge and conveyed straight to the Tower where he was lodged in that building which has ever since borne his name – the Beauchamp Tower. But the other two could not escape; Richard had been planning his vengeance too long to be cheated now. Gloucester was arrested on his manor at Pleshey. He begged the King for mercy. Bitterly, Richard promised that he should have mercy – in precisely the same measure that he had meted it out to Burley. He was conveyed to Calais and there quietly murdered. Arundel surrendered on

1a This is a reconstruction of a typical Norman motte and bailey. Almost certainly the motte of the first Tower of London was less high. The fortress had the additional protection of the Roman wall

1b The unspoilt Chapel Royal of St John the Evangelist was the heart of the Norman fortress

2a The first unsuccessful escape bid. The unfortunate Gruffydd plunges to his death from the White Tower (1244)

2b Medieval wall paintings of St John the Evangelist and an angel of judgement from a chamber in the Byward Tower

3 The earliest picture of the Tower of London from an illuminated MS of the poems of Charles, Duc d'Orléans, prisoner from 1415–40. The watergate, White Tower, Byward Tower, Great Hall (roof) and London Bridge are clearly discernible

4a Richard II being led into the Tower as Bolingbroke's prisoner shortly before his formal abdication (1399)

4b Ground floor chamber in the Bell Tower where Sir Thomas More was imprisoned and where, probably, in 1662 Samuel Pepys searched for buried treasure

5a Torture implements in the sixteenth century. The background picture on the right shows Skeffington's Irons

5b This recent picture taken during flood conditions gives some indication of what the Tower's watergate must have looked like originally

6 Edward VI's coronation procession from the Tower to Westminster (1547). Thirteen such processions took place between 1381 and 1661

7a Inscription carved by John Dudley in the Beauchamp Tower when he and his brothers were prisoners there (1553–4)

7b Hugh Peters, the great Puritan preacher, who delivered his last sermon to fellow prisoners in the Tower the day before his execution in 1661

8a The Council Chamber in the Queen's House, formerly known as the Lieutenant's Lodgings (now the home of the Resident Governor). The room was formed when a new floor was inserted in the former Great Hall. The wall monument records the examination here of the Gunpowder Plot conspirators

8b The guns of the Tower saluting the arrival of Marie de' Medici on a visit to her daughter Henrietta Maria, Queen of Charles I

receiving a promise of safe conduct. He was immediately sent to the Tower, condemned and, to the King's intense satisfaction, beheaded on the very spot where his old tutor had perished more than nine years before. Warwick, too, was brought to trial but he pleaded guilty and threw himself on Richard's mercy. In this way he preserved his life but forfeited his property and freedom, being kept in the Tower and other prisons for the remainder of the reign. A few months later the King moved against the rest of his enemies, including Bolingbroke, who was banished for ten years.

Richard II enjoyed absolute power for about two and a half years. Released at last from all restraints, he indulged in an orgy of self-glorification and wilfulness. He restored such favourites as were still alive, pursued old and imagined enemies ruthlessly, overawed parliament, rode roughshod over the law, extracted forced loans from lords and merchants, and behaved towards all suitors with an unbending haughtiness. Inevitably he made many enemies who were ready to flock to Bolingbroke's standard when he returned in the middle of 1399. The King was worsted in battle and on 2 September he was lodged, according to tradition, in the state apartments of the White Tower, this time as a prisoner.

Henry the victor was determined to have the throne but he could find no legal right to it nor could his advisers manufacture one. The only answer was to force Richard to abdicate 'freely'. This was achieved by keeping the King in close confinement and allowing him no visitors, not even his wife. By the end of a month Richard's spirit had been broken and he declared himself willing to relinquish the crown. On Michaelmas Day Henry Bolingbroke (Duke of Lancaster, since the death of his father early in the year) came to the Tower early in the morning in solemn procession with many of the leading lords spiritual and temporal and the senior justices. In the Council Chamber of the White Tower Richard II formally abdicated and urged Henry to take on the burdens of kingship.

Shakespeare based the highly dramatic renunciation scene in *Richard II* on the account by the contemporary chronicler, Froissart. Emotionally charged and poetic though it is, there is no reason to doubt that it is correct in its essentials. After dinner the King talked privately awhile with Lancaster and the Archbishop of Canterbury. Then he withdrew and reappeared dressed in his kingly robes, wearing a crown and carrying a sceptre. Standing in the middle of the chamber he laid aside the symbols of sovereignty one by one, affirming that for his part he would be content to see his cousin Henry succeed him. To this end he took a ring from his own finger and placed it on the Duke's. There was only one more simple ceremony to be performed. After parliament had ratified the deposition the two chief justices came to the Tower on 1 October and, on behalf of Lords and Commons, renounced their allegiance. Shortly afterwards this wretched king left the Tower for the last time for a quieter more secluded confinement.

He did, however, pay one more visit to the fortress. Five months later his body lay briefly there in state after he had been murdered at Pontefract Castle.

Richard II made a few changes to the Tower. The damage done by the Peasants' Revolt in 1381 made some redecoration and repair necessary. The buildings had to be made secure against looters. A new tower was built to house the royal jewels and the Keeper of the Wardrobe received enhanced powers and more prestigious accommodation. His responsibilities extended far beyond caring for sumptuous robes and kingly adornments. The term 'wardrobe' covered any strong room for the keeping of clothes, jewellery, specie, books, documents, arms, armour and furniture. As the crown accumulated possessions so the role of the Tower as a royal warehouse increased. Elsewhere, many chambers were repainted and a new house was built for the Keeper of the Wardrobe (the Wardrobe had been ransacked by the mob). The work included a new tower specifically to act as a jewel house. Many chambers were repainted and traces of this work were discovered in a room in the Byward Tower in 1953 when the removal of Tudor plaster revealed brightly coloured figures of St Mary, St John, John the Baptist and St Michael. Royal emblems also still decorate a ceiling beam in this chamber. Such discoveries show that many of the rooms in the Tower were by no means as stark and drab as they appear today. Richard also extended the wharf eastwards from St Thomas's Tower, thus bringing to an end the brief life of the Cradle Tower as a private watergate. In the south-east corner a new entrance was constructed. This took the form of a bridge and drawbridge connecting the Galleyman Tower to the new Iron Gate Tower.

Another famous name connected with the Tower during these years, though unfortunately we have no specific documentary evidence of his involvement in its life, was Geoffrey Chaucer. He grew up less than half a mile from the fortress in a house on Upper Thames Street. He was high in the favour of both Edward III and Richard II and held many offices including, from 1389 to 1391, that of Clerk of the King's Works. In this capacity the poet was responsible for all new construction and furbishment of royal buildings and his tenure of office almost certainly coincided with the painting of the Byward Tower murals and the extension of the wharf. It is tempting to search Chaucer's poems for allusions to the royal castle and it may be that we have in the *Knight's Tale* one of the earliest references to the Privy

Garden, an area within the grim battlements which the martial Edward I had embellished with several willow and cherry trees. Here king and courtiers could take their ease and (certainly in later years) highly privileged prisoners were allowed access for recreation:

> 'And in the garden as the sun arose,
> She walked up and down, and as she chose
> She gathered flowers partly white and red,
> To make a graceful garland for her head,
> And as an angel heavenly gave song.
> The great tower that was so thick and strong,
> Which of the castle was the mighty keep . . .
> Was closely joined to the garden wall.'

4

If Bolingbroke could have understood the burdens he assumed with the crown, or foreseen the toll which the worries of office would take of his health, he might well have shrunk from his act of usurpation. He ascended the throne a vigorous young man of thirty-two, he died a prematurely-aged invalid of forty-six. Nor did the change of dynasty ultimately benefit England. Henry IV, it is true, maintained his inheritance and passed it on securely to his son. That son, Henry V, in his brief reign, became the greatest warrior in Christendom and restored English prestige at Agincourt but he was succeeded by a minor, Henry VI, who had scarcely achieved manhood before he lapsed into insanity. The way was then open for the champions of the house of York, whose hereditary claim to the throne was every whit as valid as that of the Lancastrians, to take a leaf from Bolingbroke's book and usurp the authority of a king clearly unfit to wield it. Thus began the Wars of the Roses, sporadic conflicts between baronial factions complicated by the shifting support of other power groups such as parliament and the Welsh, which brought bloodshed to most parts of the country and a long period of political and economic instability.

The reign of Henry IV began amid the usual euphoria of coronation celebrations. On the eve of the ceremony the King made forty-six knights of the Bath who kept their vigil in St John's Chapel throughout the night of 11 October. The happy holiday crowds cheered Henry and his court through the streets of the City and all the way to Westminster. Yet the year was not out before the first plot of the reign was hatched. A group of Richard's friends planned to murder the usurper at Windsor and restore the deposed king. As soon as the plan was betrayed to Henry on 4 January, he went immediately with his family and court to the Tower of London where he arrived about midnight. He was not a moment too soon; within hours Windsor Castle was in the hands of his enemies. Next morning Henry's first action was to ensure the support of the City. In response to his summons thousands of Londoners assembled near the Tower and a close watch was kept at all the gates to deny access to the King's enemies. Thus strengthened, Henry was able to regain the initiative. His friends and their retainers hurried to London and Henry recruited other volunteers by offering high rates of pay. Within two days the King was able to put himself at the head of 20,000 men. The rebels were soon defeated and brought to justice, the Bishop of Carlisle and some others being lodged in the Tower.

The ghost of Richard II haunted Henry and his son for many years. Wherever there was discontent with the new regime men tended to revere the dead king as a martyr and use his memory as a pretext for opposing the crown. Some of them were given time to reflect on their folly in the Tower. One such was the Abbot of Winchelsea whose only crime seems to have been the writing of 'railing rhymes, malicious metres, and taunting verses against the King'. For which the unfortunate cleric died a traitor's death at Tyburn. It was a striking demonstration of just how nervous and insecure Henry IV felt.

Another source of concern to the King was Wales which flared into open revolt once again under Owen Glendower. For many years the Welsh enjoyed French support and, though English military expeditions were largely successful, the rebels were never totally defeated, nor their leader captured. Some important captives there were, including Glendower's son, Owen, taken in 1405 and his wife and other children who were despatched to the Tower in 1408, but the great national hero outlived his English enemy and, though his rebellion died, he ascended in a fiery chariot to the realm of legend.

Henry expended much valuable money and English blood on the Welsh campaigns. He was also frequently distracted by the need to suppress groups of powerful and dissatisfied nobles such as the Percys. Compared with these problems the persistence of Lollard heresy must have seemed a minor aggravation. Yet seen from a wider perspective it had a much greater significance.

John Wycliffe had died in 1384 but his doctrines were still very much alive. His English translation of the Bible was lovingly copied over and over again, to be read or recited in secret in the conventicles of his sporadically-persecuted followers. Most of these were men and women of humble origin – clergy, friars, students, artisans and journeymen. Occasionally they were brought to trial by the ecclesiastical authorities and forced to recant their heresies. A few obdurate Lollards were burned at the stake, refusing to deny their beliefs. Yet by no means all Wycliffites were people of little account. Merchants, gentlemen and nobles were among those who agreed with at least some of the reformer's tenets. His great protector had been no less a magnate than John of Gaunt. Richard II's first Queen possessed a copy of Wycliffe's Bible. Two members of his council were active Lollard sympathizers. It was not necessary to be a theological expert or to understand deep points of doctrine to find Lollardy attractive. Wycliffe's attacks on the power and wealth of the church attracted considerable support from secular lords and common law lawyers who resented the political power of the higher clergy, the financial exactions of Pope and parish priest and the exemption from royal justice enjoyed by all ordained men.

It was partly as a result of the protection afforded to known Lollards by influential patrons that the bishops completely failed to bring the movement under control. In 1401 they complained to the King about the situation. The result was a ferocious law, *De Heretico Comburendo*, which tidied up and reinforced existing legislation concerning the trial of heretics and their deliverance, where necessary, to the secular authorities for burning. Yet what the bishops needed most of all was a *cause célèbre*, the condemnation of some exalted heretic such as no one had yet dared to apprehend. Only this, they felt, would put a stop to influential patronage and reduce Lollardy to a working-class movement which could easily be stamped out. By September 1413 they had found their man: Sir John Oldcastle was imprisoned in the Tower pending trial on heresy charges.

John Oldcastle, Lord Cobham, was a man of considerable wealth, social standing and valour. He was also a close companion of the new King, Henry V. Now in his mid-thirties, he had already served with distinction in the Welsh campaigns, represented his shire in parliament, married a wealthy heiress, inherited a baronial title, and won a place in Prince Hal's household. It was, therefore, with some circumspection that the Archbishop of Canterbury moved against him. But close investigation convinced Archbishop Arundel that Oldcastle was 'the principal harbourer, promoter, protector and defender' of Lollards in the dioceses of London, Rochester and Hereford. The Archbishop went to the King and the King tried to reason his friend out of his errors. Only when this failed was permission given to convey the Baron to the Tower.

On 23 September the Constable escorted Oldcastle to St Paul's for his trial by the Archbishop's court. It lasted two days and attracted considerable attention. The entire area around the cathedral was packed with people, many of them sympathizers. It soon became evident that the soldier was as brave in this ordeal as in battle. He refused to recant and was, at length, handed over to the secular arm for burning. But that was far from being the end of Sir John Oldcastle. A plot to rescue him must have already been laid. As a first step the prisoner asked for leave to appear at the next meeting of Convocation in order to recant. He further requested that, because of his change of heart, he might not be kept in chains. A stay of execution was agreed and Oldcastle was lodged in one of the more comfortable of the Tower's cells. On the night of 19 October he escaped. The rescue was engineered by three of Oldcastle's London friends, though exactly how is not known. Perhaps money changed hands. Perhaps the prisoner had sympathizers or co-religionists among his guards. Whatever the details, the escape caused a panic inside and outside the Tower. While the news was kept from the King, the Constable, Robert de Morley, organized a frantic search for the fugitive, but though Oldcastle remained some time in the City, moving from hiding place to hiding place, he was never betrayed or discovered. On 28 October the news was broken to Henry V, who immediately removed de Morley from office and confined him in one of his own cells.

Not content with escape, Oldcastle now hatched a wild, Lollard plot aimed at the overthrow of the government and the despoiling of the church. Agents toured Lollard groups throughout the realm urging them to converge on London and assemble in the fields northwest of Temple Bar on the night of 9-10 January. This force would gain control of the City while a small group disguised as mummers would present themselves before the royal court at Eltham and capture the King. Too many conspirators were involved for secrecy, too few for the successful accomplishment of the ambitious plan. Several of the leaders were captured, the Lollard 'host' was disbanded in the darkness and the plot fizzled out. By morning many of the insurgents were in the Tower. They were a confused, ill-assorted collection of clerics, minor gentry and yokels. One man, a rich brewer of Dunstable, was taken with two horses complete with gold spurs and trappings. He had apparently been promised all Hertfordshire as his reward for participation in the revolt and had already provided himself with some of the accoutrements suitable to his exalted position. Oldcastle remained at large and was, indeed, not recaptured until 1417. The end of that year saw him back in the Tower under much stricter terms of confinement. A fresh trial found him guilty of both treason and heresy. This apparently made it difficult for his judges to decide exactly what form his execution should take. At length they concluded that he should be burned *and* hanged.

> . . . upon the day appointed, he was brought out of the Tower with his arms bound behind him, having a very cheerful countenance. Then he was laid upon a hurdle, as though he had been a most heinous traitor to the crown, and so drawn forth into St Giles field, where they had set up a new pair of gallows. As he was coming to the place of execution, and was taken from the hurdle, he fell down devoutly upon his knees, desiring Almighty God to forgive his enemies. Then stood he up and beheld the multitude, exhorting them in most godly manner to follow the laws of God written in the Scriptures, and in any wise to beware of such teachers as they see contrary to Christ in their conversation and living; with many other special counsels. Then he was hanged up there by the

middle in chains of iron, and so consumed alive in the fire, praising the name of God so long as his life lasted.[1]

Under the first two Lancastrian kings England reverted to a state of open hostility with Scotland and France. This brought a new selection of prisoners of war and hostages into the Tower. Two of them are worthy of special notice: King James I of Scotland and Charles, Duke of Orléans. In 1406 Robert III of Scotland sent his twelve-year-old son, James, to the French court for safety. Unfortunately the Prince's ship was taken by English pirates off Flamborough Head and young James eventually found himself in Henry IV's clutches. At that time a truce was in operation between the two countries but the opportunist English King could not sacrifice such a piece of good fortune. James was comfortably lodged in the royal apartments at the Tower. His father was shattered by the news and died of grief. Thus the captive Prince became the captive King. He remained so for seventeen years.

It was not a hard imprisonment. Only part of it was spent in the Tower, where the Constable in 1406 was allowed 6s.8d. a day for the King's keep and 3s.4d. for his suite. The lad's education was looked to and he became skilled in music and poetry as well as in martial arts. He even accompanied Henry V on campaign to France. He fell in love with, and married one of Henry IV's nieces and eventually took her back to Scotland as his Queen. Yet for all that, James was an exile and prisoner and, unlike most occupants of the Tower, he had the skill to express his longing and sorrow in poetic form. The poem called 'The Kingis Quair' was written entirely during his captivity.

> The bird, the beast, the fish eke in the sea,
> They live in freedom each one in his kind;
> And I a man, and lacketh liberty;
> What shall I say, what reason may I find,
> That fortune should do so? thus in my mind
> My case I would argue, but all for nought:
> There was no one to give my woes a thought.
>
> Then would I say, if God me had destined
> To live my life in thraldom thus and pine,
> What was the cause that he me more condemned
> Than other folk to live in such ruin?
> I suffer alone among the figures nine,
> One woeful wretch who to no soul may speed,
> And yet of every living person help hath need.

The principal reason for James's long captivity was that the regent, ruling Scotland in his name, had developed a taste for absolute power and was in no hurry to agree on a ransom. Only after the regent's death was King James restored to his land and people.

Charles, Duke of Orléans, was also a cultured man and a poet. In fact, he was one of the greatest of France's courtly poets. Nephew of Charles VI of France, Orléans was captured at the Battle of Agincourt in 1415 and remained an honoured prisoner in various English castles for no less than twenty-five years. During that time he wrote many *ballades* and love-histories in English and French. It is thanks to Charles of Orléans that we have one of our earliest and most beautiful pictures of the Tower. It features in a late fifteenth-century illuminated volume of the poet's work. In glowing colours we see the gleaming White Tower, the river busy with ships and boats, Traitors' Gate and, beyond the Tower complex, London Bridge with its multitude of shops and houses.

After these stories of long imprisonments it is pleasant to discover that some others were more fortunate: 1422 was a prime year for escapes. In April Sir John Mortimer masterminded a breakout. Sir John Brakemond, Marcellinus of Genoa, Thomas Payne and John Cobham all gained their freedom with him, though they were soon recaptured. The interesting feature of this escape is that the captives were of different categories: two were prisoners of war, one was awaiting trial for heresy, another for treason, and one had been detained on the royal prerogative. Yet all escaped together. This seems to suggest a measure of overcrowding and certainly a few years later we know that parliament was petitioning for a reduction in the number of prisoners detained in the Tower. However, the government did not react warmly to the voluntary reduction in the number of inmates carried out by Mortimer and his colleagues. The Lieutenant, and doubtless many of the warders were dismissed and it was a year before the Lieutenant was restored to favour. One might have expected that this would lead to a tightening up of restrictions but in August another Lollard, Thomas Seggeswick, was rescued by some of his London friends and remained at large for three and a half years.

It is interesting to discover that Lollards were still being incarcerated in the Tower: heresy was an ecclesiastical offence and suspects were usually detained in the bishop's prison, the City prisons or, more specifically, in the Lollard's Tower at St Paul's. Clearly their numbers were still large and their feeling of brotherhood so strong that they often made determined attempts to free their imprisoned colleagues. Some of them also had considerable influence. In 1415 a certain Richard Gurmyn was burned as a heretic by the Mayor of London. Immediately afterwards his friends claimed that the execution was illegal and that a royal pardon for Gurmyn had been deliberately suppressed. The government took the complaint seriously: the Mayor was thrown into the Tower and fined £1,000.

Nothing illustrates the persistence of Lollardy more clearly than the trouble surrounding the trial and execution of Richard Wyche in 1440. Wyche was an Essex priest with a large following both in his own locality and the City. His popularity made it necessary for him to be closely guarded in the Tower before and during his trial. After his condemnation it was thought more prudent to burn him on Tower Hill than risk conveying him through London to Smithfield which was becoming the usual place for these executions. The troublesome priest was despatched and that, as the authorities hoped, was the end of the matter. They could not have been more wrong. Sympathizers erected a cross and a stone cairn on the site which immediately became a centre of pilgrimage. The vicar of All Hallows, Barking, encouraged the custom by selling jars of the martyr's ashes mingled with sweet smelling herbs. The fact that there was very soon nothing of Richard Wyche left to sell did not for a moment bother the ingenious incumbent; he simply went out to the site at night and replenished the pile of ashes – doubtless claiming the inexhaustible nature of the relics as a miracle. For weeks the flow of pilgrims continued unabated despite royal edicts condemning this misguided devotion. At length, the Constable had the site of the stake ploughed up and deposited a pile of dung on top.

Heresy and anti-clericalism was only one aspect of the general discontent which had lingered like smoke on a still day ever since 1381. There is no smoke without fire and, in 1450, fresh breezes stirred the embers into flame again. Once more Kentishmen took the initiative in revolt, their leader being Jack Cade. The movement was more coherent and more socially representative than the Peasants' Revolt and, though it was successfully suppressed, the handling of the crisis reflects little credit on the government. Initially, Henry VI showed firmness and courage. He secured the loyalty of the City, entrusted the Tower to the veteran soldier Lord Scales, and rode forth at the head of a large force to meet the rebels at Blackheath. Outnumbered, Cade's men withdrew but when a small contingent of the royal army pursued them they turned and won an easy victory at Sevenoaks. Now the King's nerve failed him. He could not count on the loyalty of his men, many of whom had begun to echo the rebels' demands for reform. He returned to London where the Lord Mayor (properly so called since 1354) and aldermen urged him to stay and defend the City. Henry turned his back on them and withdrew to the comparative safety of his Midlands fortress, Kenilworth Castle. In an attempt to pacify the rebels he sent Lord Say, the hated Lord Treasurer, to the Tower, a fortress of which he was Constable.

Thus deserted, it is not surprising that the Londoners made little show of resistance to Cade, who entered the City on 2 July. The rebels marched straight to the Tower and laid siege to it. Scales parleyed with them from the walls and readily agreed to yield up Lord Say. Perhaps the garrison commander had received instructions to sacrifice the poor man. Perhaps he was not too sure of his soldiers. Whatever his motive the action achieved the desired tactical result. As soon as Lord Say had been thrust out of the Lion Gate he was seized by the exultant mob and borne away, leaving the Tower unthreatened and inviolate. The Lord Treasurer and his son-in-law Sir James Cromer, Sheriff of Kent, were treated to a hasty trial then beheaded. Their heads were stuck on poles and their bodies dragged through the streets at a horse's tail, the procession being led by Cade 'in a blue gown of velvet with sables furred and a straw hat upon his head and a sword drawn in his hand'.

Inevitably, success went to the rebels' heads; protest and vengeance soon gave place to indiscriminate looting. Just as inevitably, the citizens quickly became disenchanted. On 5 July the Lord Mayor and aldermen went to the Tower and sought Lord Scales' aid. Cade made his enemies' task of regaining the capital easier by his habit of withdrawing to Southwark every evening with his followers. The commander sent a detachment of troops that night to secure London Bridge. Unfortunately the alarm was given in the rebel camp and some of Cade's men swarmed onto the bridge. Fighting continued throughout the hours of darkness and the dawn brought no clear conclusion to the fray. Eventually a one day truce was agreed upon and the opposing forces withdrew to either side of the river. Now the Archbishop of Canterbury took a hand. After long discussions with other notables who, like himself, had taken refuge in the Tower, he drafted a general pardon which was sealed with the great seal of England (the Archbishop was also Lord Chancellor). Armed with this document and protected by a band of guards, he was rowed across the river to Southwark where he read the pardon to the rebels. Many of them were already growing tired of their role and eagerly took the opportunity to disperse. Cade cautiously withdrew down-river but his fate was sealed. A price was put on his head and he was captured in the Sussex Weald, dying of his wounds before he could reach London.

The rebels had called for the overthrow of many of Henry's Lancastrian officials and advisers and had declared support for the faction led by Richard, Duke of York. The scene was set for the conflict between the two noble houses but it did not begin for another five years. By then the Hundred Years' War with France had come to an end – a disastrous end for England – the King was drifting in and out of sanity and effective government had virtually ceased to exist. After various skirmishes, battles and political manoeuvrings Richard of York's son, Edward, was able to seize the crown in 1461. Henry VI and his Queen, Margaret, fled into Scotland. Henry was captured four years later and confined to the Tower of London.

'Mad Henry' must rank as the most pathetic of all the great prisoners of the Tower. He was unfitted to rule and had long since lost all desire to do so. Yet he had many admirable qualities, or rather qualities which would have been admirable in a monk but were disastrous in a king. He was obsessively devout, generous, gentle, kind and humble. He was a patron of scholars and involved himself closely with the universities. Indeed his piety and love of learning inspired his greatest achievements. Succeeding generations can forgive Henry all his stupidities and errors of judgement; for he is the King who gave us Eton College and King's College, Cambridge.

As might be expected the contemporary accounts of Henry's imprisonment vary wildly for they were all written by partisans of the red rose or the white. According to Lancastrian records, the deposed King was led through the capital an object of scorn, his legs fastened with leather thongs beneath his horse's belly and a straw hat upon his head. Once inside the Wakefield Tower, where he was confined, he was, it is claimed, ill-treated by guards, underfed, and suffered to shamble about his chamber unwashed and clothed in rags. Edward IV almost certainly made a point of parading his conquered rival through the City but he had neither cause nor desire to ill-treat the captive. Contemporary accounts show that a generous allowance was made for Henry's upkeep, he was allowed the daily ministrations of a priest in the Wakefield Tower's little oratory and he was permitted occasional visitors. If to some of those visitors he appeared shabby and underfed it was probably his ascetic frame, his hollow cheeks and his complete lack of interest in rich adornment which created the illusion, rather than any deliberate policy on the part of his captors. Henry inspired considerable loyalty and affection in his close servants and it would have been a singularly hard-hearted gaoler who could have brought himself to be cruel to this shuffling, gentle, prematurely-aged, holy man.

Edward's triumph brought other prisoners to the Tower. Prominent Lancastrians such as Aubrey de Vere, Earl of Oxford, Henry Percy, heir to the Earldom of Northumberland, Sir Thomas Tuddenham and Sir William Tyrell were now incarcerated in the fortress. Some of them ended their careers on Tower Hill, where Edward erected the first permanent scaffold. This led to a further conflict with the City authorities. Though they acknowledged that the Hill was part of the Tower Liberties they resented it being used as a permanent execution site since they would derive no benefit from the crowds who habitually flocked to witness a beheading or a hanging. Edward had no desire to annoy the City fathers, indeed, he was well aware how much his position depended on their support. He therefore yielded to them and the result was an interesting compromise: the City was granted a monopoly of executions on Tower Hill and thereafter when prisoners were led out by the Lieutenant they were handed over to the sheriffs at the gate of the Tower, and a receipt given to the royal officer.

Edward IV frequently kept court in the fortress, because of its security and partly because he wanted to maintain close contact with the capital. He incorporated into the Tower the area beyond the Lion Gate, later known as the Bulwark. This was the last extension of the castle's defences but at about the same time the outer wall was probably fortified by the building of Legge's Mount (which was known as the Old Tower throughout most of the sixteenth and seventeenth centuries). This and Brass Mount used to be ascribed to Henry VIII but recent research has proved that the building of Legge's Mount, at least, must be assigned to the fifteenth century. Within and from his strengthened palace/castle Edward IV radiated a deliberately sumptuous, showy form of majesty.

His tenure of the throne was interrupted but once. In 1470 Warwick 'the Kingmaker', the Duke of Clarence, Edward's brother, and the earls of Oxford and Pembroke staged a successful *coup* aimed at restoring Henry VI. They brought the bewildered monarch clad in a blue velvet gown in solemn procession from the Tower to St Paul's, where he received the acclamation of his subjects. It was a short-lived restoration. Edward immediately regained possession of London and the Tower and inflicted a final defeat on his enemies at Tewkesbury the following spring. Queen Margaret was captured and taken to the Tower whither her husband had already been returned. Their son, the Lancastrian heir, was murdered. Edward returned to London on 21 May. The next day Henry was found dead in the oratory of the Wakefield Tower.

Exactly how the wretched political puppet was thrown aside can never be known. Legend ascribed the murder to Richard of Gloucester (the future Richard III) and claimed that it was carried out with needless brutality. But then every possible foul crime was laid at Richard's door by contemporary chroniclers. The Constable of the Tower was John Dudley, a veteran soldier, a violent man and one who had turned his coat when he realized that the Yorkists were unassailable. He must have been privy to the assassination and may well have attended to it personally. Ultimate responsibility, of course, lay with Edward IV. With the Lancastrian heir dead, the Lancastrian ex-king was the only focal point of plots and rebellion. His death was regrettable but necessary.

The same was true of George, Duke of Clarence. Edward forgave his shallow, headstrong brother his part in the Lancastrian coup of

1470 but Clarence refused to be warned. He hated playing second fiddle. He hated Edward's Queen, Elizabeth Woodville, and he hated her family whose members were rapidly monopolizing most of the positions of power and influence. Clarence was openly insulting to his brother and the Woodvilles. He arrogated royal powers to himself. He plotted with Edward's enemies at home and abroad. The King was patient – until June 1477. Then he summoned brother George to Westminster, confronted him with his crimes and had him instantly rowed down river to the Tower. It was seven months before the Duke was brought to trial. Perhaps his brother was hoping for some sign of contrition. If so he hoped in vain; Clarence remained truculent and defiant. In January 1478 he was condemned to death by the Lords in parliament. Again, the King could not bring himself to give the necessary order until parliament itself urged that sentence should be carried out immediately. On 18 February the Duke of Clarence was executed privately in the Tower of London.

But was he drowned in a butt of Malmsey wine? Two things need to be said about this extraordinary story. First, it was a widespread rumour vouched for by contemporary chroniclers. Second, some of those chroniclers, while giving the popular version of Clarence's death clearly found it difficult to believe. For example, Polydore Vergil, Henry VII's official historian, reports that the Duke 'was drowned (as they say) in a butt of malmsey'. Various explanations have been offered. Some historians suggest that Clarence's bloody corpse was removed from the Tower in a barrel of wine after his conventional execution. Others believe that the braggart Duke may have requested this form of death as a last piece of contemptuous bravado. Like so much that happened in the secrecy of the Tower of London, we shall never know the complete truth. What can be said with definite conviction is that the execution was perfectly legal, that Clarence was accorded all the usual rites of the condemned, and that his death was fully merited.

The deaths of Henry VI and Clarence ushered in a bloody century marked by frequent dynastic murder and execution at the Tower of London. Edward IV, Richard III, Henry VII and Henry VIII did not scruple to remove every possible obstacle to their security and they found the Tower the most useful setting for carrying out their ruthless, judicial murders. It was a brutal age but it was one in which strong, centralized government emerged from the chaos of the Wars of the Roses. The mortar used in the creation of that state was mixed with blood. The Tower was well equipped for its work. The instruments of torture were increasing in number and versatility. It was probably in the middle of the fifteenth century that the most feared of all these implements, the rack, arrived. John Holland, Duke of

Exeter, who was Constable in 1446, is believed to have invented it, and for some years it was known as the Duke of Exeter's Daughter. Appropriately the remains of the Duke now rest in the Tower, though they have only come there after a long and eventful history. Holland and two of his wives were originally interred in an elaborate chantry tomb in St Katharine's Hospital. In 1825 the building was demolished to make way for St Katharine's Docks. The remains and the benignly smiling effigies found a new home in a chapel at Regent's Park. Still their journeyings were not over. In 1951 it was thought appropriate to move them once again. So, the Duke came back to the Tower where his 'daughter' had ceased her activities centuries before.

We now come to the year 1483 and the most notorious event in the history of the Tower of London – the murder of the little princes. Popular legend and biased chroniclers have built up an account of an elaborate, cold-blooded crime planned by a depraved monster whose mind was as twisted as his deformed body. Scholars have removed the layers of myth and fallen to argument about how the small kernel of fact should be interpreted. Yet despite all the heated debate and the countless words written on the subject, when we ask the question 'What happened to Edward IV's sons?' we receive no clear answer. The Tower keeps its secrets well.

Edward IV died at Westminster on Wednesday 9 April, 1483, after a sudden and unexpected illness. He was succeeded by his twelve-and-a-half-year-old son, Edward. Once more the throne was occupied by a minor. Once more powerful factions immediately began mustering their powers. The Queen and her family, the Woodvilles, seemed unassailable. They were under no illusions about their unpopularity and they had made preparations against the day when their provider and protector, Edward IV, would no longer be available. Their chief mainstay was the Tower. Elizabeth's son, the Marquess of Dorset, was Constable. He immediately secured the fortress with its massive arsenal and removed the greater part of the royal treasure, which he divided between the leading members of the faction. They would need cash to secure the allegiance of some of the nobles and, if necessary, to buy troops. Their first objective was to bring Edward V to London as quickly as possible and lodge him safely in the Tower. Then he must be crowned immediately so that all the great men in church and state could swear allegiance to him. Only then could the Woodvilles feel secure: they would have the King under their control.

But the King was at Ludlow. Urgent orders went to Earl Rivers, the Queen's father, to bring young Edward to London by 1 May. His coronation was fixed for 4 May. Yet, for some reason, the royal party did not set out until 24 April. The delay proved fatal. At Stony Stratford they were intercepted by Richard, Duke of Gloucester, and

Henry Stafford, Duke of Buckingham, with a body of armed men. Richard, as Edward IV's only surviving brother, demanded the right to be the Protector of his heir. He had served faithfully throughout the preceding reign and he was determined that the country should not now fall into the hands of the Woodvilles. He arrested Earl Rivers and informed Edward V that he had intervened to stop a conspiracy against the crown. He then sent messengers hurrying ahead of him on the London road. One went to the Archbishop of Canterbury urging him, if possible, to gain control of the Tower and the royal treasure. Another commanded the Lord Mayor of London to be ready to receive his sovereign.

The sudden turn of events completely demoralized the Woodvilles. Elizabeth and Dorset sought sanctuary at Westminster. The Council, led principally by William Hastings, the Lord Chamberlain, refused to sanction their unconcealed ambition. It was, indeed, Hastings who rallied the City and most of the great magnates to support the proper, legal arrangement – that authority be vested in the King's uncle as Protector until a Council of regency was formed. Richard's supporters gained possession of the Tower and recovered much of the treasure; Elizabeth Woodville escaped to France with the rest. The King entered his capital on 4 May and a few days later he took up residence in the Palace in the Tower.

The Protector was judicious in his appointments to the major offices of state. He did not only appoint his friends. He wanted the support of all the important men and hoped to avoid creating factions. Guardianship of the Tower did, however, go to a trusted supporter, Sir Robert Brackenbury, who was also created Master of the Tower Mint. As Constable he was paid £100 a year and when, later, he was appointed Keeper of the Lions and Leopards he received another 12d. a day. Many other perquisites came Brackenbury's way during Richard's short tenure of power and Sir Thomas, for his part, supported his patron loyally to the end.

During the weeks that followed the Protector's quiet but triumphal entry to London, the Tower was alive with activity. The King's Council met there, making plans for the coronation as well as for the day to day administration of the realm, while an army of workmen under the command of Peter Curteys, Keeper of the Wardrobe, prepared clothes, trappings and accoutrements for the forthcoming ceremony. But beneath all the bustle the atmosphere was changing, becoming more tense. Richard was growing anxious about his own position after the coronation. Then, the Council would technically rule during the minority and there was no guarantee that they would continue to follow his leadership. On the contrary it seemed inevitable that the government would collapse in political and personal feuding. Hastings and some of his colleagues, for their part, were worried about the power wielded by Richard and Buckingham and feared that they would try to overawe the Council. All the leaders were afflicted by misgivings about the accession of a minor. Twice had it happened in the last hundred years and on both occasions it had been the prelude to disaster. A weak king could be nothing but the embodiment of a token royalty to legitimize the rule of one or another baronial faction.

The manoeuvring had begun by the beginning of June. Hastings and some of his friends opened secret negotiations with Elizabeth Woodville. Had these plans succeeded Richard would probably soon have found himself a temporary tenant of the Tower *en route* for Tower Hill. But Richard got wind of the plot. By 10 June he was sending messengers galloping to his friends in the country, urging them to gather in London with soldiers. Richard of Gloucester was a man who saw issues clearly and acted decisively. Had his plans not ultimately miscarried, he would have been hailed by history as a strong-willed and successful king. Failing, it was inevitable that the record would be written by his enemies and that he would be portrayed as a cynical, ruthless tyrant.

On the morning of 13 June the Protector summoned a meeting in the Council Chamber at the Tower. He informed the assembled lords that a treasonable conspiracy had been uncovered. It involved the Queen and the Woodvilles *and* some men seated around the table with him. He named Hastings, Lord Stanley, Bishop Morton and the Archbishop of York. At Richard's signal, armed men rushed in to arrest the four. Stanley and the two ecclesiastics were immediately taken away and locked up. Not so Hastings; angrily Richard told him that he was to be executed immediately for treason. A priest was found to shrive the Lord Chamberlain and he was then hurried out onto the Green. A balk of timber for repair work lay conveniently to hand and on this Hastings was forced to lay his neck. He thus became the first of seven people to be privately executed on Tower Green.

Later that day the Protector summoned a full Council meeting and explained his actions. The death of Hastings was a brutal and calculated act, and it had the desired effect of overawing Richard's colleagues and deterring them from rebellion. To the other conspirators he felt he could be generous. After only short spells of imprisonment they were restored to their positions.

Richard was now resolved to take the crown for himself. The decision was forced upon him by a genuine desire for political stability as well as by ambition. It was the decision his friends had been urging him to take for some weeks. It was also a decision for which he seemed to have justification. He had received information that

Edward's sons were not the rightful heirs to the throne. The story was that the late King had been pre-contracted to another woman before his marriage to Elizabeth Woodville. Despite the fact that the latter had lived with Edward for years as his wife and had borne him children, their relationship was technically adulterous. Since there were therefore no legitimate heirs of the King's body the crown devolved upon his only surviving brother, Richard of Gloucester. Whether the story was true and whether Richard believed it are now both beyond proof. What matters is that it presented a way out of the potentially dangerous political situation in which England found herself. The Protector had already had nine-year-old Richard of York brought to the Tower to join his brother and now he caused the boys' bastardy to be proclaimed throughout the country.

And that is almost the last statement that can be made with certainty about the unfortunate princes. At the end of 1483 an Italian who had been in England until the previous July wrote:

> After Hastings was removed, all the attendants who had waited upon the King were debarred access to him. He and his brother were withdrawn into the inner apartments of the Tower proper, and day by day began to be seen more rarely behind the bars and windows, till at length they ceased to appear altogether. A Strasbourg doctor, the last of his attendants whose services the King enjoyed, reported that the young King, like a victim prepared for sacrifice, sought remission of his sins by daily confession and penance, because he believed that death was facing him . . . I have seen many men burst forth into tears and lamentation when mention was made of him after his removal from men's sight; and already there was a suspicion that he had been done away with. Whether, however, he has been done away with, and by what manner of death, so far I have not at all discovered.[2]

By 'the inner apartments of the Tower proper' Mancini probably meant the White Tower to which very few people had any access. It was only natural that Londoners should have put the worst possible complexion on the princes' disappearance; a mere twelve years had passed since the death of another king in the hated fortress. In July word was going around the City taverns that the fate of the princes was sealed. But popular belief that the boys were already dead does not appear to have been widespread until October at the earliest. In August the Woodville interest was stirring again and there was a move throughout the home counties to rescue young Edward and Richard. It failed (see below), and thereafter opponents of Richard III claimed the allegiance of Englishmen, not in the name of Edward V but in that of the latest Lancastrian claimant, Henry Tudor. By then most men believed what only a handful of men knew for certain, that Edward IV's sons were dead and their remains buried somewhere in the Tower.

A gap of a hundred and ninety-one years intervened before any more facts came to light. In 1674 the accretion of medieval buildings along the south front of the White Tower was demolished. Part of this complex was a stair turret giving access to the original entrance. Ten feet below the foundations of the staircase workmen discovered a wooden chest containing the skeletons of two children. These were hailed as the remains of the princes and interred in Westminster Abbey. When the bones were examined in 1933 experts concurred in the probability that they were, indeed, of the right age and period. Some scientific doubts have been raised since but most historians accept the original identifications as the most likely. It is, after all, improbable that two other children were laboriously buried in this spot at about the same time that the princes disappeared.

The two boys, therefore, perished probably in the White Tower and probably in 1483. (There is no reason whatsoever to associate the Bloody Tower with this double murder, which was known as the Garden Tower until late in the sixteenth century.) Any attempt to reconstruct the crime or apportion responsibility rests almost entirely on circumstantial evidence. Henry VII claimed to have received a confession to the crime from Sir James Tyrell, a claim which can safely be disregarded (see below, p. 90). Sir Thomas More wove this confession together with strands of Tudor propaganda and popular myth to create a story as elaborate as it is false. Polydore Vergil gave a similar account. According to these versions of the events surrounding the death of the boys Richard III was the villain, Tyrell his willing tool and Constable Brackenbury an honourable man who refused to do the deed but who did yield up the keys to the eventual perpetrators. Later historians intent on rescuing Richard's good name have fastened the blame on one or other of two possible culprits, the Duke of Buckingham and Henry VII. Child murder is a particularly horrible crime yet when we speculate what might have happened to Edward V and Richard of York had they lived we may conclude that their reasonably speedy end was a merciful release from a world which can only have held nightmarish terrors. Most of their surviving cousins and nephews suffered periods of imprisonment which terminated in gruesome death.[3]

Richard had himself proclaimed King by Lords and Commons and then planned to treat London and all who crowded into it to a coronation procession such as they had never seen before. He held court in the Tower and made seventeen knights of the Bath. On 6 July he took the traditional route to Westminster wearing a doublet of blue cloth of gold 'wrought with nets and pineapples' beneath a long gown of purple velvet, edged and speckled with fur, and attended by an unprecedented array of nobles, knights, esquires and ladies. It seemed and was meant to seem as though all men of rank supported him.

Within weeks the illusion was shattered. The mainstay of his usurpation and his new power – Henry Stafford, Duke of Buckingham – defected. He had probably decided that he had backed the wrong side. The new King was unpopular, for Englishmen set great store by legitimate succession.* They were not convinced by the official story about Edward IV's marriage and they were suspicious of the fate of his two sons. Buckingham also knew that all the forces opposed to Richard were cohering around the figure of Henry Tudor. By October large areas of East Anglia, Kent and Surrey had declared for Buckingham. However, thanks to Brackenbury and the Duke of Norfolk, London was denied to the rebels. With his capital secure Richard was able to take the field. He soon appeared so strong that the opposition melted away leaving Buckingham to plead, in vain, for mercy.

Richard was magnanimous enough, and foolish enough, to pardon most of the Duke's confederates. He ruled for a little over two years, which brought him no satisfaction. His wife and his only son died, his enemies gathered their powers, his subjects murmured against him and indulged in the most obscene and malicious gossip. He was within himself a defeated man before Henry Tudor met him at the battle of Bosworth Field.

There is a story told about the Tower of London at this time which may or may not be true. It is, however, so charming and makes such a pleasant contrast to the saga of insecure princes that it is worth repeating. Sir Henry Wyatt fell foul of Richard III and found himself in the Tower, where he was kept on short rations. When he complained to his gaoler the man replied that he had his orders and dared not exceed them. Wyatt had a frequent visitor in the shape of one of the castle cats who took such a liking to him that she brought her trophies to show him. She must have been an excellent huntress for from time to time she jumped in through the window with a pigeon in her mouth. Sir Henry persuaded his keeper to cook the birds and, thus provided for, he passed the days in better spirits until a change of regime returned his freedom to him. The story would be easier to accept if it were not repeated almost identically in relation to Lord Southampton, a century later. But then who is to say that Southampton's champion had not inherited her skills from an ancestor?

*A fact demonstrated again in 1553 when they made the appalling blunder of preferring Mary Tudor to Jane Grey.

5

Before considering the part played by the Tower in the involved and sanguinary political history of the period 1485–1547 we should, perhaps, pause to consider some of the less spectacular events and activities in which its officers and their families were concerned. The executions and atrocities perpetrated in and around the Tower by the first two Tudors, when catalogued, make a lengthy and appalling list but we should not forget that long periods of time passed during which no one was beheaded on the Hill or the Green and more mundane matters than the fate of royal wives and ministers loomed large in the lives of Tower personnel.

The officers and workmen of the Mint were certainly kept busy. Within days of gaining the crown Henry VII decided on a complete reform of the currency. The work, entrusted to Sir Giles Daubeney and Bartholomew Reed who were jointly appointed to the offices of Master and Worker of Monies and Keeper of the Exchange in the Tower, was, according to one expert, the 'first step in the transition from medieval to modern currency', and produced some of the most beautiful coins ever designed in England. The new gold coins were the rial (ten shillings), the half and quarter rial, the angel (six shillings and eightpence), and the angelet (three shillings and fourpence). Fresh dies were also produced for the silver pieces, the groat (four-pence), half groat, penny, halfpenny and farthing. In 1489 the first gold sovereign appeared and about the same time the first shilling (or testoon). The designs and workmanship of these coins and particularly the portrait of the King which appeared for the first time on the shilling were of the highest standard and rivalled anything currently being produced in the great centres of Renaissance Italy.

Elegant currency was more than just a pleasant form of exchange; it symbolized the stability and magnificence of the monarchy. Henry VII was determined that no careless workman should mar the royal image. Strict rules were laid down concerning the standard he required – no off-centre coins with broken rims nor coins with indistinct legends would in future be tolerated. For a time the King closed all provincial mints in order to ensure a rigid standard. He also had other ways of achieving his ends: in 1505 one of the Tower coiners was hanged at Tyburn for malpractice.

Henry VIII's French wars greatly increased the demand for currency and the work load of the Tower Mint increased in direct proportion. In 1526 Mint Street was cleared of ordnance and cannon so that the carts travelling to and from the workshops should be unimpeded. In the same year £480 was spent on extending the premises, an improvement which included the considerable luxury of glazed windows. Part of the work was concerned with issuing a new debased silver coinage in order to bring English currency into line with continental standards of fineness. Towards the end of the reign a more wholesale debasement took place and this time there was no defensible fiscal motive. Henry had run through one fortune bequeathed by his father and another plundered from the monasteries (which were dissolved between 1536 and 1540) and now there was no money left. He therefore set about defrauding his subjects. There is something conspiratorial about the way the new issue of coin was prepared. The Master of the Mint and his subordinates were sworn to secrecy and amply rewarded for their work so that the Mint could buy a large quantity of bullion before the price went up – the inevitable consequence of the drop in the value of money.

Another department which was kept very busy was the Ordnance. This had separated from the Wardrobe during the course of the fifteenth century. In the 1450s the Master of the Ordnance established gun foundries on Tower Wharf but he continued to have various storehouses within the fortress (as well as elsewhere), principally in a building inside the north inner wall. The Master, himself, lodged in the Brick Tower. These facilities proved inadequate to feed Henry VIII's martial ambitions. In 1512–13 the enlargement and improvement was completed of a 'tower standing on the backside of the house of the Ordnance within the Tower of London'. There were, as we have already seen, other buildings belonging to this department near the Mint and this is confirmed by an order of 1536 for a new storehouse to be constructed 'upon the north side of the Mint where was wont to be an house for the selfsame purpose'. This document also reports that the bridges leading into the Tower had been weakened by the carts carrying the heavy Ordnance stores in and out. The Master at that time urged the need for a new, much larger building which could house all the military stores kept at the Tower. This suggestion was not taken up until 1545 when the Lieutenant of the Ordnance (this was a new post) was given permission to 'erect and new build one house wherein all the King's majesty's stores and provision of artillery ordnance and other munitions may be kept guarded and bestowed in the Artillery Yard'. The new building must have been very large, for, as well as fulfilling its principal function it contained a special room for the King's personal collection of 'rich weapons' as well as offices and lodgings.

All this activity reflected the changing face of warfare. Cannon had made their appearance in the fourteenth century but it was a long time before their versatility was appreciated. Originally they were only used in siege warfare: field battles continued to be dominated by the armoured knight and the foot soldier equipped with bow and pike. By the mid-sixteenth century the situation had changed radically. A wide range of cannon was used from the massive 'twelve apostles' taken by Henry VIII to the siege of Thérouanne, each of which could fire a sixty-pound shot, to the tiny eight-inch calibre robinet. There were falconets, falcons, culverin, demi-culverin, sakers, minions and demi-cannon, most of which were capable of discharging both large balls and small shot. By this time also hand guns were coming into use, while naval warfare was being revolutionized by the design of gun-carrying ships.*

For all this equipment the Master of Ordnance at the Tower was ultimately responsible. Nor did his concerns embrace only the offensive weapons. Captains about to embark on a campaign might well indent for heavy guns, small arms, bows, pikes, match, shot, bandoliers, bullet moulds, melting ladles, musket rests, powder, powder flasks, touchboxes, shovels, spades, crowbars, pickaxes, felling-axes, hedging bills, scythes, reaping hooks, tarred and white rope, canvas for binding halberds, chests for muskets and calivers, nails, tallow, and timber.[1] There must have been times when his small permanent staff at the Tower (6 clerks, 1 bowyer, 1 fletcher, 1 cooper, 1 carpenter and wheelwright, 1 blacksmith, 1 plumber – for making shot – and 2 furbishers, who polished weapons and armour) were rushed off their feet.

Even when there were no armies in the field to be supplied the Ordnance office had other tasks to attend to. As well as storage and repair they had to test armour, gunpowder and saltpetre. They had to make new weapons and equipment. The depots at the Tower and elsewhere were never adequate to keep the army and navy fully supplied. Arms and armour had to be bought from private manufacturers at home and abroad. Even this was the responsibility of the Master of the Ordnance.

It is in this period that we begin to get a clear picture of the major personnel of the Tower. By 1485 the office of Constable was habitually bestowed as a mark of favour on a favourite courtier or important member of the royal household. Throughout Henry VII's

* A sad memorial of one of the first great English fighting ships can still be seen at the Tower. In 1545 the *Mary Rose* heeled over in a squall of Portsmouth. Her gunports had been left open and as a result she sank with her complement of 700 men. In 1836 some of her guns, still loaded for action, were retrieved and taken to the Tower.

reign the Constable was John de Vere, Earl of Oxford, the soldier to whom more than anyone else the Tudor victory at Bosworth was due. Such men did not reside in the Tower. The Lieutenant had by this time definitely taken over all responsibility for the day to day running of the fortress. About 1530 it was decided that he should be more comfortably housed. A pleasant, timber-framed building, known as the Lieutenant's Lodging (now the Queen's House), was erected in the corner of the Inner Ward adjacent to the Bell Tower. Its most impressive feature was its central hall which was two storeys high. The house was of a type with many merchants' town dwellings of the period and seems to rank the Lieutenant on a par with the wealthy burgesses of the capital.

Henry VII was responsible for organizing the custodians of the Tower into a distinct body. 'In the first year of his reign, the Yeomen of the Guard was first ordered of which the Yeoman Waiters or Warders of the Tower hath the seniority.' The Yeomen of the Guard was an élite corps of about two hundred picked men who had a two-fold function; they provided a trustworthy bodyguard for a King who at the beginning of his reign felt far from secure, and they enhanced that King's prestige. With many Yorkist sympathizers still at large and a number of Yorkist prisoners in the Tower, Henry felt it to be particularly important that the castle should be very securely guarded by his own appointees.

Daily duties were assigned by the two senior warders, the Gentleman Porter and the Gentleman Gaoler. The latter was responsible for the security and welfare of the prisoners. His colleague (who eventually emerged as the senior of the two officers) kept the gates and organized the guard duties. Membership of the band of Yeoman Warders was much sought after, being both a privilege and a not inconsiderable source of income. Some of the lustre wore off in 1539 when Henry VIII's chief minister, Thomas Cromwell, created a new royal body-guard, the Band of Gentlemen Pensioners, and the Yeomen of the Guard were largely restricted to keeping the Tower and augmenting the royal entourage on ceremonial occasions. However, places were still eagerly sought by courtiers and noblemen on behalf of relatives and retainers. Originally appointments were strictly controlled by the sovereign but the recommendations of the Lieutenant carried increasing weight, and aspiring patrons were prepared to pay handsomely for the exercise of the Lieutenant's good offices.

In addition to all these permanent officers of the Tower there were, from time to time, hundreds of other people staying in the fortress. Troops were garrisoned in permanent quarters in the Outer Ward whenever the need arose and when the King kept his court there the population of the Tower increased very considerably. With soldiers,

Yeoman Warders, servants, royal officials, prisoners, visitors, work-men of the Mint and countless others constantly coming and going, the Tower of London was obviously a busy place and its officers had quite enough to occupy their minds.

From time to time there were unexpected diversions and excite-ments. In 1501 Henry VII held a tournament in the Tower, perhaps in celebration of the forthcoming marriage of his elder son to a Spanish princess. In the year 1512 St Peter's Chapel was badly burned. In 1518 a riot arose in London between native and foreign merchants. This was not an infrequent occurrence but the latest affray seems to have been particularly serious, or so the Lieutenant of the Tower thought: 'Whilst this ruffling continued Sir Richard Cholmondeley, Knight, Lieutenant of the Tower, no great friend to the City, in a frantic fury loosed certain pieces of ordnance, and shot into the City, which did little harm, howbeit his good will appeared.[2] In April 1544 a gunpow-der magazine in East Smithfield exploded 'whereby five men, a boy and a woman were destroyed',[3] an event which caused the Lieutenant to complain at the large number of small manufacturers of powder and ordnance who had set up their workshops near the Tower. 'In the year 1546, the 27 of April, being Tuesday in Easter week, William Foxley, Potmaker for the Mint in the Tower of London, fell asleep, and so continued sleeping, and could not be wakened, with pricking, cramping or otherwise burning whatsoever, till the first day of the term, which was full fourteen days and fifteen nights . . . The cause of his thus sleeping could not be known, though the same were diligently searched after by the King's physicians, and other learned men: yea, the King himself examining the said William Foxley, who was at all points found at his wakening to be as if he had slept but one night. And he lived more than forty years after in the said Tower . . .'[4] On a November night in 1548 the peace of the Tower was shattered by a curious demonstration: 'a Frenchman lodged in round bulwark, betwixt the west gate and the Postern, or drawbridge, called the warder's gate, by setting fire on a barrel of gunpowder, blew up the said bulwark, burned himself, and no more persons.'[5]

The accidents referred to above together with general dilapidation made necessary a considerable amount of rebuilding. One large account survives for the year 1532, although it cannot have been the only one occasioned by workmen at the Tower:

Work done by carpenters and taking down old timber, etc., at St Thomas's Tower [this explains the half-timbered north face of St Thomas's Tower as it now appears]; and for alterations in the Palace . . . There has also been taken down the old timber in the four turrets of the White Tower; and the old timber of Robin the Devil's

Tower [i.e. the Devereux Tower]; and of the Tower near the King's Wardrobe. Half of the White Tower is new embattled, coped, indented, and dressed with Caen stone to the extent of 500 feet.[6]

The cost of this work was £3,593.14s.10d.

Henry VIII commissioned a major rebuilding of St Peter's Chapel after the 1512 fire. Most of the windows were replaced by wider, lighter ones in the prevailing Perpendicular style. The arches and the roof also date from the sixteenth century. It is interesting to note that from the time of the rebuilding St Peter ad Vincula became a 'respectable' place for Lieutenants of the Tower to be buried. The first such to build an impressive memorial for himself was Sir Richard Cholmondeley (he who was 'no great friend to the City'). He died in 1544 but appears not to have been interred in the fine tomb he had erected.

Henry VIII may also have caused the last addition to the Tower's defences to be built.* This was the artillery platform at the north-east corner of the outer wall called Brass Mount (probably because of the brass cannon installed there). This construction and the location of ordnance on the roof of the White Tower was little more than a gesture: it did not bring the Tower up to date as a piece of military architecture. It was in this period that the castle reached its last stage of development. Changing patterns of warfare had rendered it almost obsolete. In so far as stone fortifications were needed at all it was as massive artillery platforms. Henry built some of the new style forts along the south coast. They still exist at places like Deal, Walmer and St Mawes. But the Tower of London could not be transformed into such a defence work. Nor was there any further need for a great castle to guard the capital. No English magnate could now martial a force large enough to threaten London and the City never had to face a foreign army.

The Tower had always been essentially a castle–palace complex, and by the time it was no longer effective as a defence it had also ceased to be used as a palace. Architectural fashion was changing rapidly. The fortified manor house was becoming a thing of the past. In their new buildings kings and noblemen rejected the medieval concept of great hall and offices built round one or more enclosed courtyards all protected by a moat. They sought new standards of comfort and elegance. This meant smaller, warmer private rooms, and public ones made grand by wide windows, carved wainscots and moulded ceilings. By 1547 the palace at the Tower had become old-fashioned. The Tudors provided themselves with a number of more modern and appealing homes in and around the capital such as Bridewell, Whitehall, Hampton Court, Richmond, and Greenwich.

* See also above, p. 69

The Tower of London c. 1547 showing later Medieval and Tudor Developments

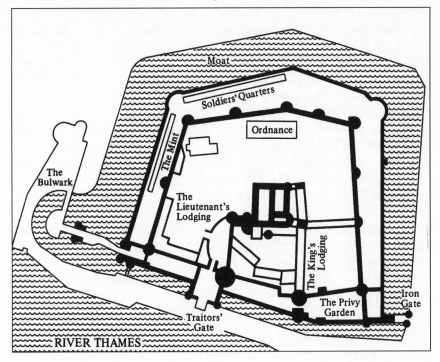

Nor did the monarch need to use the Tower as a refuge. Henry VII and Henry VIII by their ruthless establishment of autocratic power gave England a greater measure of internal stability than she had known for decades. No baronial factions now threatened the crown. Henry VII was the last English sovereign to use the Tower as a principal residence. In the time of his grandchildren the medieval palace buildings began to fall into decay.

We can say that the death of Henry VIII in 1547 marks the point at which the close personal contact of the sovereign with the Tower ceased. It remained a royal building; it continued to play a vital and complex role in the life of the nation; but its essential character had changed to meet the requirements of a new age. The first half of the sixteenth century was an age of violence (as events in the Tower luridly testify) because it was an age of revolution. A powerful nation state was forged with a strong, centralized government. Medieval household administration disappeared to be replaced by the beginnings of modern bureaucracy and parliamentary participation. England had severed her links with European Christendom and become a Protestant country. The redistribution of monastic land had created a much more graded social structure comprising free landowning peasants, yeomen and gentlemen. The Renaissance had drastically changed men's thinking about art and politics. The Tower reflected the new patterns of monarchy, government and social order.

But we must now take up the story at 1485 and chronicle the major events which occurred during the reigns of Henry VII and his wilful son. Like every usurper Henry VII's first concern was to impress his people with the magnificence and strength of his regime. His creation of the Yeomen of the Guard must be seen partly in that light. So must the splendour of his coronation. The new King was determined to outdo the festivities which had marked Richard III's accession two years before. The feasting was longer (the celebration lasted from 27 October to 13 November), the pageantry more elaborate, the clothes and hangings more costly. On his first coming to the Tower Henry rewarded his supporters in the recent conflict, creating one duke, two earls and seven knights of the Bath. The ritual bath for the latter was prepared 'in the dungeon as of old time hath been accustomed'.[7] After the procession through the City and the Abbey coronation it was to the Tower that the court returned for the banquet and not to Westminster Hall. The event in the Great Hall of the Tower lacked nothing of its traditional impressiveness.

> At the table next to the wall, on the right side of the hall, sat the Barons of the Cinque Ports and the Benchers of Chancery; next to the wall on the left-hand side were the Mayor and Aldermen of London, and other important citizens; in the middle of the hall, on the right, sat the prelates and abbots and Barons of the Exchequer; while at the table on the left were lords temporal with other knights. The Earl of Arundel waited at the cupboard as Chief Butler of England 'by his inheritance', and 'because of his age he had a chair made to sit in at this coronation'. When the King had been served the second course the minstrels struck up a song after which the Kings of arms, heralds, and pursuivants came down from a stage at the end of the royal table and went to the nether end of the hall, 'the middle room voided'. The Earl of Oxford set the crown on the King's head; the officers of arms made their obeisance thrice; and Garter thanked Henry for his largess that day amounting to one hundred pounds. The heralds then remounted the stage, and there followed the voidee of spices, when the Mayor of London was accorded the honour of serving the King with *Ipocras* and of retaining the cup as his fee. So ended the coronation banquet of Henry VII . . . it appears to have been a sumptuous repast, and one can well imagine Henry retiring that night very satisfied with his day's work.[8]

Henry VII often kept his court at the Tower and it was the scene of a number of other celebrations hardly less sumptuous than his coronation banquet. In November 1487 his Queen, Elizabeth of York, was brought thither by water from Greenwich to prepare for her own crowning. Henry received her at Tower Wharf and a water pageant (one of the first recorded royal pageants on the Thames) was presented. All the City guilds paraded in richly-decked barges but the prize was taken by the 'Bachelors' Barge' which was 'garnished and apparelled, passing all other, wherein was ordained a great red dragon spouting flames of fire into Thames'.[9] The royal party then entered the castle by the Cradle Tower drawbridge, which had replaced the watergate as the private entrance of the sovereign since the extension of the wharf. Two years later Henry's three-year-old son, Arthur was brought down river from Sheen with great ceremony to be installed as Prince of Wales.

Henry VII's greatest diplomatic triumph was the marriage of Arthur to the Spanish Princess, Catherine of Aragon, and her arrival in London in 1501 was greeted by the most lavish and prolonged celebrations. She was brought by barge to the Tower, attended by a multitude of other gaily-adorned boats and there entertained privately by the King for two days before setting out with her young bridegroom on a tour of the City, which had been preparing for three years the costly series of pageants with which the couple were now entertained. Rejoicing would not have been so unbridled if the Mayor and aldermen could have foreseen that within five months Prince Arthur would be dead.

Not all the royal ceremonial centred on the Tower was of a jubilant nature. In February 1503 Henry VII's much loved Queen was brought to bed there of a daughter. The child survived but a few days and was swiftly followed into death by the mother. For some days she lay in state in St John's Chapel before being taken to Westminster for her solemn and costly funeral.

The lavish court and public entertainments indulged in by Henry VII from time to time go some way towards dispelling the popular myth of the King as mean and avaricious. Yet they were not for the first Tudor (as they undoubtedly were for his son) spontaneous expressions of an extravagant pleasure-loving spirit. They were calculated displays which had their place in the achievement of Henry's three major objectives – to make the dynasty secure, internationally respected, and solvent. He was successful in all three, yet he never felt himself to be completely safe. This goes some of the way towards explaining why Henry VII spent so much of his time in the Tower and also why he filled its prison quarters to overflowing with enemies, real and imaginary. Throughout his reign he was confronted by rebellions, by potential claimants to the throne, some of whom had a better title than himself, and by pretenders. Persistently, ruthlessly, successfully he tracked down all who might prove a threat to himself or his heirs. One by one they came to the Tower. Most of them never left.

The senior Yorkist heir was the fifteen-year-old Edward, Earl of Warwick. Immediately after the Battle of Bosworth Henry had the lad brought from his Yorkshire confinement and accommodated in the Tower. At the same time Elizabeth, Edward IV's elder daughter, was brought out of the castle where she had been kept by King Richard. Next time she entered its portals it was as Henry's Queen. Poor young Warwick was so closely confined, as indeed his unfortunate cousins had been, that rumours of his death were soon circulating. This gave some of the leading Yorkists an opportunity to unseat their enemy. They tutored Lambert Simnel, the son of an Oxford tradesman, to impersonate the Earl. With this impostor as their figurehead, they raised the standard of revolt in first Ireland, then in northern England. Henry immediately brought Edward out of his prison and paraded him at St Paul's where he spoke with a number of people who knew him well and would vouch for the fact that he was still alive. This made no impression on the leaders of the revolt. What mattered to them was not who the real Warwick was, but that he was alive and that his claim to the crown was better than the usurper's. Soon the leader, John de la Pole, had a large army at his back and was offering the Tudor a very serious threat. It all ended at the Battle of Stoke where de la Pole was killed and Simnel captured. The impostor was contemptuously set to work in the royal kitchens. Even so his fate was preferable to that of the real Earl who, after a brief glimpse of the outside world, was back in his prison.

The next attempt to supplant Henry VII with a Yorkist 'prince' was more carefully planned. Perkin Warbeck claimed to be Richard, Duke of York, one of the boys who had disappeared at the Tower in 1483. He toured the Continent in an effort to impress England's enemies and gain their backing. Finally he went to Scotland where the King promised his support. Meanwhile his claim was being canvassed throughout England, where Henry's vicious financial measures against the nobility were creating widespread discontent in high places. Even Sir William Stanley, Lord Chamberlain of the Household, and the King's step-uncle, was becoming disenchanted. It was largely his intervention at Bosworth which had won the day for Henry but the determination of the new monarch to break the power of the nobility and to resurrect all manner of feudal financial exactions eventually forced him to switch his allegiance. He used his position as Councillor and intimate of the King to provide information for the schemers abroad. He reckoned without Henry VII's counter espionage system. The King was soon informed of Stanley's treasonable dealings. At the beginning of 1495 the Lord Chamberlain was imprisoned in the Tower and shortly afterwards he ended his days on the Tower Hill scaffold. His not inconsiderable estates reverted to the crown. By their involvement in or sympathy for the long drawn out and abortive Warbeck rebellion many of the nobles played into Henry's hands. Wherever he discovered the slightest suspicion of disaffection he acted quickly and ruthlessly, imprisoning, extracting fines or recognizances (sums paid as assurance of good behaviour), thus enhancing his Treasury and reducing the potential of the magnates for independent action. Warbeck's first attempt at invasion was made at Deal that summer. It was a complete fiasco and the Sheriff of Kent was soon leading some eighty prisoners through the streets of London to the Tower, 'railed in ropes like horses drawing . . . a cart'. They were executed, some on Tower Hill and some on selected sites throughout the country.

It was not only the wealthy and powerful who resented Tudor financial measures. In 1497 the men of Cornwall rose in revolt and a sizeable army reached Blackheath before the King was able to send troops against them. Two thousand Cornish dead were left upon the field of battle while ringleaders were lodged in the Tower and the City prisons before trial and execution. Lord Audley was sent to his death on Tower Hill clad in a suit of paper armour. The Tudors had a penchant for using ridicule as a means of dissipating any sympathy which might have been felt for their enemies.

The end came for Perkin Warbeck's rebellion shortly afterwards. Thinking, no doubt, to turn the discontent of the West Country to his advantage, he came by boat to Land's End in September and marched north gathering an army of a few thousand poor countrymen. Near Taunton the whole enterprise fizzled out when the insurgents were confronted by royal troops. Warbeck was soon captured but, like Simnel, was treated leniently. After he had made a full confession he was honourably confined within the royal household. It was only when he tried to escape, a year later, that he was moved to a Tower cell where he found conditions very different. After two months in the royal prison he was seen by an old acquaintance who remarked 'he is so much changed that I, and all other persons here, believe his life will be very short.'

What happened next has never been entirely clear. The government claimed that Warbeck conspired with the real Earl of Warwick to escape from the Tower and to do considerable damage there by blowing up the gunpowder store (presumably in the Ordnance building against the north side of the Inner wall). Both of them were tried on this charge and both were executed. But there are certain questions which need answering satisfactorily before we can accept the official story. Why was a practised troublemaker like Warbeck allowed access to the Earl, who had always been completely isolated from political personalities? Why were a few London burgesses, found guilty of abetting the escape bid, subsequently pardoned? What would have become of Henry's plans for a Spanish marriage for his son if Warwick had remained alive? King Ferdinand had put a complete block on the negotiations because Warwick's claim to the throne was stronger than Henry's. When diplomacy failed the English King had no alternative but to remove the obstruction. He may have used the heaven-sent opportunity of an actual escape bid or he may have engineered the whole plot himself. Perhaps the truth lies somewhere between the two. Here is a possible reconstruction of the events which destroyed these two young men. Warwick was allowed to meet his 'double' and talk with him, probably in the grounds of the Tower palace. They would have had much to discuss including the amount of Yorkist support still existing in the country. The Earl, who by now had spent almost half of his young life inside the Tower, must have listened, fascinated, to his eloquent companion's reports of life outside and of his travels abroad. Then via the Lieutenant or some visitors the outline of a possible escape plan was fed to Warbeck. The vain adventurer, who enjoyed conspiracy and had revelled in being the centre of attention for so long, could be relied on to do the rest. Warwick must have grabbed at any opportunity to get away from the Tower. The plot was given several weeks to mature and then the authorities 'discovered' it. Both men were tried (Warwick by his peers) and found guilty. Warbeck was hanged at Tyburn. The Earl, the last direct male descendant of Richard of York, was beheaded on Tower Hill.

But still the Tudor succession was not secure. The next in line was now Edmund de la Pole, Earl of Suffolk, brother of John de la Pole who had fallen on the battlefield at Stoke. He fled the country in 1499 but was persuaded by the King to return. It was an uneasy situation for Edmund, who knew that Henry could and probably would, sooner or later, find some pretext for arresting him. In 1501 he left the country again with his brother Richard.* His worst fears were immediately realized when the King seized William de la Pole, his other brother, and put him in the Tower, where he was to stay for the remaining thirty-eight years of his life.

The death of Prince Arthur a few months later placed Henry VII's dynasty in jeopardy. All now depended on his one remaining son, Prince Henry. Hasty negotiations were made for the ten-year-old boy's engagement to Catherine of Aragon and the King himself looked around the courts of Europe for a new bride capable of presenting

* Such was Henry's reputation for deviousness that one contemporary chronicler saw the King's hand in the flight and downfall of the de la Poles. Polydore Vergil claimed that Henry used an *agent provocateur* to frighten Edmund and Richard into decamping so that he could seize their property and imprison them.

Potential Rivals Disposed of by the Tudors

Edward III

Richard D. of York — Edward D. of Buckingham (1521)

Edward IV — George D. of Clarence — Richard III — Elizabeth == John de la Pole E. of Suffolk

Henry VII == Elizabeth

Henry VIII

Edward V   Richard D. of York — Murdered 1483 'The Princes in the Tower'

Catherine == Wm. Courtenay M. of Exeter

Henry E. of Devonshire (1538)

Edward E. of Warwick (1499)

Margaret == Sir R. Pole Countess of Salisbury (1541)

Henry Pole Ld. Montague (1538)

Reginald Cardinal Pole

Geoffrey

Ursula == Henry Ld. Stafford

John E. of Lincoln

Edmund E. of Suffolk (1513)

William   Richard

Thomas (1557)

Dorothy

Of the other people close to the succession in the above table:

John de la Pole died in battle against Henry VII, 1487.
William de la Pole was imprisoned in the Tower in 1501 and died there in 1539.
Richard de la Pole was killed at the Battle of Pavia, 1525.
Reginald Pole lived most of his life in exile and as a priest was debarred from the succession.
Geoffrey Pole was arrested by Henry VIII but bought his freedom by giving evidence against his mother and brothers.

him with sons in his old age. At the same time he made repeated, earnest efforts to bring back the renegade de la Poles. His first step was to arrest Sir James Tyrell, Governor of Guisnes, and certain persons who had aided the runaways. Tyrell, who throughout the reign had served the King faithfully, was convicted of treason and beheaded on Tower Hill on 6 May 1502. Immediately afterwards the official story was circulated that before his death Tyrell had confessed to the murder of the two princes in 1483. This account, later embroidered upon by Tudor historians and Shakespeare, was long accepted at face value. When examined critically certain problems emerge. First of all no written confession seems to have been produced by the government and certainly none has survived. Furthermore it is difficult to see why, whether guilty or not, Tyrell should have volunteered the confession so long after the event. If Tyrell did 'reveal all' why did he not indicate the spot where the two boys lay buried? It scarcely seems credible that the King would have allowed him to carry to the grave the one piece of evidence which would have corroborated the story. Finally the clearing up of the nineteen-year-old mystery benefited one person and one only. By spreading this account Henry VII scotched once and for all the rumours that Edward IV's sons were still alive and he did so at a time when it had suddenly become a matter of urgency to clear away all possible rivals and pretenders.

Another person close to the throne (though by marriage) who attracted Henry's displeasure at this time was his brother-in-law William Courtenay, heir to the earldom of Devon. Courtenay found himself in the Tower for the rest of the reign. Meanwhile the objects of all this activity, the de la Pole brothers, had taken refuge in Flanders where they enjoyed the protection of the Archduke, Philip of Burgundy. Repeatedly Henry asked Philip to return the fugitives but all to no avail. Then, in 1506, fortune favoured the bold. Philip was *en route* for Spain when his ship ran aground on the Dorset coast. For over three months the Archduke and his wife were the unwilling recipients of Henry's lavish hospitality. The King simply would not allow his guests to depart – before they had concluded a treaty which included among its terms the surrender of the de la Poles. Richard escaped to Hungary before the Archduke's orders could be carried out but Edmund was brought back to England and joined his brother in the Tower.

Three years later Henry VII was dead and England waited hopefully for the advent of its new youthful and vivacious sovereign. 'Heaven and earth rejoices; everything is full of milk and honey and nectar. Avarice has fled the country. Our king is not after gold, or gems, or precious metals, but virtue, glory, immortality.'[10] So wrote one entranced courtier in the first heady months of the new reign

90

when the cultured King was delighting everyone with many evidences of a complete contrast to his father's style of government. Yet there may have been some men in England who were alarmed at the evidence Henry provided that he was breaking with his father's methods of administration.

On the day after Henry VII's death his son came up the river from Greenwich to the Tower. Two other men soon found themselves heading for the same destination. Sir Richard Empson and John Dudley had been the principal instruments of the late King's financial policy. As a result they were enthusiastically if unfairly hated. Their arrest and imprisonment was an easy means of pleasing the populace and demonstrating that the miser's son was not after their gold. The two ministers, whose only crime was that of serving their royal master too faithfully, languished in prison for sixteen months. Dudley, though he made one vain attempt at escape, devoted his time to writing a political treatise *The Tree of Commonwealth*. This allegorical exposition of the roles of King and estates was dedicated to Henry VIII and urged him to shun avarice and rule with firmness tempered by mercy. The trial of Empson and Dudley was typical of the mish-mash of injustice and expediency that passed for judicial procedure in Tudor state hearings. The defence put into Sir Richard's mouth by a later historian is probably reliable in substance. He pointed out that he was being condemned for enforcing those very laws which some of his judges had helped to put through parliament, and concluded:

> . . . whoever yet saw any man condemned for doing justice? Especially when by the King, the chief dispenser of the laws, the whole frame of the proceeding hath been warranted and confirmed . . . In what well governed country do the infractors of national laws escape punishment, and they only suffer who have laboured to sustain them? Or if any such thing were read or heard of, could there be imagined a more certain sign of ruin to that commonwealth? And will you alone hope to escape this heavy judgement? If contrary to all equity and example, you not only make precedents for injustice and impunity, but, together with defaming, would inflict a cruel death on those who would maintain them, what can we then expect but a fatal period to us all ? . . . Only, if I must die, let me desire that my indictment be entered on no record, nor divulged to foreign nations; lest, from my fate, it be concluded, that in England all law and government are dissolved.[11]

Empson was right and his judges knew that they could not sustain their original charges without impugning the administration of the late King. So they trumped up a charge of conspiracy to treason and on this the two lawyers were executed on Tower Hill in August 1510.

It is, perhaps, a mark of the Council's lack of conviction in the justice of their actions that the 'traitors' heads were not exposed to public view but given decent burial with the rest of the dead men's remains. Both victims went to the obscurity of the tomb but the Tower of London had by no means seen the last of the remarkable house of Dudley.

While Empson and Dudley fretted in their prison apartments Henry VIII and his Queen returned to the Royal Lodgings in the Tower in June 1509 for their coronation procession. The festivities which inaugurated the new reign were more sumptuous than anything the City had seen before and they were but the prelude of fifteen or so splendid years during which the spendthrift monarch lost no opportunity to stage spectacular entertainments. Every political and diplomatic event, every ambassadorial reception, every military triumph was celebrated publicly and enthusiastically, as were the annual round of Christian festivals. This was the great period of the tournament and Europe boasted no more ardent exponent of the military arts than Henry VIII. Throughout his early manhood jousts and tournaments were held frequently and the King took an active part in them. Henry was determined that English armour should rival the elegant and intricately-decorated suits being produced in the workshops of Innsbruck, Nuremburg and Milan. Thanks to his patronage the workshops at Greenwich under the aegis of masters such as Martin van Royne and Erasmus Kyrkenar produced some of the finest armour ever made. The King's own collection, housed at Greenwich, was both large and magnificent, nor was his enthusiasm a whit diminished when he came within an inch of death while jousting with his friend Charles Brandon, Duke of Suffolk.

The Suffolk title had become vacant in 1513 with the death of Edmund de la Pole. Throughout seven years of imprisonment the Earl had given no trouble to his guards, no cause why his life should be suddenly terminated. However, political events made it expedient that Suffolk should die, and in expediency Henry VIII was very much his father's son. The King was about to go campaigning in France where Richard de la Pole had enlisted with the enemies of England. Henry thought it unwise to leave alive the leading Yorkist claimant to the throne while he himself was out of the country, so Edmund took the short walk from the Byward Tower to the top of Tower Hill.

Still the weeding out of possible rivals had not finished. The next to perish was Edward, Duke of Buckingham, a descendant of Edward III. Sometime in 1520 Henry wrote with his own hand (a rare occurrence) a private memorandum to his chief minister, Thomas Wolsey.

To this that followeth I thought not best to make him [i.e. the messenger] privy, nor none other but you and I, which is that I would you should make good watch on the Duke of Suffolk, on the Duke of Buckingham, on my lord of Northumberland, on my lord of Derby, on my lord of Wiltshire and on others which you think suspect.[12]

What the occasion was which had given the King reason to suspect even his close friends we do not know but the letter indicates that Henry VIII had inherited in large measure his father's sense of insecurity. In eleven years of marriage Catherine of Aragon had given him stillborn sons, sons who died in infancy and one daughter. The Queen was thirty-five and gossips were already whispering that the kingdom would have no male heir. Prior Hopkins of Merton had gone further; he had prophesied to the Duke of Buckingham that the crown would one day devolve upon him. The Duke was an arrogant and forthright young man unsparingly critical of government policy and especially of Wolsey whom he hated as a low-born upstart. Hopkin's words went to his head. He began boasting of his lineage and the changes he would make when he was king. It was enough to seal his fate. Wolsey interrogated the Duke's servants and confidants and laid the information before the King at Greenwich. On 8 April 1521 Buckingham received a royal summons to come to court. He set out down river in his barge but as he drew near to the capital he was intercepted by the captain of the guard and escorted not to Greenwich but to Queenhythe, whence he was marched to the Tower.* On 13 May he went in solemn procession to Westminster accompanied by the Constable and the Lieutenant for his trial, conviction and sentence. Four days later he was beheaded on Tower Hill.

Buckingham's fate was the result more of his own foolhardiness than of the King's cruelty: by the standards of the day he deserved to die. Henry VIII's reputation as a bloodthirsty and lecherous tyrant derives from the events of the last dozen years of his reign. By 1533 he was conscious that his most vigorous years were passed; he already suffered occasional bouts of pain from ulcerated legs; he was genuinely worried about the succession to the throne; he was harassed by an empty treasury which hampered his desire to play an active role in European affairs; he was perturbed by the growing religious discord in the country stemming from the growth and spread of native and foreign heresy. He thought he had solved the

---

* Passengers passing up and down river usually disembarked at Queenhythe or Billingsgate and walked from one landing stage to the other in order to avoid the dangerous rapids swirling around the piers of London Bridge. Boatmen often offered to 'shoot the bridge for sixpence' but it was a hazardous undertaking as Thomas Rempston's fate demonstrates (see above, p. 49).

problem of the succession when he decided to set aside Catherine of Aragon in favour of the young, beautiful and presumably fertile Anne Boleyn. But his plans foundered on the rock of the Pope's unwillingness to comply with the formality of granting an annulment. It was at this point that the King was fortunate in acquiring 'the most devoted, laborious and efficient servant of the crown in the long history of England.'[13]

If we envisage Henry VIII as an immense, potentially destructive force, we may fairly picture Thomas Cromwell as an engineer attempting to harness that power for constructive and lasting purposes. Indeed he once described himself in almost those terms: 'My prayer is that God give me no longer life than I shall be glad to use mine office in edification and not in destruction.'[14] It was Cromwell who cut the Gordian knot of the 'King's great matter', brought Anne and Henry together and severed the English church from its papal obedience. In doing so he won the bulk of the country's Protestants and many others who, though no heretics, were bitterly dissatisfied with the corruption and wealth of the clergy. Thus strengthened, Cromwell was able to solve the King's financial problems by closing down the monasteries and diverting their wealth into the Treasury. These negative policies* were only one aspect of an enormous programme of social and administrative reform which covered government, religion, education and commerce. It was nothing short of a revolution – a social revolution led from above. Inevitably it provoked widespread antagonism and opposition. Inevitably it necessitated a tightening up of the state's security system if it was to be carried through. And that largely explains the unprecedented number of prisoners brought to the Tower between 1534 and 1547.

The setting aside of Catherine and the marriage to Anne were widely unpopular. Preachers declaimed against them; men sang bawdy songs in taverns about them; tinkers sold crude pictures of the royal lovers at fairs; foreign ambassadors reported that all England was scandalized. In the face of this opposition Anne Boleyn's coronation acquired a considerable propaganda significance. Henry was determined that the event should conform in every particular to ancient custom and be staged with a magnificence rivalling even his own crowning. In 1532 Cromwell was ordered to carry out a complete survey of the Tower's palace buildings and to order any necessary refurbishings and repairs. The Mayor and aldermen of London were advised that the King looked for a lavish display of loyalty to his 'most dear and well beloved wife Queen Anne' and that

*It should be stressed that only a man of exceptional vision could have conceived so radical an undertaking; only a man of immense application and stamina could have operated the vast administrative machine the Dissolution made necessary.

the City should be 'ordered and garnished with pageants in places accustomed, for the honour of her grace'.[15]

On 19 May 1533, the Queen was brought up from Greenwich to be greeted by a spectacular water pageant and a salute of ordnance. Anne might be unpopular but there were few citizens who disdained to line the river banks or venture forth in boats to see the barges glowing with heraldic colour, filled with 'minstrels continually playing'; the aquatic float carrying 'terrible monsters and wild men' casting fire and making hideous noises; and the simulated mountain decorated with red and white roses among which virgins sang and played musical instruments. Within the Tower there was the usual banquet and the making of knights of the Bath and many other celebrations throughout the next eleven days. It would appear that Cromwell's workmen had made all the necessary repairs to enable the court to be accommodated in the palace. However, Anne Boleyn seems to have been lodged in the Lieutenant's house which suggests that the decay of the royal apartments noted in the 1532 survey had not been completely arrested. During Henry VII's reign the Coldharbour Tower had been the Queen's usual quarters. This was by now so derelict that only demolition and rebuilding would, it was believed, save it.

On 31 May the crowd gathered on the Hill and around the Bulwark saw the splendid procession emerge. Two by two they rode out – gentlemen, knights and esquires in their costly coronation robes, then the judges followed by the knights of the Bath 'in violet gowns with hoods lined with miniver', the Lord Chancellor preceding the Archbishop of York with the Venetian Ambassador and The Archbishop of Canterbury with the French ambassador. After them came the Mayor followed by the heralds and the peers of the realm in crimson velvet. The Queen in an open litter drawn by two palfries was dressed in white and ermine. An escort of knights held over her a canopy of cloth of gold fastened to silver staves. The rear of the procession was brought up by servants, guards and ladies of honour borne in chariots.

The court had scarcely left before the Tower began to fill with suspected opponents of the Cromwellian revolution. There was Robert Dalyvell who was arrested for uttering seditious words, racked on suspicion of being a spy, and eventually set at liberty minus his ears; Sir William Essex, closely examined because of sundry writings he had disseminated and only protected by his rank from being tortured; and William Hubberdyne, a flamboyant Catholic priest, who opposed religious innovations and sparked off riots in Bristol by his contest of pulpit oratory with Hugh Latimer, the great Protestant preacher. He spent at least five years in the Tower, where according to the complaint of a fellow prisoner he continued his 'popish talk'.

Another inmate, Abbot Thomas Marshall of Colchester, who opposed the King's marriage and the breach with Rome, broke down under interrogation and begged for mercy but was eventually hung, drawn and quartered for treason. From all over the country they came, as Cromwell's agents, determined to root out all opposition to the Reformation, sent under guard to the capital men and women whose offences varied from a few unguarded words to definite Catholic conspiracy.

What was fundamentally at stake was national security, and the government felt justified in threatening or using torture to extract confessions and information. It comes as no surprise that Leonard Skeffington who was Lieutenant in the 1530s provided the Tower with one of its most fearful implements. This was Skeffington's Gyves or the Scavenger's Daughter. Its effects and manner of operation were described by a seventeenth-century writer. It was, he said,

> in all respects the opposite of the rack, for while that draws apart the joints by the feet and hands tied, this, on the contrary constricts and binds into a ball. This holds the body in a threefold manner, the lower legs pressed to the thighs, the thighs to the belly, and thus both are locked with two iron cramps which are pressed by the tormentor's force against each other into a circular form; the body of the victim is almost broken by this compression. By the cruel torture, more dreadful and more complete than the rack, by the cruelty of which the whole body is so bent that with some the blood exudes from the tips of the hands and feet, with others the box of the chest being burst, a quantity of blood is expelled from the mouth and nostrils.[16]

As well as being extremely unpleasant this instrument also commended itself to the gaolers because it was very portable. Unlike the rack it could be taken to a prisoner's cell and the unfortunate man could presumably be locked into it and left until his shrieks and groans indicated that he was prepared to tell his tormentors what they wished to know.

The mention of Leonard Skeffington tempts us to diverge briefly from our gruesome narrative to mention an interesting fact about the intimate side of life at the Tower. That is the number of families which were associated with the castle over many generations. Occupations and offices were often passed on from father to son. Grandparents and grandchildren might live and die in the same quarters. A community spirit developed within the Tower which with its church, shops and ale-houses must have had a daily life very much like that of an English village. The Skeffingtons were one of the 'Tower families'. Sir William Skeffington, Leonard's father, was Master of the

Ordnance until 1529 when he was appointed Lord Deputy of Ireland. Another William, Leonard's son, obtained a post as gunner in the Tower in 1527. The register of births, marriages and deaths in St Peter's Chapel does not cover this period, it dates from 1550, but the frequency with which certain names occur within its pages indicate quite clearly that while traitors, state prisoners and discarded royal servants were suffering in the cells an ordinary English community was living within the walls of the Tower and experiencing all the simple joys and sorrows of humble men, women and children.

The most celebrated popular opponent of the King's policies was Elizabeth Barton, the 'Holy Maid of Kent'. She was a simple girl given to epileptic fits and 'visions', whose utterances created more interest than they might have done in less troubled times and who was exploited by unscrupulous men. In 1533 she was attracting large crowds by her prophecies of the disasters that were about to befall the King because of his marriage to the 'Bullen whore'. Wild-eyed and fervent, she declaimed that 'Harry shall no longer be king of this realm and will die a villain's death.' Elizabeth was telling the people what many of them wanted to hear and the government could not allow her to continue spreading her sedition. Together with her mentors she was arrested and locked up in the Tower. Whatever befell them there was so terrifying that they all broke down completely, confessed that the Holy Maid was an impostor and begged for mercy. They were ordered to make their confession in public at St Paul's Cross and again in Canterbury so that their movement would be totally discredited. But that did not conclude their punishment. They were returned to the Tower while Cromwell and the King calculated what other advantages might accrue to the regime from the Elizabeth Barton affair. A number of prominent Catholics had either supported the Maid or at least listened to her ravings and it was decided to take the opportunity of striking at these. Early in 1534 Elizabeth and six of her colleagues were attainted of treason while Sir Thomas More, John Fisher, Bishop of Rochester and four others were accused of misprision of (concealing) treason. The Maid and her associates perished at Tyburn, More was acquitted, the others were fined.

Thomas More, ex-Lord Chancellor, had been a close friend of the King but he could not accept the royal supremacy over the church and his stubbornness turned Henry's affection to hatred. Fisher was another confirmed papalist and both men were widely popular with the people. Henry had to have their support. The King and his parliament were tightening up the treason laws in order to act more firmly against those who opposed the supremacy *by word*, but More was very careful to say nothing which might be construed as criticism. In order to isolate and identify the opposition quite clearly Henry had the Act of Succession passed in 1534 and obliged his subjects to take an oath in support of it. Anyone taking the oath not only swore fealty to the heirs of Henry and Anne but acknowledged that the King's first marriage had never been valid. This meant that they accepted that Henry was right and the Pope was wrong. More, Fisher and the handful of other opponents of the King's religious policy were now driven into a corner from which they could only escape by compromising their consciences.

There is no direct connection between the ground floor and first floor chambers of the Bell Tower where More and Fisher were lodged in 1534. They are roomy, light, airy and, judged as prison quarters, not unpleasant; there were certainly far worse cells in the Tower. There were also many considerably better lodgings. Places such as the Beauchamp and Bloody Towers where prisoners of rank were often kept afforded greater comforts. The Bell Tower was chosen as the place of confinement for More and Fisher partly because conditions there could be made unpleasant and partly because the Lieutenant could personally keep a close watch on the prisoners as the Bell Tower cells opened directly from the Lieutenant's Lodging.

The object of their confinement was to induce them to submit. Henry, affronted by their opposition and the sympathy they commanded in England and abroad, would happily have hastened them to execution but there is evidence that Cromwell, Archbishop Cranmer and other members of the Council laboured hard to abate the royal wrath and to persuade their erstwhile colleagues to accept the *status quo*. They had a genuine affection for More and Fisher and they also knew that it would be politically undesirable to make martyrs of them. For seven months through the summer and early autumn they were afforded most of the usual privileges of high ranking prisoners – a reasonable diet, exercise, some visits from family and friends, and the attendance of personal servants. More walked in the Lieutenant's garden with his wife and daughters. He had books, ink and paper and was able to occupy himself writing short, devotional treatises. Once or twice his privileges were suddenly removed as part of his captor's technique of interrogation but, apart from occasional visits from members of the Council and theological experts brought by them to argue with him, he was largely unmolested until November. Much the same was true of Fisher, although the case against him was stronger. He had certainly compromised himself with the Maid of Kent, had been less discreet than More in expressing his opinions concerning the King's matter, and had unwisely opened his mind to the Imperial ambassador, a notorious Catholic intriguer and spymaster.

In November parliament attainted the two men of misprision of treason and their conditions of imprisonment changed drastically.

They were now convicted offenders serving official sentences of detention at the King's pleasure. Papers, books and ink were removed. They were put on short rations. As the winter drew on they were denied adequate heating and clothing. The objectives of the government seem to have been to increase the rigour of their detention so that they either died (Fisher was an old man of seventy-five and More, at fifty-six, was well past his prime) or were forced into submission, as happened in the case of Dr Nicholas Wilson, another opponent of the supremacy imprisoned in the Tower at the same time. Suffering they certainly inflicted, as both prisoners confessed:

> 'I am dying already, and have since I came here been divers times in the case that I thought to die within one hour. And I thank our Lord I was never sorry for it, but rather sorry when I saw the pang past.' More to Cromwell.[17]

> 'I beseech you to be good master unto me in my necessity; for I have neither shirt nor suit, nor yet other clothes that are necessary for me to wear, but that be ragged, and rent so shamefully. Notwithstanding, I might easily suffer that, if they would keep my body warm. But my diet also, God knoweth how slender it is at any times, and now in mine age my stomach may not away but with a few kind of meats, which if I want I decay forthwith, and fall into coughs and diseases of my body, and cannot keep myself in health.' Fisher to Cromwell.[18]

But they did not undermine either man's resolve.

Fisher and More languished in the Bell Tower until the following spring, the government apparently taking little interest in them. The Lieutenant of the Tower, Sir Edmund Walsingham was embarrassed by his strict orders and apologized that he was unable to improve the prisoners' conditions. But their continued resistance was well known and served to strengthen Catholic opposition. It was, indeed, one of the prisoners' friends, no less a person than Pope Paul III, who forced the King's hand. In May he appointed Fisher a cardinal. This unequivocal support from the head of the Roman Church drove Henry into one of his frightening rages. He was now determined that the two men should die, not as martyrs but as traitors clearly exposed in open court. Thus there began another series of interrogations in the Tower as Cromwell and his colleagues tried to gather or concoct evidence which would stand up before a jury. In the case of Fisher they had little difficulty and his trial on a charge of oral treason took place on 7 June. It was altogether a different matter with Thomas More, the experienced and infinitely subtle lawyer who had never in public or private voiced his opinion concerning the King's Supremacy.

The ex-Chancellor was eventually convicted on the evidence of Richard Rich. This Councillor came with others to the Tower on 12 June to collect More's books. The conditions of Sir Thomas's imprisonment had been once more relaxed and he was able to set down on paper his spiritual reactions to his sufferings. His last work was the little, unfinished treatise on Christ's agony in Gethsemane. It ends abruptly at the words *tum demum primum manus iniectas in Iesum* ('then, after all this, did they first lay hands upon Jesus'). As More wrote those words the cell door was unlocked. Richard Rich strode in and engaged his old patron in conversation while his companions packed More's precious volumes into a chest. The two men talked, as lawyers often will, of hypothetical cases.

'If it were enacted by parliament that I should be king, and whoever say nay it should be treason, would it be an offence to say "Rich is king"?'

'No', replied More, 'but let me put a higher case. If it were enacted by parliament that God were not God and if any repugned at the same Act it should be treason, would it be proper for you, Master Rich, to deny that God is God?'

'Nay, but that is not a true case for parliament hath no competence to decide on the existence of God. But now I will put you a middle case. Our King has been made Supreme Head by parliament. Will you not take him as such as you would take me for king?'

'A king may be made by parliament and a king deprived by parliament and to such an Act a subject must give his consent. But on the matter of the supremacy a subject is not free to consent to the Act of parliament.'[19]

At the trial More claimed that in this account of the conversation Rich, who was certainly one of the more odious and untrustworthy politicians of the age, had perjured himself; whether he had or not is still a subject of debate among historians.[20] In any event the Councillor's evidence was the government's only weapon, and a fairly blunt one at that. Yet it was sharp enough to sever More's head from his body.

Both men met their ends bravely though perhaps not with quite the panache later ascribed to them by Catholic propagandists. They were condemned to be hung, drawn, and quartered at Tyburn but their sentences were later commuted to beheading on Tower Hill. Fisher went forth to his death on 22 June. His headless body was interred in All Hallows Barking-by-the-Tower but was soon after brought back to St Peter ad Vincula, presumably because his tomb had become a centre of pilgrimage. On 6 July More was brought out of his prison and handed over to the Sheriff of London at the Bulwark Gate. His celebrated witticism at the foot of the scaffold 'I pray you, Master Lieutenant, see me safe up, and for my coming down let me shift for myself', if it was spoken at all, must have been spoken to the Sheriff's officers. More, too, was brought to rest in St Peter's.

Within a year the cause of all the trouble and bloodletting – Anne Boleyn – lay within feet of the Catholic martyrs. In January 1536 the Queen miscarried. Of the babies she had conceived only one had survived and that was a girl. Henry was three years older than when he had married her. He had set all Europe by the ears. He had done good men and women to death. And all for nothing: he still had no heir and he had tired of the woman who had once inflamed his passions. In January 1536 Catherine of Aragon died. Henry must have reflected often that were it not for Anne he would be free to marry without any of the complications that had attended his last wedding. Sometime in the early part of that year, 1536, the King realized that what he had done once he could do again. The callousness with which he disposed of Anne Boleyn is more shocking than the long drawn out affair of the annulment of his first marriage. Then he could at least claim that his conscience troubled him about the morality of his union with his dead brother's widow. But the murder of Anne Boleyn and her 'lovers' was pure, calculated expediency. Henry knew that the Catholic world did not recognize his second marriage and that no diplomatic difficulties would ensue upon his breaking it.

It was all accomplished very quickly. On 24 April a secret commission was appointed to find means of disentangling the King from his marriage. By the end of the month they had laid their plan. On 1 May Henry Norris, a courtier and one time friend of the King, was seized suddenly at Greenwich and rowed to the Tower. The next day other arrests followed – Lord Rochford, the Queen's brother, Sir Francis Weston, William Brereton and Mark Smeaton, a musician. Then, in the afternoon, Anne was confronted with her husband's command that she proceed immediately to the Tower. In a state of hysterical collapse she was conveyed up river by Cromwell, the Lord Chancellor and Sir William Kingston, Constable of the Tower. On her arrival she asked nervously where she was to be lodged. It was a natural question; she knew that she had completely lost Henry's affection and that his spite might well display itself in the issuing of instructions concerning her imprisonment. Kingston reassured her; she was to live in the rooms she had occupied on her last visit to the Tower in the days preceding her coronation. She was still Queen and would be afforded the honours appropriate to her position. The Constable himself was appointed her guardian and Lady Kingston was installed in Anne's suite so that she could report to her husband every word spoken by the prisoner.

Mark Smeaton, socially the least important of the arrested courtiers, was tortured. He confessed adultery with the Queen and, on promise of release, signed a written statement to that effect. Rochford was accused of incest with his sister and the others of carnal knowledge of the Queen. They denied the charges but they were convicted on perjured or circumstantial evidence. All except Rochford were tried on 12 May. Three days later twenty-six peers assembled in the Great Hall to adjudicate on the charges against the Queen and her brother. Anne was as good as condemned already: the convictions of her 'lovers' left her no means of proving her innocence. The men were all beheaded (except the commoner, Smeaton, who was hanged) on Tower Hill on 17 May and buried in the churchyard of St Peter ad Vincula.

The volatile girl hovered between tearful despair and wild hope that the King would intervene to save her. But towards the end she found a serene resignation. She made her confession to her old friend Archbishop Cranmer and not once did she admit to any marital infidelity. Fearing that Anne would maintain her innocence even on the scaffold, careful arrangements were made that her execution should be a very private affair, as a letter from the Constable to Cromwell indicates:

Sir, this shall be to advertise you I have received your letter wherein [you say] you would have strangers conveyed out of the Tower, and so they be . . . [including] the ambassador of the Emperor . . . [who was] honestly put out. Sir, if we have not an hour certain and known in London I think here will be but few, and I think a reasonable number were best: for I suppose she will declare herself to be not a woman for all men but for the King [only] at the hour of her death. This morning she sent for me that I might be with her at mass as she received the good lord . . . At my coming she said 'Mr Kingston, I hear say that I shall not die afore noon, and I am very sorry therefore; for I had thought to be dead this time and past my pain.' I told her it should be no pain, it was so subtle, and then she said, 'I have heard say the executioner was very good, and I have a little neck,' and put her hand about it laughing heartily. I have seen many men and also women executed, and that they have been in great sorrow; and to my knowledge this lady has much joy and pleasure in death.[21]

It was, therefore, in front of a small official gathering on Tower Green a little before noon on 19 May 1536 that the first execution of the consort of a reigning English monarch took place. It was accomplished by the public executioner of Calais who performed his office with a sword, after the French fashion. Before Anne was blindfolded she must have been able to see quite clearly the freshly turned earth on the graves of her unfortunate friends. Then her eyes were bandaged. She knelt and carefully arranged the folds of her dress. She bent forward her 'little neck' and said aloud 'O Lord God have pity on my soul'. Thus, perfectly composed, she died. Afterwards her body made the very short journey to St Peter's where it was buried beneath the altar.

Cromwell had already begun his purge of the smaller religious houses, many of which were so badly run or had so few numbers that dissolution was entirely appropriate. That was not the pragmatic view taken by ordinary folk in many parts of the country. In the north this spoliation came as the final straw to a people burdened and bewildered by social change, heavy taxation and an unprecedented degree of interference in their lives by the central government. In the winter of 1536–7 rebellion broke out in Lincolnshire, Yorkshire, Westmorland and Cumberland, the most serious being Yorkshire's 'Pilgrimage of Grace'. First reports of the troubles were garbled and alarming. Hasty preparations were made to combat the ill-defined menace. Horses were commandeered in London and the Tower garrison was strengthened. On 8 October Richard Cromwell (the minister's nephew) came to the Tower to collect arms for despatch to the troubled area. Among other items he took '34 little falconets of those made by the King last year.' They were loaded onto waggons and immediately Cromwell set out northwards. He got no further than a mile beyond the City. There the heavy carts were completely bogged down in roads made quagmires by the autumn rains. Loads were redistributed but it became obvious that there was no way of transporting all the cannon. Eighteen had to be sent back to the Tower.[22] After the first panic was over the government organized its transport of munitions rather more effectively. On 23 November a large quantity of ordnance was taken out to Tower Wharf and loaded onto ten warships in order to be conveyed up the coast and delivered to the army currently being mustered by the Dukes of Suffolk and Norfolk.

The risings failed but not before they had severely shaken Henry VIII's throne. In the end the rebels were defeated less by military might than by subtle negotiations based on false promises of pardon and redress of grievances. Hundreds of prisoners were taken and over two hundred men and women were executed. Most of this activity took place in the northern shires but the ringleaders were brought to the Tower, whose cells, by the spring of 1537, were filled with rebels awaiting trial. They were a motley collection – nobles, gentlemen, abbots, priests and commoners – for all conditions of men had joined the revolt in pursuance of a variety of special interests. Torture was freely used in the many interrogations which took place within the Tower, for the government had to know how widespread the disaffection was, how much trust they could repose in the leading men of the north, and where to look for further possible outbreaks.

103

The most tragic of these figures was Robert Aske, Yorkshire gentlemen and London lawyer. He took the leadership of the main revolt but was tricked by the King and the Duke of Norfolk into travelling to London to present the rebels' petition in person. Aske was an idealist and, perhaps, somewhat naive. When Henry received him cordially, listened to his point of view and sent him back to Yorkshire with soft words he believed the King, disbanded his forces and even helped to suppress a fresh outbreak of revolt. When Norfolk began unleashing severe reprisals Aske realized that he had failed his cause. Yet resolving to try persuasion once more and relying on the pardon the King had granted, he travelled south again to speak personally with his sovereign. For his credulity he was thrust into the Tower and submitted to the rigours of interrogation. His pleas from prison for the common necessities of life make touching reading:

> I most humbly beseech you all to be so good unto me [that] . . . I might know whether I might send for my rents or fees or not without any displeasure to any man, for unless the King's highness and my Lord Privy Seal [Cromwell] shall be merciful and gracious unto me I am not able to live, for none of my friends will do nothing for me, and I have need to have a pair of hose, a doublet of fustian, a shirt (for I have but one shirt here) and a pair of shoes. I beseech you heartily that I may know your mind herein and how I shall be ordered that I may trust to the same for the love of God.[23]

His appeal was ignored and two or three weeks later he was obliged to write again.

> Good master Doctor I beseech you to send me money and my stuff [such] as a shirt, a pair of hose, a doublet and a pair of shoes, for neither I have money nor gear to wear as ye saw yourself. For the reverence of God send me the same or else I know not how to do nor live . . .[24]

The demeanour of another prisoner was very different. Lord Darcy was a truculent member of the old baronage who would not be cowed by his interrogators.

> Cromwell it is thou that art the very original and chief causer of all this rebellion and mischief, and art likewise causer of the apprehension of us that be noble men and dost daily earnestly travail to bring us to our end and to strike off our heads, and I trust that or thou die, though thou wouldst procure all the noblemen's heads within the realm to be stricken off, yet shall there one head remain that shall strike off thy head.[25]

Darcy was beheaded on Tower Hill and Aske taken to York to be hanged in chains.

The Pilgrimage of Grace provided the opportunity and the sort of reason a totalitarian regime required for removing more of the surviving Yorkists. The Courtenays and most of their Pole relatives attended at court and demonstrated their loyalty to the Tudor regime while being ever conscious that their position was fundamentally precarious. Not so Reginald Pole the young priest who had lived most of his life abroad and advanced himself in the service of the papacy. He put himself at the head of a Catholic crusade to win England back to the old religion. At the height of the northern rebellions he was appointed cardinal and papal legate with secret instructions to help organize the government which, it was expected, would be established on the successful outcome of the Pilgrimage. While his brothers and cousins were leading royal troops against the insurgents, Cardinal Pole was in treasonable communication with the enemies of the crown.

Cromwell made several attempts to have Pole arrested or assassinated. He also planted spies to report on the Cardinal's communications with his family. It was known that his brothers, Geoffrey and Lord Montague, as well as Henry Courtenay, Marquis of Exeter, were bitterly opposed to the new religious order. There were many, especially in the West Country, who looked to them for leadership. The investigation went on for months. Then, without warning, Geoffrey Pole was arrested.

Geoffrey was a weak man, which was probably why he was chosen. He was thrown into an unpleasant cell and every kind of psychological torture was used to break him down – poor and irregular meals, frequent and intense interrogation, the threat of the rack, the promise of pardon in return for implicating others, the hint that the King knew the truth anyway so that it was useless to keep silence. The wretched man was soon in a black fit of terror and despair. Indeed, his examiners did their job almost too well: 'His keeper being absent, a knife at hand upon the table, he riseth out of his bed, and taketh the knife, and with full intent to die, gave himself a stab with the knife upon the breast.'[26] Soon after this Geoffrey Pole was ready to say whatever his tormentors wished. On his evidence Lord Montague, the Marquis of Exeter, Sir Edward Neville, the Marchioness of Exeter and her young son and several others were brought to the Tower. All the men were convicted of verbal treason and were executed. Geoffrey was released. While all this was happening the 68-year-old Countess of Salisbury, mother of the condemned Montague, was apprehended. Failing to satisfy her examiners, she was eventually brought to the Tower in March 1539. She was attainted of treason but little molested and was probably kept largely as a hostage to ensure Cardinal Pole's good behaviour. With her in the Tower were her young grandson, Henry, and his playmate, Edward Courtenay. There she remained until 27 May 1541 when, suddenly and without warning, she was led out onto the Green and decapitated. Whether this needless act of barbarism was a result of a vicious royal whim or a calculated blow at Cardinal Pole it is difficult to say. It was carried out immediately before Henry left on a tour of the north and there is reason to believe that the decision was a hurried one. According to an early account, the official executioner was not available and the job was badly bungled by an inefficient stand-in. A later gruesome story tells of the shrieking Countess being chased around the block by the headsman but this exaggeration may safely be put down to Catholic propaganda. Young Henry Pole apparently died in the Tower about a year later and Edward Courtenay was not released until the beginning of Mary Tudor's reign in 1553.

It is pleasant to be able to relieve this catalogue of political butchery with the story of one Tower servant who, in so far as he was able, acted with humanity and pity. So many of the noble and wealthy prisoners in the Tower at this period complained of inadequate treatment that we cannot avoid the conclusion that most of the money provided for their keep was being appropriated by the Lieutenant and the Yeoman Warders. But there was at least one gaoler who was cast in a different mould. Thomas Philips was a convinced Protestant and a man who displayed commendable Christian charity. He was either the keeper of, or had access to, the Countess of Salisbury and the Marchioness of Exeter. When the prisoners had appealed without success to the Lieutenant for some alleviation of their discomfort, Philips, presumably not without some risk of reprisal, went over his superior's head and wrote directly to a member of the Council. 'By reason that I am daily conversant with them I can no less do but utter' their complaints. The Marchioness 'wanteth raiment, and hath no change but only that your lordship commanded to be provided'. One of her gentlewomen 'hath no manner of change and that that she hath is sore worn'. The Marchioness's servants were faithful to her 'and very sorry is she that she hath not [that with which] to recompense them, at least their wages'. She 'maketh great moan for that she wanteth necessary apparel both for to change and also to keep her warm.'[27] The warder's appeal brought a response and some, at least, of the ladies' wants were attended to.

Another prisoner, Sir Nicholas Carew, who was executed on Tower Hill in March 1539, actually regarded himself as fortunate to have been brought to the Tower. On the scaffold, 'he made a goodly confession, both of his folly and superstitious faith, giving God most hearty thanks that ever he came in the prison of the Tower, where he first savoured the life and sweetness of God's most holy word, meaning the Bible in English, which there he read by the means of one Thomas Philips, then keeper.'[28]

Not all Tower officers had such pure motives for helping prisoners. In 1534 John Bawde, a servant of the Lieutenant Sir Edmund Walsingham, made the acquaintance of Alice Tankerville, a prisoner in the Coldharbour. He found her very attractive and was soon seduced by her into helping her make a bid to escape. Their plan was very elaborate and involved Bawde in having duplicate keys cut and obtaining lengths of rope. On a dark night the pair made their way over the roofs until they reached St Thomas's Tower from which they let themselves down by rope to the Wharf. Unfortunately they got no farther than Tower Hill before being seen and recognized. What happened to the lady we do not know but Bawde felt the full force of Walsingham's anger. He was thrown into the Little Ease, the vilest dungeon in the castle. Later he was racked and, after a trial, hanged in chains.

The story is interesting for a number of reasons. It is the first and one of the very few references to the Little Ease which has become an entrenched feature of the legend of the Tower. It is supposed to have been dark, noisome and narrow with no room for a man to stand or lie down. Among the prisoners who were believed to have been kept there is Sir Walter Raleigh. There is no truth whatever in that story and a great deal of mystery about the cell itself. Despite a persistent tradition situating it in the White Tower, there is no chamber there which answers to the description. The most likely location seems to have been in the base of the old Flint Tower. This was rebuilt at the end of the eighteenth century, so even that solution to the problem must remain conjectural.

The other interesting feature of the Bawde saga is its illumination of Walsingham's character. Sir Edmund served as Lieutenant of the Tower right through the period which many would regard as the blackest in its history. He was appointed about 1525 and resigned on the death of Henry VIII in 1547. Throughout he was the ideal royal servant. He identified himself closely with the regime from his earliest years. He was almost an exact contemporary of the King. He fought and distinguished himself in Henry's early battles and was knighted on the field of Flodden. He was a member of the pliant jury which condemned Buckingham in 1521. By 1525 he had shown himself to be a man the government could trust. And so he proved. Walsingham administered the fortress efficiently and carried out his instructions scrupulously. Few, if any, men escaped from the Tower during his Lieutenancy and from the savagery of Bawde's treatment

107

it is not difficult to see why. In that case Walsingham may well have felt that the actions of his servant reflected upon himself and he was therefore determined not only to make an example of Bawde but also to demonstrate his loyalty beyond any doubt. With such a master Bawde may well have been as anxious to escape from the Tower as Alice Tankerville. Walsingham presided unfeelingly over the tortures, the harsh treatment of prisoners and the few executions which took place on the Green. He might, as in the case of More and Fisher, express regret for the harsh conditions imposed but he never deviated from his instructions in the name of humanity. Thomas Philips knew that it was useless to appeal to the Lieutenant on behalf of the noble ladies in his charge. Walsingham's attitude kept him in office for twenty-two years (except, apparently, for two periods when his job was performed by a deputy or substitute) and made him a wealthy man able to buy land in his native Kent and elsewhere. Only once in that period do we read of the Lieutenant protesting about anything that happened in the Tower and that was during one of the two times when someone else was deputizing for him (see below p. 110).

By 1540 such an enormous pressure of hatred had built up against Cromwell that it took only a slight faltering of royal favour for the full force of it to be suddenly released. Cromwell's foreign policy had failed and, moreover, he had inveigled the King into marriage with Anne of Cleves, a woman who was as plain as she was dull. Henry was angry and Cromwell's enemies on the Council, led by Stephen Gardiner, Bishop of Winchester and the Duke of Norfolk, grasped their opportunity. Young pretty Catherine Howard was paraded before Henry's eyes and the Norfolk faction concocted evidence upon which to base treason charges against Cromwell. Henry was persuaded that Anne could be set aside and the whole disastrous episode blamed on his minister. He knew that to throw Cromwell to the wolves would be the most popular act he could perform and he was so besotted with Catherine that he did not pause to consider the results of that act. On 10 June Cromwell was arrested at a Council meeting, taken to a waiting barge and rowed straight to the Tower.

For forty-eight days he waited for a reprieve reflecting angrily on the way he had been paid for faithful service and just as angrily that the task he had begun seemed destined never to be finished. He wrote, in vain, to remind his ungrateful sovereign of what was no less than the truth:

Mine accusers your Grace knoweth. God forgive them. For as I ever had love to your honour, person, life, prosperity, health, wealth, joy and comfort, and also your most dear and most entirely beloved son, the Prince his Grace, and your proceedings, God so help me in this mine adversity, and confound me if ever I thought the contrary. What labours, pains and travails I have taken according to my most bounden duty God also knoweth. For if it were in my power – as it is in God's – to make your Majesty to live ever young and prosperous, God knoweth I would. If it had been or were in my power to make you so rich as ye might enrich all men, God help me . . . I would do it. If it had been or were in my power to make your Majesty so puissant as all the world should be compelled to obey you, Christ he knoweth I would . . . Sir, as to your common wealth, I have ever after my wit, power and knowledge travailed therein, having had no respect to persons (your Majesty only excepted) . . . but that I have done any injustice or wrong wilfully, I trust God shall be my witness, and the world not able justly to accuse me . . .[29]

On 28 July Thomas Cromwell went patiently to his death on Tower Hill, only to suffer appallingly from the ministrations of a 'ragged, butcherly miser, which very ungodly performed the office'.

If the execution of Thomas More was Henry VIII's foulest crime, the execution of Thomas Cromwell was his most stupid. England was in the grip of the greatest social and religious upheaval in her history and the King had thrown away the one man who had exercised a measure of control over the situation. The conflict between Catholic and Protestant had grown rapidly more intense and widespread. Now the divisions were reflected even within Henry's Council. For the remainder of the reign conservative and radical factions struggled for power within the government of the ailing king. Their objective was to secure control of the regency council which must inevitably be appointed to govern the country on the accession of Henry's son, Edward, who was still a child. Norfolk and Gardiner, leaders of the conservative group, had triumphed in the overthrow of Cromwell. Their opponents, led by the Earl of Hertford, Viscount Lisle and Archbishop Cranmer were not slow in fighting back.

They directed their attack against Queen Catherine Howard, Norfolk's niece and protégée. By encouraging servants to gossip and friends to break confidences they pieced together an unsavoury story of Catherine's loose living before her marriage. Then, more by accident than design, they discovered that the Queen had been carrying on an adulterous affair in recent months with Thomas Culpepper, a gentleman of the King's Privy Chamber. A later age may sympathize with a high-spirited young woman of normal appetites who found some relief from the attentions of a bloated, ill-tempered old man whose legs were a mass of suppurating sores, but all Henry could see was that he had been cuckolded and by one of his own servants.

On 10 February 1542 Catherine Howard was taken to the Tower with Lady Rochford, who had aided her in arranging her secret assignations. Both ladies had been confined for several weeks at Sion House since the arrest and execution of Culpepper and her pre-marital lover, Francis Dereham. They were only brought to the Tower for their execution, which took place three days later in the seclusion of the Green. Catherine's body was interred in St Peter's beside that of the other Queen who had perished under almost identical circumstances a mere six years before.

Henry was wary about contracting a sixth marriage but in the middle of 1543 he wed the devout, patient, scholarly Catherine Parr, a widow who had already nursed two ageing husbands. Surely here was no flighty girl who would humiliate him. No, but she was a sympathizer with the new religious ideas. Gardiner and Norfolk, who had come very close to ruin at the downfall of his niece, saw in this a possible opportunity of destroying her and of destroying their political rivals along with her. For Henry was no Protestant. He may have turned the Pope out of England, set up the English Bible in parish churches and relied heavily on Protestant preachers to spread his antipapal propaganda, but he believed firmly in his own orthodoxy. As if to demonstrate the fact, the Tower and other prisons frequently housed both Catholics accused of treason for rejecting the supremacy and Protestants awaiting death at the stake for heresy.

In 1545–6 the Bishop of London was troubled by a most pestilential heretic. She was Anne Askew, an outspoken Lincolnshire gentlewoman with friends and relatives at court. She was pert, she knew her Bible better than most priests knew theirs and she was not overawed by ecclesiastical authority. In March 1546 Bishop Bonner interrogated her and after several exhausting hours extracted a recantation from her and released her. She returned to Lincolnshire but was soon back in the capital again where she faced renewed heresy charges. This was part of a purge of Protestants in high places which filled the Tower and the City prisons with suspected heretics throughout the summer. This time Anne refused to recant. She was condemned to be burned as a relapsed heretic. *Then* she was conveyed to the Tower.

Gardiner and his friends had been taking a close interest in Anne. They knew of her close connection with the Queen's circle. They were almost ready to strike at the Queen. All they needed was a little more evidence. They did not doubt that, terrified by the Tower and all it meant, Anne Askew would tell them what they wanted. Lord Chancellor Wriothesly and Richard Rich went there and questioned her for hour after hour. Anne told them nothing. Their next decision indicates just how desperate they were to make her talk. They sent for the Lieutenant and asked him to have the rack prepared. The

Lieutenant was Sir Anthony Knyvett who was deputizing for Walsingham, perhaps because the latter was occupied with his duties as M.P. for Surrey (he had been elected the previous year). Sir Anthony was nervous; he knew that the racking of a woman was unprecedented (there is certainly no other account of it in the records of the Tower), but he was assured that a light 'pinching' would be sufficient to terrify Anne into revealing all she knew.

He was wrong. Mistress Askew had the martyr temperament. She had already embraced death and could now endure any pain as a part of her suffering for truth's sake. In the basement of the White Tower she was stretched on the rack and the screw was turned. Rich and Wriothesly put their questions. Silence. The ministers ordered more pressure to be applied. Still they got nothing from the prisoner. Knyvett now ordered his men to release the woman. The Chancellor turned on him angrily and told him not to interfere. The Lieutenant pointed out the irregularity of what they were doing. Wriothesly ordered him in the King's name to continue the torture. He refused. At that point the two councillors removed their gowns and with their own hands worked the rack themselves. 'And so quietly and patiently praying unto the Lord, she abode their tyranny, till her bones and joints were almost plucked asunder.'[30]

When Anne was released she fainted and when she recovered she no longer had the full use of her limbs. Still her tormentors continued their questions. But Knyvett had long since left. He hurried by boat to Westminster, exercised his right of access to the King, and gave Henry a full report. What Henry's reaction was or how far he was privy to his minister's actions we do not know but within days the plot against Catherine Parr had collapsed. There would never be another English queen discreetly done to death on Tower Green.

Anne Askew had to be carried in a chair to Smithfield where she was burned.

The courtier poet Thomas Wyatt shall sum up for us this epoch in the Tower's history. He was a prisoner there in 1536 and witnessed Anne Boleyn's execution from his cell 'grate' (window grating).

> The Bell Tower showed me such sight
> That in my head sticks day and night
> There did I learn out of a grate,
> For all favour, glory or might,
> That yet *circa Regna tonat*.*

* It thunders round the throne.

6

In the *Survey* made by Hayward and Gascoyne in 1597 a broken wall appears in the forecourt of the White Tower and against it the legend 'The Hall decayed'. John Stow, writing in the very next year observed:

> . . . in the east by the Tower of London, is the Hospital of St Katharine . . . from this precinct of St Katharine to Wapping . . . was never a house standing within these 40 years: but since the gallows being after removed farther off, a continual street, or filthy straight passage, with alleys of small tenements or cottages builded, inhabited by sailors victuallers, along by the river of Thames almost to Ratcliff . . . Now for Tower Hill, the plain there is likewise greatly diminished, by encroachments for building of small tenements, and taking in of garden plots, timberyards, or what they list . . .[1]

In 1590 a commission was appointed to inquire into 'houses lately erected against the Tower walls or near to the Tower ditches or wharfs, and whether they are fit to be continued or not and who dwells in them and to whom they pay their rents.' The waterfront from London Bridge to a point far to the east of the Tower was a strand of bustling wharfs and quays and the river thick with merchantmen, warships and galleys. Occasionally a foreign visitor came up the Thames and landed at Tower Wharf but the reception committee of noblemen and City dignitaries did not lead him to the royal lodgings within the castle; he was offered hospitality in some great house belonging to a minister or bishop within the capital or its western suburb. Within the fortress more and more buildings were taken over to house ordnance, records and other stores. As the Tower became increasingly a warehouse complex it was sometimes difficult for its function as a prison to be sustained; often cells and chambers had to be hurriedly cleared of chests and lumber in order to accommodate an influx of detainees.

There are many reasons for this radical change which came over the life and appearance of the Tower of London. We have already mentioned the fact that royal visits declined in frequency and this may well be fundamental. The 'charisma of monarchy' about the Tower must have dwindled as steadily as the gorgeous palace buildings decayed or were taken over for mundane purposes. Late sixteenth-century records give us the first hint that the Tower was acquiring an antiquarian and curiosity interest. Distinguished visitors, such as the German traveller Paul Hentzner who came in 1597, were shown around the building which was now one of the sights of London. From Hentzner's description one gets the impression that there was already an established itinerary:

Upon entering the Tower we were obliged to quit our swords at the gate and deliver them to the guard. When we were introduced we were shown above a hundred pieces of arras belonging to the crown, made of gold, silver and silk; several saddles covered with velvet of different colours; an immense quantity of bed furniture, such as canopies and the like, some of them most richly ornamented with pearl; some royal dresses are so extremely magnificent as to raise one's admiration at the sums they must have cost. We were then led into the armoury, in which are these peculiarities: spears out of which you may shoot; shields that will give fire four times; a great many rich halberds, commonly called partisans, with which the guard defended the royal person in battle; some lances covered with red and green velvet; and the body armour of Henry VIII. Many and very beautiful arms, as well for men as for horses in [tournaments] – the lance of Charles Brandon, Duke of Suffolk, three spans thick; two pieces of cannon – the one fires three, the other seven balls at a time; two others made of wood, which the English had at the siege of Boulogne, in France. And by this strat-agem, without which they could not have succeeded, they struck a terror into the inhabitants, as at the appearance of artillery, and the town was surrendered upon articles; nineteen cannons of a thicker make than ordinary, and, in a room apart, thirty-six of a smaller; other cannon for chain shot, and balls proper to bring down masts of ships; crossbows, bows and arrows, of which to this day the English make great use in their exercises; but who can relate all that is to be seen here. Eight or nine men, employed by the year, are scarce sufficient to keep all the arms bright.[2]

Hentzner obviously had a good tour and an experienced guide – the role of the Tower as a tourist attraction had begun.

The battle fought by successive monarchs to prevent encroachment by other buildings was finally lost in the second half of the sixteenth century. Population pressure and the growth of trade created an unprecedented clamour for housing, workshops and business premises. The number of people living in London more than doubled between 1560 and 1600 to stand at some 200,000. Despite the efforts of the government to stop them, vagrants crowded into the City in search of work and settled to a life of honest labour, beggary or crime. Prospering merchants extended their premises on or near the waterfront and as trade expanded a host of ancillary craftsmen – coopers, carpenters, sail-makers, tailors, cordwainers, blacksmiths, and others – established themselves as near as possible to their prospective patrons. This was the development which sustained England's establishment of maritime supremacy. It also engulfed the Tower of London in a sprawl of unplanned dwellings and workplaces, many of which rapidly turned into slums.

It was the dissolution of the monasteries which accelerated this urbanization. When Henry VIII took into his own possession the lands, churches, cloisters, farms and cottages belonging to the religious it was in order to sell most of them again through the specially created Court of Augmentations. Never in the history of England has so much property come onto the market at one time. The resulting orgy of speculation led to the piecemeal dismemberment and amalgamation of estates. Buildings were demolished, converted or abandoned. In the towns and cities quick fortunes were made by splitting up monastic sites into small building plots. The appearance of the Tower environs certainly changed. The Crutched Friars' house at the top of Tower Hill was transformed into a town mansion for Lord Lumley who established on part of the site a factory for making glass after the Venetian fashion. The King kept the Abbey of the Nuns of St Clare (the Minories) and turned it over to the Ordnance Office which constructed there 'divers fair and large storehouses for armour, and habiliments of war, with divers workhouses serving to the same purpose'.[3] It was in this new Minories complex that the Lieutenant of the Ordnance had his lodging. The farm adjoining the abbey was divided and leased out as 'garden plots'. St Mary Graces Cistercian Abbey was torn down by Sir Arthur Darcy, Lieutenant of the Tower, who had obtained a monopoly of supplying food to the King's ships in the port of London and who now built a victualling depot. It was probably these changes of land ownership which made necessary a restating of the boundaries of the Liberty of the Tower in 1536. They were now defined as running north from the Ram's Head in Petty Wales to the new brick wall at the edge of Lord Lumley's property, thence east by 'the nine gardens' to the City wall. The boundary followed this southwards a short distance then turned eastwards once more to cut across the top of East Smithfield to the corner of Hog Lane. From there it ran due south along the outer scarp of the Tower moat to the river. This settlement did not bring peace. Indeed (as we shall see later), as the number of buildings within and near the Liberty increased so did the friction between City and Tower authorities, until Londoners and freemen of the Tower came to blows.

It is against this changing background that the major events of the period 1547–1603 must be seen. After many false alarms, spread over

114

a period of four or five years, Henry VIII finally succumbed to his illnesses and died in January 1547. In his last hours he appointed a regency council for his young son which confirmed that the progressive/Protestant faction had triumphed over the conservative/Catholic group. The preceding months had seen the downfall of the Howards. Thomas Howard, Duke of Norfolk, had for years lived a politically charmed life. Opposed to religious change, the new learning and the new men, he had schemed and plotted for power near the throne. Often his plans had come undone. Colleagues and relatives had gone to the block. Yet Norfolk had survived. A fresh crisis arose in the concluding months of 1546 when accusations of treason were laid against his son, the Earl of Surrey. That 'foolish, proud boy' had boasted openly about the power which would come to the Howards when the King died and had even quartered the arms of Edward the Confessor with his own. The abuse of a strictly royal privilege seemed to indicate very clearly the extent of his ambition. On 12 December Surrey and his father were taken to the Tower. On 21 January the Earl was beheaded on Tower Hill and his body interred in All Hallows Church.* Norfolk was attainted of treason and was condemned to share his son's fate. He threw himself on the King's mercy but in vain. His execution was fixed for the morning of 28 January. At seventy-three the Duke did not find it easy to sleep; he wrote from the Tower 'unless I have books to read ere I fall asleep, and after I wake again, I cannot sleep, nor have done these dozen years.' Did slumber elude him even more than usual on that night of 27–28 January? If so, it was a discomfort he shared with other members of the Council. They were with the King at Whitehall and the King was dying. Norfolk had no way of knowing why he was not led out to the block shortly after that winter dawn. It was some days before he was informed that Henry VIII had passed away in the small hours of 28 January and that England's new rulers had decided to postpone the execution. It remained 'postponed' and Howard remained in the Tower throughout the six years of Edward VI's reign.

Once again the throne of England was occupied by a minor and there was little reason to suppose that the experiment which had always failed before would this time succeed. Baronial factions were a thing of the past but religious division and social discontent were creating a state of unrest that even the late self-willed autocrat had had difficulty in controlling. Henry had done his best to provide his heir with a united regency council. He deliberately excluded Bishop Gardiner who, he knew, would never work with men who did not share his convictions. Henry was right: for the next eighteen months the Bishop of Winchester denounced, intrigued against and urged

* It was later moved to the family church at Framlingham, Suffolk.

115

general disobedience to the new government until, at last, he was shut up in the Tower. The Council itself took the step of appointing Edward Seymour, Earl of Hertford as the young King's Protector. It was an obvious choice: Seymour was Edward's uncle, a close friend of the late King, an experienced soldier and one of the leading figures in the old Council. He had no ambitious rivals anxious to claim authority, save Norfolk and Gardiner, both of whom were effectively excluded from office. The Protector hurried to inform the nine-year-old King of his father's death and to bring him immediately to the safety of the Tower.

On 31 January Londoners had their first glimpse of their new monarch as they cheered him through the streets to the castle. As his small entourage approached the Tower there was 'great shot of ordnance in all places there about, as well as out of the Tower as out of the ships.'[4] Edward established his court in the ancient palace buildings and his ministers sent out messengers to secure universal assent to the *fait accompli*. During the next few days most of the leading men in church and state came into the Presence Chamber to pledge their loyalty to the small figure perched on the chair of state. Young, Edward may have been, but he had been trained to kingship from his earliest years and he did not fail his tutors now. Having received his nobles and bishops at his first audience he addressed them with gracious solemnity, 'We heartily thank you, my lords all; and hereafter in all that ye shall have to do with us for any suit or causes, ye shall be heartily welcome to us.'[5]

On 17 February the new King held an investiture at which he created his uncle Duke of Somerset. Other titles were also distributed, most significant of which was that of the earldom of Warwick, now conferred on John Dudley, Lord Lisle, son of that Edmund Dudley who had perished on Tower Hill thirty-seven years before. Two days later the court, obedient to tradition, conveyed Edward VI through the City of Westminster. London welcomed the new sovereign with enthusiasm if with rather less magnificence than usual. The authorities had had little time to prepare their decorations and rehearse their pageants. In fact they had to fall back on a series of tableaux that had been used for the last coronation of a child king, that of Henry VI, a hundred and fifteen years before. Thus Edward VI left his Tower to be greeted with this rather unfortunate omen. He never returned.

We have said that Somerset had no rivals but it was not long before one emerged: his own brother, Thomas. The bizarre case is, in many respects, similar to that of the Duke of Clarence, seventy years earlier. Thomas was jealous of Edward's unlimited power with a jealousy which possessed him to such an extent that he talked wildly of unseating the

Protector and gave his name to the most hairbrained plots. Thomas Seymour married Catherine Parr, Henry VIII's widow and, when she died in childbirth (or probably before), he played the most outrageous court to Princess Elizabeth. He ingratiated himself with the young King by bringing him presents and lending him money. Somerset knew all this and was well aware of the scandal gathering round his brother's name, but he could not bring himself to take firm action. Then Thomas was detected in a plot to obtain possession of the Bristol mint to finance a *coup d'état*. The Protector's colleagues protested against his continued leniency and, in January 1549, Somerset consented to allow his brother to be imprisoned in the Tower. When he was questioned in his cell he haughtily refused to answer, perhaps relying on his brother or his nephew to rescue him from the consequences of his actions. When the truth dawned on him that he could expect no salvation from that quarter he grew morose. Despondently he confided in his gaoler, Christopher Eyre, that once he had thought he had friends in the Council but now he knew he had been wrong. He was attainted of treason and his death warrant was signed but for several days Somerset could not bring himself to enforce it. As well as his natural revulsion against killing his own brother he calculated that the act would soil his reputation. He had deliberately cultivated the popularity of the commons and was loath to damage his image. But he had no choice. Thomas Seymour, Baron Sudeley, went to the block on Tower Hill on 20 March 1549. It apparently required two strokes of the axe to despatch him.

There is a story (and in the absence of proof it can never be any more than a story) which indicates that Thomas Seymour was an unrepentant schemer to the end. It seems that the Council thought it advisable to deny the prisoner any writing materials. However, Seymour devised a form of invisible ink and, tearing a metal aglet from his doublet, wrote with it upon two scraps of paper. The letters were addressed to the two princesses, Mary and Elizabeth, and were sewn into the lining of one of Seymour's velvet slippers with instructions that his body servant was to see that they were delivered. Even as he laid his head upon the block the intriguer could think of nothing but his conspiracy and urged his man to attend to the delivery of his notes without delay. In so doing Seymour ensured that even his last plot should fail. The servant was questioned and the letters discovered. They were found to contain encouragement to the King's half-sisters to try to put an end to Somerset's tutelage of Edward. The tale is so typical of Thomas Seymour in every respect that it could well be true.

There was no doubt about the direction of the new regime's religious policy. Edward VI had been brought up by Protestant tutors. He was a convinced, even a bigoted, adherent of the evangelical faith and most of his Council were also committed to further reform. Archbishop Cranmer abolished the mass as well as other 'superstitious' ceremonies and drew up the first English Prayer Book. He advanced Protestants to important ecclesiastical offices, insisted on the regular preaching of sermons (even providing a book of 'homilies' for parsons to read to their congregations if they felt unable to preach) and sent out his own licensees to exhort the people from pulpit and village cross to espouse biblical religion. In London and in many parts of the country this unequivocal move towards full Reformation was welcomed. But there were still conservative areas where change was greeted with hostility. One such was the extreme south-west. In 1549 the men of Cornwall rose in revolt against Cranmer's Prayer Book. Since many of them spoke Cornish the new services were as meaningless to them as the old Latin ones. They were joined by thousands of other malcontents from neighbouring regions. The government was thoroughly alarmed and sent a hastily gathered contingent of troops to face the rebels.

But the Prayer Book Rebellion was only one of their problems. In sundry parts of the country men were on the verge of revolt. There were many causes of discontent: changes of land ownership had resulted in the discarding of old relationships and work patterns; there was unemployment resulting from enclosure and other new farming methods; there were complaints about taxation and debasement of coin; there was anger at rising prices; and there were always purely local grievances. Somerset was very sympathetic to the suffering of the commons. He was the patron of a radical group of political and religious thinkers called the commonwealth party who wished to revolutionize society by means of a redistribution of wealth which they believed was sanctioned in the New Testament. Ironically, the Protector's known support for these new ideas only served to fan the revolt. Peasant leaders believed or affected to believe that they had government support. Some even took matters into their own hands by tearing down hedges and drawing the plough over enclosed land they believed was rightly theirs. This brought obvious reaction from the landowning class upon which the government relied for the maintenance of law and order in the shires. Locally there were arrests and ugly incidents. Centrally there was a growing demand that the Council should take firm action in putting down incipient revolt.

Caught between his ideals and the inevitable results of implementing those ideals, Somerset temporized. His colleagues urged him to mobilize troops, to make examples of troublemakers before it was too late. By July it was too late: the government had two major revolts, in the south-west and Norfolk, as well as several minor outbreaks on its hands. Now panic prevailed. The Master of the

118

Ordnance was besieged with orders for artillery, harness and equipment from the commanders who were hurriedly despatched to the various trouble spots. As well as that there were brass cannon to be allocated for the defence of the City gates. By the end of September it was all over; the Earl of Warwick had put down Robert Kett's revolt in Norfolk. The Lords Russell and Herbert had, after a bitter and far from easy campaign, reduced Devon and Cornwall to submission. There were hundreds of on-the-spot hangings but, as usual, the worst offenders were sent up to the Tower to be examined, tortured and to await trial. After conviction Robert Kett and his brother were delivered to the Sheriff of Norfolk. Robert was bound in chains and swung out over the wall of Norwich Castle 'and there hanged for a continual memory of so great villainy until that unhappy and heavy body (through putrefaction consuming) shall fall down at length.' William Kett was similarly hanged from the tower of his own village church.[6]

The convicted leaders of the western revolt were taken to Tyburn for their execution on 27 January 1550, being led thither by Sir John Gage, the Constable, who was a Catholic and who sympathized with much that the rebels stood for. Religious considerations weighed little with officials when it came to cases of civil disorder. Rebellion and anarchy were feared and hated more than any other crime in Tudor England. In 1549 there were few men and women still living who remembered the chaos and bloodshed of the Wars of the Roses but the unrest of those years had bitten deeply into English folklore and few men would have disagreed with Stephen Gardiner's dictum, 'The contempt of human law, made by rightful authority, is to be punished more heavily and more seriously than any transgression of the divine law.'[7] This largely explains the terrible conditions in which these prisoners and their comrades were kept while in the Tower. Among the detainees were several men who could not be detected in any treasonable acts but about whose loyalty there was considerable doubt. They were held in the Tower for shorter or longer periods and subjected to rigorous examination. Some were released; some remained in prison until the end of the reign; at least one died in his cell.

The most interesting case is that of the Cornish brothers Sir John and Sir Thomas Arundell. They were related to one of the leaders of the western revolt and they failed to respond when summoned by Russell to the royal standard. Sir John was examined in the Tower in July 1549 but managed to maintain his innocence. He was bound over on bail and ordered to remain in London. When the troubles in Devon and Cornwall were over he was released unconditionally. But the 'commotion' had inflamed old rivalries and before the end of the year a neighbour had laid fresh evidence against the Arundells.

They were both placed in the Tower as 'close' prisoners (i.e. they were confined to their cells and allowed very few privileges).The brothers were men of spirit. Believing themselves to be innocent and therefore wrongly imprisoned, they made their protest in the only way open to them: they refused to pay for their food.* This was, doubtless, an annoyance to the Lieutenant, who could not let his charges starve. We may be sure that, in retaliation, the prisoners were allowed only the minimum fare. On the suit of their friends, the Arundells' conditions were relieved sometime in 1550. They were allowed to take exercise and Sir John was frequently visited by his wife. Then, in April 1551, by order of the Council all these privileges were again removed. Just as suddenly, Sir Thomas was released on bail in early October. From this point the Arundells' story is closely bound up with that of the Duke of Somerset, to which we must now turn.

The Protector's credibility had been severely shaken by the revolts and his inefficiency in handling them. The landowning classes, whose support was vital, disliked him and he had alienated his Council colleagues by his arrogance and his increasing unwillingness to consult them. He had lost control of the Scottish border, his foreign policy was in shreds and the country's economic plight was steadily worsening. The Council now resolved to revoke Somerset's virtually sovereign powers and resume control into its own hands. The man who took the lead in opposing the Protector was John Dudley, Earl of Warwick. In mid-September 1549, Dudley returned to London from Norfolk with the greater part of his army at his back. Somerset was at Hampton Court with the King. As soon as he heard of the meetings Warwick was having with his colleagues he summoned other captains to join him with their forces. His opponents could now spread the story in London that the Protector was seeking to bolster his authority with military might and that the King's life was in danger. There was little need to draw the parallel between Edward VI and another twelve-year-old king who had been murdered by a power-seeking uncle.

One of the first actions Warwick's party had to take was to secure the Tower. On 6 October the Council sent for the Lieutenant, Sir John Markham and 'required him to suffer certain others to enter for the good keeping [of the Tower] to his Majesty's use; whereunto the said Lieutenant [agreeing], Sir Edmund Peckham, knight, and Leonard Chamberlain, esquire, with their servants, were commanded to enter into the Tower, as associates to the said Lieutenant, for the better presidy and guard of the same.'[8] Quite clearly Markham was not deprived of his office but the Council probably felt that he was too

* Though allowances were still made by the government for important state prisoners, lesser fry were expected to pay cash for their keep.

much Somerset's man for them to be sure of him.* The men appointed to help him were prominent courtiers who had close connections with the Tower: Peckham was Master of the Mint and Chamberlain was (a few years later, if not in 1549) Gentleman Porter. The move should not, therefore, be seen as one of securing the fortress by introducing 'new' men.

Within days the great Protector himself was in the Tower. He had tried to raise the common people around Hampton Court and when that had failed he had fled by night to Windsor with the King. From there he had sent out propaganda broadsheets and appeals for aid. But his position was hopeless and on 11 October he yielded to representatives of the Council. On the fourteenth he was escorted through the City by the earls of Southampton and Huntingdon, Sir Anthony Wingfield, the Lord Mayor and sheriffs of London and 300 cavalry while the City militia lined the route.

By the following February it was considered that the Duke had been sufficiently chastened. He was released and by late spring most of his former possessions and privileges had been restored to him, except, of course, the Protectorship. Warwick earnestly desired a *rapprochment* and arranged a marriage between his eldest son and Somerset's daughter to cement it. But the Duke was incapable of sharing power. He tried to force his opinions on the Council and when he failed to gain his own way he was not averse to using other means to do so. It was Somerset who was largely responsible for helping the Arundells and in getting their prison conditions alleviated. He also left a permanent mark on the Tower: during his stay there the ex-Protector was apparently impressed by the conduct of the Yeoman Warders. On his release he recommended that the guardians of the Tower should be permitted to wear royal livery. The Yeoman Warders' dress – unique and famed throughout the world – has been modified over the centuries but remains essentially true to its Tudor pattern.

For a year the Council tried to rule a divided and bankrupt country while being itself divided and bankrupt of agreed policies to solve the nation's ills. Within the government and in the kingdom as a whole there were those who supported the attractive, impractical idealism of Somerset and others who backed Warwick's harsh pragmatism. In his attempt to outmanoeuvre the widely-popular Seymour, and to re-establish peace and stability, Dudley sought the alliance of two

---

* At about the same time the Council stated in a letter to the two princesses that Somerset had tried to seize the Tower. It is very doubtful that this was an entire fabrication. Indeed, it was an obvious course for the Protector to take. Probably he sent a message to Markham instructing him to hold the castle for him, a message which was either intercepted or betrayed.

groups of people. One was the wealthy landowners who alone had the power and authority to prevent further peasant revolt. The other was the Protestants (foremost among whom was the young King) who, drawing much of their inspiration from Geneva and Zurich, were pressing for further reform and who constituted by far the most energetic pressure group in the country. The Reformation moved into a more virulent phase. Churches were stripped of superstitious images; wall paintings were whitewashed over; stained glass windows were smashed; altars were replaced by communion tables; vestments and other 'relics of popery' were sold for profane use. It was probably at this time that the two Tower chapels were stripped of all their medieval adornments. In the 1550s or soon after the Norman Chapel of St John ceased to be used at all for divine worship and became just another store room for records. Warwick was unpopular with Catholics, religious moderates and the vast mass of humble Englishmen. This goes a long way to explain why he has traditionally been ranked second only to Richard III among the arch-villains of English history. That he was not an ambitious, devious, unscrupulous schemer concerned merely to grasp and hold political power is clear from any objective study of the events of 1549–53. For a year he tried to obtain the co-operation of his old comrade in arms, Edward Seymour, but the ex-Protector and, still more, some of his misguided friends made this impossible. The means by which Somerset was brought to his arrest, condemnation and death were shabby in the extreme, a typical example of Tudor state trial procedure. Yet two facts need to be remembered: all Tudor statesmen had learned the arts of totalitarian rule from a consummate master; what was at stake was not merely the fortunes of a few ambitious nobles but the security of the realm.

Throughout the summer of 1551 foreign observers were forecasting the imminent collapse of conciliar government but there was a tense calm in the courts of power until October when Warwick 'uncovered' to the King a plot by Somerset to re-assert his power with the help of armed force. Part of this plot involved Sir Thomas Arundell. He was suddenly, unaccountably released from prison on 4 October, the same day that Somerset returned to court from a stay on his country estates. Within a week it was being claimed that he had taken the earliest opportunity of seeking out Somerset to inform him that the Tower was 'safe' (i.e. that its officials were sympathetic towards the ex-Protector and would support his planned *coup*). He was immediately re-arrested. The Duke, too, was returned to the Tower with several of his supposed accomplices. It may have been as a result of Arundell's revelations that the Lieutenancy of the Tower now changed hands. We hear nothing more of Sir John Markham;

it was to Sir Arthur Darcy that strict orders were given concerning his new charges. They were to be closely guarded in their cells, to have no access to one another, no writing materials and no visitors save their examiners whom Darcy was to assist by 'putting the prisoners, or any of them, to such tortures as they shall think expedient'.[9] These instructions might only be superseded by written warrant signed by at least six members of the Council. Somerset, of course, was not tortured but he was questioned closely and repeatedly about conversations with the conspirators and with the Earl of Arundel, a councillor known to dislike Warwick. The Earl was also shut up in the Tower, while Dudley, to place himself on an equal footing with his adversary, took the title Duke of Northumberland.

By mid-November the Council believed it had amassed sufficient evidence to go to court. Somerset, who had previously been honourably lodged either in the palace complex or the Lieutenant's house was now placed in more 'secure' accommodation (perhaps in the Beauchamp Tower). This meant that he was removed from the company of his wife who had been imprisoned with him. If we accept the common judgement of Anne Seymour as a haughty, overbearing shrew we may believe that Somerset's closer confinement was not altogether unwelcome. The Duchess continued to enjoy a standard of life which was certainly more than adequate. She and her entourage of two gentlewomen and a manservant were allowed almost £5 per week for their food, fuel, candles and such necessaries as 'napery, plate, pewter vessels, spices, the roasting of her meat, butter to baste the same, with other different charges which be needed, as vinegar, mustard, various onions, salads and other.'

Somerset's trial was fixed for 1 December and the most elaborate precautions were taken to avoid trouble. Seldom if ever had the citizenry of London been more favourably disposed towards a state prisoner. The Imperial ambassador reported that the people, 'are particularly dissatisfied with this manner of procedure, calling the Duke of Northumberland a tyrant, hating him, saying that his one object is to lord it over all.'[10] The Lord Mayor was sent instructions that he was to have armed men ready to quell any spontaneous uprising. Lieutenant Darcy had detailed orders for the safe conduct of the prisoner to Westminster. Long before dawn Somerset was brought from his chamber and surrounded with a large guard of Warders and soldiers. He was taken to a waiting barge and rowed away from Traitors' Gate. It was unusual for travellers to make the journey from the Tower to Westminster Stairs entirely by water but Somerset and his escort not only did so, they 'shot the Bridge' at five o'clock on a dark winter's morning. The peers listened to the poor evidence brought against the accused and acquitted him of treason. It was the custom of the Gentleman Gaoler of the Tower to accompany accused traitors to their trial bearing before them his axe, the symbol of his office. Usually he made the return journey with the weapon's blade pointed towards the prisoner as a sign that the man was condemned. When the Duke of Somerset was acquitted of high treason the Gentleman Gaoler left the hall to return to the Tower. Whey they saw him the enormous crowed outside raised a shout of triumph believing that their hero was safe. There was much confusion on this score for several hours. What actually happened was that Seymour, though excused of treason, was found guilty of felony, a crime which also carried a capital sentence. The government decided to wait until darkness had fallen before returning Somerset to his prison. It was gone five o'clock before the procession set out.

> After the Duke was thus condemned, he was again returned to the Tower, through London, where were both exclamations, the one cried for joy that he was acquitted, the other cried out that he was condemned. But howsoever they cried, he was conveyed to the Tower, where he remained until the 22 day of January next following.[11]

The courtiers and gentlemen cast in the role of conspirators were also tried and condemned, though the government had some difficulty securing a conviction against Sir Thomas Arundell:

> Sir Thomas Arundell was likewise convicted of felony in treason, after long controversy; for the matter was brought in trial by seven of the clock in the morning . . . at noon the inquest went together; they sat shut up together in a house, without meat or drink, because they could not agree, all that day and all night; [the next] day in the morning they did convict him.[12]

The mood of the City remained ugly as the festive season drew near.

> Wherefore as well to remove fond talk out of men's mouths, as also to recreate and refresh the troubled spirits of the young King, it was devised that the feast of Christ's Nativity . . . should be solemnly kept at Greenwich with open household . . . what time of old [custom] there is always one appointed to make sport in the court, called commonly lord of misrule . . .[13]

The Tower witnessed a considerable part of this desperate play for popularity on the part of Northumberland's regime. On 4 January 1552 the lord of misrule

> landed at Tower Wharf and with him young knights and gentlemen, a great number on horseback . . . and on the Tower Hill there they went in order, first a standard of yellow and green silk with

St George, then guns and . . . trumpets and bagpipes . . . and flutes, and then a great company all in yellow and green . . . then came my lord with a gown of gold furred with fur of the goodliest colours as ever you saw . . . and after came also a hundred in red and white, tall men of the guard, with hoods of the same colour, and came into the City . . .[14]

The procession bore a hogshead of wine which was broached at 'the cross in Cheap' for all the people to drink, while Misrule and his courtiers scattered largesse.

If they thought that the approbation of the London mob was so easily bought, the Council were wrong. Thousands of citizens flocked to Tower Hill early on 22 January, despite orders that no man was to stir from his house before 10.00 a.m. The scaffold was ringed with armed men called out by the Lieutenant from the Tower Liberty as well as contingents from the villages and suburbs around. The Duke had already composed himself for the coming ordeal. A note in his hand has survived, written on a pocket calendar (presumably the only paper he had in his cell):

> Fear of the Lord is the beginning of wisdom.
> Put thy trust in the Lord with all thy heart.
> Be not wise in thine own conceit, but fear the
> Lord and flee from evil.
> From the Tower the day before my death.[15]

The execution passed off quietly with only one mishap: a contingent of mounted militia reporting late for duty tried to force a way through the crowd immediately causing confusion and panic. Some believed that the soldiers brought a last minute pardon and a great cheer went up.

For eighteen months England knuckled down grudgingly under the governance of a Council controlled rather than dominated by the hated Northumberland. Many of them looked forward to the day when King Edward would rule in his own right. It was a vision John Dudley shared. He had never enjoyed the work of day-to-day administration and the strain was making inroads on his health. He brought a bill into parliament advancing the age of the King's majority from eighteen to sixteen. In a series of marriage alliances linking Northumberland and his friends with outlying members of the royal dynasty, Dudley's son, Guildford, was married to Lady Jane Grey, daughter of the Duke of Suffolk and granddaughter of Henry VIII's sister, Mary. He had done very well for himself and for his family and he could now look forward to withdrawing gradually from the position of supreme power.

Then, in the summer of 1553, within a few months of his sixteenth birthday, the King began clearly and distressingly to fall victim to the tuberculosis which had possessed his body for years. Edward had for some time been quite determined that his virulently Catholic half-sister, Mary should not succeed him and had drawn up a 'devise' instructing that, in the event of his dying without issue, the crown was to pass, in the first instance, to his favourite (and firmly Protestant) cousin, Jane Grey. When he knew that he was dying Edward summoned the judges and the members of the Council to his bedside and forced them to endorse his will settling the succession. It was not a legal document but it was a royal command. Northumberland, out of loyalty and a desire to preserve the religious and political *status quo*, swore to uphold Edward VI's dying wishes.*

In the event he did so in a very half-hearted, blundering fashion, as though he knew that his own unpopularity and the widespread sympathy felt for Mary ever since Henry VIII's abandonment of Queen Catherine, were insurmountable obstacles. Edward VI died on 6 July at Greenwich. By the next day rumours of his death and the plan to change the succession were already circulating in the capital. Mary was given plenty of time to escape deep into East Anglia where the gentry and people were soon rallying to her standard. Not until 10 July was Jane Grey brought to the Royal Lodgings in the Tower and there proclaimed Queen. She was a slim, palely beautiful girl of sixteen. She had no wish to wear the crown. She had no love for her new husband. But she would address herself to her royal and marital responsibilities in a spirit of Christian duty.

While Queen Jane discussed material for coronation robes, received homage from courtiers and bishops and ordered her household in a way which indicated she would be no political pawn, the members of the Council held frequent meetings and listened to messengers bringing the latest news from Suffolk. It was not good: Mary, who had already written demanding the surrender of the Tower and the City, was gathering forces steadily. It was obvious that someone would have to lead an army out against her. It was equally obvious that none of Dudley's colleagues wanted to commit themselves so irrevocably. Northumberland himself must go. Then the others could sit securely in the Tower and await the outcome of events. On 12 July the Duke submitted to the inevitable. He mustered men and equipped them from the armoury. He checked the fortifications of the Tower and left Suffolk in charge of the castle and the Queen (his daughter). He demanded a further pledge of loyalty from the Council and every man affirmed that he supported Queen Jane. 'I pray God it be so,' muttered

* Had he only been concerned to save his skin he could have immediately proclaimed Queen Mary.

the Duke, 'let us go to dinner.' On the 14th he set out northwards. Immediately some of the lords of the Council sought means of escaping from the Tower and changing their allegiance. On the 19th a group of them met at the Earl of Pembroke's house, pledged their support for Mary and had her proclaimed throughout the City. They sent a force of 150 men back to the Tower which the now dispirited Suffolk immediately yielded. He went to his daughter and told her that her nine days' reign was ended. She begged him to take her away from that dreadful place. Suffolk explained that that was not possible. It never would be.

Jane was obliged to move out of the royal apartments. She was installed, temporarily, in the Lieutenant's Lodging and later (perhaps as accommodation more suited to her station) in the Gentleman Gaoler's house, next door. It was comfortable, but a prison. As the ringing of church bells and the cheers of the people floated up from the City, Guildford Dudley was also moved. His new quarters were in the Beauchamp Tower. Did he there carve his wife's name – JANE – as legend suggests? If so he must have been capable of warm feelings and was not the spoiled, callow youth some historians have described. During the next few weeks 'all change' was the prevailing order in the Tower. Gardiner, Norfolk, Bishop Bonner of London and others detained as inimical to the Protestant Edwardian regime were released and their cells were filled with Northumberland's supporters and with prominent Protestants. On 25 July the defeated Duke was brought through London 'all the streets as he passed by standing with men in harness afore every man's door till he came to Tower Wharf, all the streets full of people, which cursed him, and calling him traitor without measure.'[16] He was placed in the Bloody Tower (then known as the Garden Tower). His four other sons, John, Ambrose, Henry and Robert, joined their brother in the Beauchamp Tower. Archbishop Cranmer, Bishop Ridley and the celebrated preacher, Hugh Latimer also came to the Tower as did an increasing number of outspoken Protestants in succeeding months for, significantly, religious as well as political prisoners now began to feature prominently in the annals of the castle.

On 3 August Mary Tudor entered the Tower of London, amidst scenes of wild rejoicing, to begin one of the most disastrous reigns in the history of England, and one totally devoid of positive achievement. The Queen had inherited from her mother two great passions – Spain and the Roman Catholic faith. She tried to force both on her people. She was not in herself vindictive or hard-hearted but in issues involving religion or foreign policy her judgement was always clouded, and she too often allowed herself to be swayed by advisers such as Gardiner and Cardinal Pole who were bent on vengeance and the return of the Old Religion. She married Philip of Spain, an act which affronted most of her countrymen, made England another Hapsburg satellite and introduced the prospect of a Catholic heir. She instigated a religious tyranny similar in many respects to the Spanish Inquisition and sanctioned the burning of over three hundred Protestant martyrs. She dispossessed thousands of parish clergy who had had the temerity to get married as soon as the injunction to celibacy had been lifted. Civil unrest continued throughout the reign and hundreds of Englishmen fled abroad to avoid religious persecution. One symptom of the rule of this unsuitable and unhappy sovereign was that for long periods of time the Tower's prisons were fuller than they had ever been before.

Only three men perished immediately for their part in the recent *coup*. Northumberland was taken forth to his trial at Westminster on 18 August. His execution together with that of his two henchmen, Palmer and Gates, was fixed for the 21st. On the Hill the scaffold was ready, the Tower Liberty militia were in position, the Sheriff and his officers were prepared to receive the prisoners. But the prisoners did not appear. The Duke had obtained a stay of execution by asking permission to hear mass. For Bishop Gardiner this was too good an opportunity to be passed up. His revenge and triumph were about to be made complete. Not only was his old enemy (a man he had once come to blows with at the Council table) to be executed as a traitor, he was going to make a complete and public volte-face, renouncing his heresies and being reconciled to the Roman church. Hastily plans were made for the service. As well as prisoners and Tower personnel, courtiers and representatives of the City were brought in by the exultant Gardiner. Jane Grey did not attend. She watched from her window the little procession cross the Green to St Peter's. Dudley's change of mind was probably made in the hope of saving his skin, although Jane found this difficult to believe, according to a visitor who dined with her at Nathanial Partridge's (the Gentleman Gaoler):

... though other men be of that opinion, I utterly am not; for what man is there living, I pray you, although he had been innocent, that would hope of life in that case; being in the field against the Queen in person as general, and after his taking, so hated and evil spoken of by the commons ... Who was judge that he should hope for pardon, whose life was odious to all men? But ... like as his life was wicked and full of dissimulation, so was his end thereafter. I pray God, I, nor no friend of mine, die so. Should I who am young ... forsake my faith for the love of life? Nay, God forbid! Much more he should not whose fatal course, although he had lived his just number of years, could not have long continued. But life is sweet, it appeared. So he might have lived, you will say, he did not care how. Indeed, the reason is good, for he that would have lived in chains to have had his life, [by the same token] would leave no other means [un]attempted. But God be merciful to us, for he saith, 'Whoso denyeth him before men, he will not know him in his Father's kingdom'.[17]

The three men died on Tower Hill on 22 August. Northumberland was buried beneath the altar of St Peter's beside his old friend and rival Edward Seymour. Near them were the bodies of Anne Boleyn and Catherine Howard – so that, as Stow says, 'there lieth before the high altar in St Peter's Church two dukes between two queens'.

On 28 September the reigning Queen was back at the Tower for the formalities preceding her coronation. With her was her half-sister Elizabeth, a fiery-haired twenty-year-old who, being next in the succession and also a Protestant, was highly vulnerable. Both women knew that Elizabeth was the focus of the hopes of all men who loathed Mary's attempt to put the clock back. The Queen laboured hard for the Princess's conversion and Elizabeth was careful to conform outwardly to the restored ceremonial. But Mary was unsure how to treat her potential rival and her close advisers whispered in her ear that Elizabeth should go to the Tower. Mary, like Edward, tried to alter the succession debarring Elizabeth in favour of some other candidate of unimpeachable religious views, but she was rightly told that parliament would never sanction such a move. For the time being the Princess was allowed her request to retire into rural seclusion.

On 16 November Jane, her husband and two of her brothers-in-law, Ambrose and Henry, were led out to their trial at the Guildhall. With them went Thomas Cranmer. All were condemned of treason and returned to their prison quarters. No date was set for their execution and it may well be that Mary intended to release most of them. Cranmer and the other religious leaders were, in any case, only being held pending proceedings for heresy. On 17 December orders were given for some improvement in the prisoners' conditions. Jane and Cranmer were permitted the liberty of the Tower, including the Queen's Garden (in the south-east corner between the inner and outer walls). The Dudleys were allowed to exercise on the wall-walk between the Beauchamp and Bell Towers.

It was Wyatt's Rebellion which deterred the government from any show of leniency it might have been contemplating. Sir Thomas Wyatt, son of the poet, was one of a circle of prominent men who were appalled at the Queen's plan for a Spanish marriage and resolved to balk them. At the end of January 1554 he raised a force in Kent and marched towards the Thames. Despite the failure of other contingents to materialize, Wyatt continued and was soon at the head of four thousand men. A force sent out under Norfolk to block his path laid down their arms and joined him, obliging the octogenarian Duke to flee. The government was severely shaken but Mary personally ensured the loyalty of London and the insurgents found the Bridge closed against them. When the Tower cannon opened up a bombardment from across the river Wyatt had to move on eastwards. Crossing the Thames at Kingston, he proceeded steadily through the suburbs to Ludgate but several of his followers had lost their nerve and deserted.

The confused events of the next few hours were recorded by one of the officers at the Tower in his pocket diary:

> The said Wyatt, with his men, marched still forward all along to Temple Bar, also through Fleet Street along, till he came to Ludgate, his men going not in any good order or array. It is said that in Fleet Street certain of the Lord Treasurer's band, to the number of 300 men, met them, and so going on the one side passed by them coming on the other side without any whit saying to them. Also this is more strange: the said Wyatt and his company passed along by a great company of [harnessed] men, which stood on both sides, without any withstanding them, and as he marched forward through Fleet Street, most with their swords drawn, some cried 'Queen Mary hath granted our request, and given us pardon'. Others said, 'The Queen hath pardoned us'. Then Wyatt came even to Ludgate, and knocked, calling to come in . . . but the Lord William Howard, standing at the gate, said, 'Avaunt, traitor! thou shalt not come in here'. And then Wyatt awhile stayed, and, as some say, rested him upon a seat at the Bellsavage Gate; at last, seeing he could not come in, and belike being deceived of the aid which he hoped out of the City, returned back again in array towards Charing Cross, and was never stopped till he came to Temple Bar, where certain horsemen which came from the field met them in the face; and then began the fight again to wax hot.[18]

It was soon over and the captured rebels were being marched into the Tower to the taunts of the garrison, which probably included the writer of the above account. The prisoners strained the already well-occupied accommodation and many of them were thrust into the crypt of St John's Chapel. It was conveniently near the rack. Thus ended the last military action in which the Tower of London was directly involved.

About 680 people were taken with Wyatt or arrested on information obtained from the prisoners, among them was Henry Grey,

Duke of Suffolk. Mary and her Council now had to decide how much blood was necessary to wash away the stain of rebellion. They could not agree: Mary wanted to win the people's hearts by leniency; Gardiner and her Spanish advisers were all for making examples and removing possible rivals in the accepted Tudor fashion. Whoever made the decision to execute Jane and Guildford Dudley, the final responsibility rested with Mary. It was a decision as unnecessary as it was brutal. Even if Suffolk's daughter had consented to be used once again as a royal pawn no one would have bowed the knee to her, not, at any rate, while Elizabeth was still alive. Yet the decision was made sometime in early February and the execution fixed for the 12th.

The way the two young people went to their death was an example to those of whose scheming they had been the innocent victims. The Queen committed the final insult of trying to wean Jane from her faith. She sent a priest to talk with the girl and for some hours they were engaged in theological debate. The outcome is worth quoting for it indicates clearly how deep were the religious divisions running through English society.

'Madam, I am sorry for you,' said the priest finally, 'for I am now sure that we shall never meet'. [i.e. in heaven.] The young girl replied, with equal sadness, 'It is true, Sir, we never shall meet, except God turn your heart; for I am assured, unless you repent and turn to God, you are in a sad and desperate case; and I pray God, of his infinite mercy, to send you his Holy Spirit; for he hath given you his great gift of utterance, if it pleases him also to open the eyes of your heart.'[19]

Neither of the young people had wanted their marriage but shared suffering had brought them closer to each other. Guildford begged to be allowed to see his wife before he went out to the scaffold. Jane refused, but not out of indifference: 'If the meeting would benefit either of their souls,' she said, 'she would see him with pleasure, but in her opinion it would only increase their trial; they would meet soon enough in the other world.' From her window Jane saw her young husband led out across the Green to disappear from view through the Bloody Tower gateway about ten o'clock in the morning. A while later a cart lumbered through that same gateway bearing towards St Peter's Guildford's body and his head 'in a cloth'. She saw that too.

Shortly afterwards the Lieutenant called upon her to inform her that all was ready for her own execution. With complete composure, though her two gentlewomen wept profusely, she walked from Mr Partridge's house to the scaffold on the Green. In her short speech to the little crowd there was no grovelling self-effacement. She admitted her crime but vowed 'before God and the face of you Christian

131

people' that the conspiracy had been none of her desiring. She made a simple affirmation of her Protestant faith, allowed herself to be blindfolded, and submitted herself to Mary Tudor's headsman.

For some weeks the blood-letting went on: a hundred or so Kentish rebels – forty-five of them hanged in London on one day, the Duke of Suffolk beheaded on Tower Hill, and his brother, Lord Thomas Grey. Other prisoners, such as Robert Dudley, were now tried and condemned. Last of all to die was Wyatt, beheaded on 11 April and immediately hailed as a martyr by many who had failed to rally to his standard.

By then Elizabeth had been brought to the Tower. The Queen was convinced of her complicity in the recent rising but repeated examinations of Wyatt and his confederates had failed to produce damning evidence. Elizabeth was ill in bed when the royal officers arrived to fetch her to London. That did not deter them. She was brought first to Westminster. Three weeks later she heard she was to be taken to the Tower. The Princess was horrified by the implication of being sent to 'a place more wonted for a false traitor than a true subject'. She wrote to Mary, begging her to change her mind

> I protest before God, who shall judge my truth whatsoever malice shall devise, that I never practised, concealed nor consented to anything that might be prejudicial to your person in any way, or dangerous to the state by any mean . . . Let conscience move your Highness to take some better way with me than to make me be condemned in all men's sight, afore my desert known.[20]

She might as well have appealed to her bedpost. Elizabeth landed at Traitors' Gate on a rainy Palm Sunday. Her mother, as she well knew, had entered this gloomy portal nineteen years before. Dejectedly she mounted the steps but not without a word for the Lieutenant and his men who had come to meet her:

> Oh Lord! I never thought to have come in here as a prisoner; and I pray you all good friends and fellows, bear me witness that I come in no traitor but as true a woman to the Queen's majesty as any now living: and thereon will I take my death.[21]

The Princess was lodged in the Bell Tower with permission to exercise on the 'leads' between there and the Beauchamp Tower. Later she was allowed to walk in the Privy Garden, but only with an escort. Elizabeth's pacing of the narrow wall-walk brought her close to the door behind which lay a childhood friend, Robert Dudley. It is very unlikely that the two prisoners were allowed to meet but the shared captivity was another bond between them. After two months the government gave up trying to find evidence against the Queen's half-sister and realized that her continued confinement in the Tower was only making her the object of popular sympathy. On 19 May she was conveyed to the country again, to Woodstock, Oxfordshire.

The surviving Dudleys whiled away the long hours of their captivity in a variety of ways. They played at cards and dice, read books and made up poems in their common room on the first floor of the Beauchamp Tower. They also carved figures and legends in the stonework. This pastime was indulged by hundreds of prisoners before and after the 1550s but very few of them showed the patient skill and draughtsmanship of John Dudley, elder of the four brothers. Around his heraldic devices, the bear and the ragged staff of Warwick and the double-tailed lion of Dudley, he carved an intricate border of leaves and flowers, designed to be a puzzle as well as a decorative motif, as the legend below indicated:

> You that these beasts do well behold and see
> May deem with ease wherefore here made they be
> With borders eke wherein [there may be found]
> 4 Brothers names who list to search the ground.

The 'names' are represented by carved plants: roses for Ambrose, gillyflowers for Guildford, oak leaves for Robert (Latin *robur* = oak), and honeysuckle for Henry. It is a pity that John Dudley did not live to leave us other examples of his art. The four brothers were released on 11 October 1554. John died ten days later, whether as a result of his confinement, we do not know.

The enlargement of the Dudleys was one of the many calculated political manoeuvres designed by the government to win popular support from a people most of whom had come to loathe Philip and Mary and all they stood for. Northumberland had been hated but for the new regime Englishmen felt not only antipathy but also contempt. London apprentices pelted Spanish courtiers with snowballs as they rode through the capital and minor rebellions continued throughout the reign. Under these circumstances *raison d'état* demanded a fine balance of ostentatious clemency and equally ostentatious punishment. Thus, 400 of Wyatt's rebels were led through London from the Tower all roped together in order to receive personal pardons from the Queen at Westminster. In January 1555 another batch of his confederates was released from the Tower but not by the simple process of unlocking their doors and permitting them to walk out: the Lord Chancellor and several of the Council rode up to the castle and brought the prisoners forth personally, 'and after there was a great shooting of guns'.[22] On the other hand the failure of a jury to convict Sir Nicholas Throckmorton of treason for his complicity in the rising drew forth angry reprisals from the Queen. Not only was Throckmorton returned to the Tower, he was joined by the two foremen of the 'unco-operative' jury (the other ten were thrown into the Fleet prison).

Disaffection even invaded the court. Yet another member of the Dudley family, Henry Dudley (a distant cousin of Guildford and his brothers), was organizing abroad a widespread and sophisticated rebellion. Among his English agents was Henry Peckham, courtier, M.P. and son of no less a person than Sir Edmund Peckham, Master of the Tower Mint and member of the royal Council. Henry was detected in a plan to obtain funds by robbing the Exchequer. He soon found himself a prisoner in the building which he must have visited often on happier occasions. In July 1555 he and his assistant were 'hanged on the gallows of Tower Hill for treason against the Queen . . . and after cut down and headed and their bodies carried unto London Bridge and there set up and their bodies buried at All Hallows, Barking.'[23]

Due to the overcrowding in the fortress Thomas Cranmer was obliged to share his quarters in the Bloody Tower with his Protestant friends Nicholas Ridley, Hugh Latimer and John Bradford. For some weeks they enjoyed pleasant comradeship in adversity, praying together, studying their New Testament together and planning the defence they would have to make at their heresy trials. They left for other prisons on 12 March 1554 and within little more than a year all of them had perished at the stake. They were among the first of the many brave men and women who were burned to death during the last three and a half years of the reign. There was no moderation in this sphere of government policy, no careful thought for the effect of the executions on public opinion. As one London Protestant told Bishop Bonner, 'You have lost the hearts of twenty thousand that were rank papists within these twelve months.' Then, at last, on 17 November 1558, it was all over. Mary Tudor died – unhappy, unloved and unmourned.

Before we leave the story of this reign we must say a few words about one of the more distinguished Lieutenants in the history of the Tower. Sir John Brydges was already in his sixties when Mary appointed him on her accession. He had proved himself as a soldier in Henry's wars, was a staunch Catholic and a man Mary trusted implicitly. He presided over the Tower during one of its most difficult periods. The mere day-to-day administration of the castle must have been a headache when it was strained to bursting point with prisoners of every social class and every degree of culpability. He had to show sensitivity towards Lady Jane Grey and supervise the torture of Wyatt's ruffians. In the crisis of January 1554 it was his prompt decision to use the Tower battery against the rebels which forced them to abandon any attempt to capture London Bridge. Yet he was not just a rough, efficient soldier. No word of complaint about him from prisoners in his charge has ever come to light and he was certainly responsible for alleviating the conditions under which some of them were held. Indeed, he incurred the Queen's displeasure over his leniency towards Princess Elizabeth. Jane Grey was moved to present the Lieutenant with a memento of her, a prayer book in which she had inscribed a brief devotional exhortation. By the spring of 1554 he was finding his duties quite a strain and was being assisted by his brother Thomas (who later succeeded him). It was then that his grateful sovereign elevated Brydges to the peerage as Baron Chandos of Sudeley. He thus became the founder of one of the most distinguished and certainly one of the richest noble houses in England. One of his descendants was known as the 'king of the Cotswolds' and an eighteenth-century Brydges became the first Duke of Chandos, a byword for ostentatious wealth and the patron of Frederick Handel.

It is not surprising that Queen Elizabeth I should have disliked the Tower of London. She came there on 28 November to take possession of her fortress but did not remain until her coronation, leaving by water on 5 December 'with trumpets playing, and melody and joy and comfort to all true English men and women'.[24] She came back on 12 January for the formalities preceding the coronation on the 15th. Throughout the rest of her long reign (1558–1603) she never again slept within the walls of the Tower. For almost two centuries the Tower had sent a monarch forth to be crowned in every generation. Every one had been greeted with exuberant enthusiasm and eager hope as the champion of a new and better age. It was the same in January 1559; Elizabeth, 'was of the people received marvellously entirely, as appeared by the assembly, prayers, wishes, welcomings, cries, tender words, and all other signs, which argue a wonderful earnest love of most obedient subjects towards their sovereign.'[25] Doubtless all men hoped that this time the bright light in the sky was not a false dawn, that this slip of a girl would give England a new lease of stability and national pride. Few can have foreseen that the reign would be adorned with many splendours and see the kingdom safely through one of its longest and most telling crises.

This is not the place to tell again the story of the many achievements of Gloriana's reign – the establishment of English naval power, the beginnings of long-distance seaborne trade and empire, the religious settlement, the masterpieces of art, poetry and music, the restoration of financial stability and the devotion which the Queen personally inspired in her subjects. But we do well to remind ourselves of these accomplishments, for the story of the Tower is

135

largely the story of the dark side of the reign – of men and women made prisoners by rebellion, rumour and royal caprice.

Elizabeth's first Lieutenant was a man who knew the Tower well. Sir Edward Warner had held the position at the end of Edward VI's reign only to be dismissed by Queen Mary and later imprisoned in the Tower for a year on suspicion of complicity in Wyatt's Rebellion. He was now reinstated but his tenure of office was not to be an altogether happy one. In 1560 his wife died and was buried in St Peter's. The following year Lady Catherine Grey was delivered into his keeping. This young lady had a history scarcely less tragic than that of her sister, the 'nine days' queen'. She was next in line to the throne and as such governed by a law which made it treason for her to marry without royal consent. During Mary's reign she fell in love with the young Earl of Hertford and the two were quietly married in 1560. Catherine, who was a daily attendant upon Elizabeth, was able to keep her secret only as long as she was not obviously pregnant, a condition which came to an end in August 1561. The Queen was furious. Like her father and grandfather she was sensitive about all potential rivals and she knew too well from her own experience how a woman close to the throne could become the instrument of political schemers. Poor Catherine was very soon enjoying one of Elizabeth's own ex-lodgings – the apartments in the Bell Tower. There she was delivered of a son on 24 September. He was baptized with the name of Edward in St Peter's Chapel.

The boy's father was by now in the White Tower and both of the young people were closely and repeatedly questioned to see if they were part of a plot. Lieutenant Warner was assured by his superiors that 'many persons of high rank are known to have been privy to the marriage' but he had to confess complete failure in extracting any useful information. A judicial enquiry meanwhile had declared the marriage null and void. Warner was, of course, charged to ensure that the couple were kept apart. He was either soft-hearted or inefficient for, in February 1563, the Seymours had another baby. That news sent Elizabeth into a volcanic rage. She levied a swingeing fine upon Hertford, dismissed Warner from office and, for good measure, gave him a spell in one of his own cells. The star-crossed lovers continued in captivity, though, no doubt, enjoying reasonable comfort. Catherine's apartments were furnished with tapestries, Turkish carpets, curtains, velvet covered chairs and a bed with 'a bolster of down'. She was allowed to keep pet monkeys and dogs. She must have needed such distractions. From her windows she could see her lover's prison and perhaps, even, catch occasional glimpses of him. Yet they could not speak or be close to each other. It was a more excruciating torment than anything inflicted by Skeffington's Gyves.

Because of a severe outbreak of plague in the summer of 1563 the Seymours were moved into the country – to different places of confinement. Catherine was taken to various houses over the next few years. She made repeated requests to see her husband, all of which fell on deaf ears. In January 1568, broken in health as well as spirit, she died at the Suffolk home of Sir Owen Hopton (later Lieutenant of the Tower). Edward lived quietly in the country and it was many years before he remarried. He never forgot Catherine. In 1595, thirty years after his clandestine wedding, he asked for the invalidity of his marriage to be set aside so that his heir might inherit the earldom. All he received for his pains was another spell in the Tower. Elizabeth also had a long memory.

The Queen was obsessively sensitive on the subject of marriage, whether it was her own, a relative's or a close friend's. She only ever loved one man, Robert Dudley (created Earl of Leicester in 1564), and she had to forswear all thoughts of marrying him, for reasons of state. She toyed with various diplomatic marriage alliances but could never bring herself, though urged by Council and parliament, to yield herself to another man. Her high sense of duty forced upon her the role of 'virgin queen' and she expected the same self-sacrifice of those close to her. Dudley, Raleigh, Hatton, Essex and all her great courtiers had to play the role of lovers, competing for her favours, loyal to her alone. When any of them were lured off this mad whirligig and sought consolation in the arms of another woman, Elizabeth was beside herself with outrage, self-pity and scorn. That is why Sir Walter Raleigh first came to the Tower.

In 1591 Raleigh was forty years old, a courtier of long standing, Captain of the Guard and patron of many maritime ventures, including an abortive attempt to found a colony in Virginia. In 1591 this captive planet of the Sun Queen put one of her maids of honour in the family way. Bess Throckmorton insisted on marriage and the two were secretly wed. Bess was able to absent herself from the court for some weeks to have the baby without the Queen knowing. Of course, it all had to come out eventually and the longer the deception was carried on the worse would be Elizabeth's anger when she discovered the truth. Raleigh lied and brazened it out with his friends. He tried to escape to sea on an Indies venture. It was too late; the Queen knew. For days, weeks perhaps, she waited for her errant lover to grovel, to apologize, to beg forgiveness but Raleigh was not cast in that mould. On 7 August 1592 Elizabeth's patience was at an end. Sir Walter and Lady Bess went to the Tower.

As Raleigh sat in the Brick Tower he pondered over his years in the service of his magnificent, infuriating sovereign. All his self-pity, pride and devotion were poured out in a long poem, his *Book of the*

Ocean to Cynthia. Here is part of his description of Elizabeth:

> So hath perfection, which begat her mind,
> Added thereto a change of fantasy,
> And left her the affections of her kind,
> Yet free from every evil – but cruelty.

Only the press of urgent royal business saved the poet from the enforced leisure which would have enabled him to finish his epic. He was released on 15 September but his wife remained under lock and key until the end of the year. However it was a long time before Sir Walter was fully restored to the Queen's favour.

During the years of England's life and death struggle with Spain there were many prisoners in the Tower guilty of worse crimes than breaking the Queen's heart. When, in 1570, the Pope issued a bill of excommunication against Elizabeth he transformed every devoted English Catholic into a latent traitor. Each faithful son and daughter of the church had to believe that their Queen was dethroned and no longer held any claim to their obedience. The majority, of course, compromised, conforming outwardly to the new religious ceremonies and occasionally hearing secret masses performed by recusant priests. But there were considerable pockets of hard-line Catholics who wanted to get the heretic off the throne and were prepared to help in the achievement of that goal. Their resolve was stiffened by Jesuits and priests given special training at Catholic colleges in Rome and France, then smuggled into England. Across the northern border (until her eventual capture and detention by Elizabeth) was Mary, Queen of Scots, the woman the Catholics hoped to put on the throne. And in Madrid there was Philip II, the most powerful man in Europe, who prayed daily for the conversion of England and did all in his power to hasten it. There were four serious Catholic revolts (serious, that is, in the sense that they were well planned and involved prominent men; none of them came near to success), a number of attempts to raise insurrection in Ireland, and a plethora of ill-conceived plots by individuals and small groups of fanatics. Elizabeth's ministers and local officials needed all their vigilance. For three decades they kept the prisons filled with suspected traitors. The 250 Catholics* who went to the scaffold or died in prison during Elizabeth's reign have been claimed as martyrs though they were executed for treason and not for what they believed. Some of them were indeed saintly men whose only crime was preaching their faith and seeking to win converts. But no line could be drawn between religion and politics in the sixteenth century. Those men were agents

* This figure excludes those executed for their complicity in major rebellions.

138

of a foreign power, the papacy, which had declared war on the Queen of England.

Hundreds of prisoners falling into this category were kept in the Tower between *c.* 1570 and 1603. Many of them have left carved mementoes – initials, religious emblems, brief homilies in verse and prose, simple aids to devotion. Some were scions of ancient families. The majority were anonymous. A few were released. A few were executed. Most spent long, lonely years in their cells. Some died there. There is no space here to attempt any kind of survey of these forgotten men; all we can do is consider some of the more interesting among them.

Thomas Howard, Duke of Norfolk, was the son of the Earl of Surrey who had been executed in the last few days of Henry VIII's reign. In 1568 he was thirty-two years of age, an accomplished courtier, the first and probably the richest nobleman in England. But this was not enough for him; he possessed all his father's headstrong pride and believed that he should be a more potent influence in the government. He resented Dudley's hold on the Queen's affections and William Cecil's supremacy in affairs of state. In brief he saw himself as the champion of the ancient Catholic nobility whose right it was to be the sovereign's principal body of advisers. In 1568 Mary, Queen of Scots fled into England and Norfolk was appointed to lead the delegation charged with examining her and deciding what to do with her. Very soon he was drawn into a plot which seemed to solve all England's and Scotland's problems and which also pandered to his vanity: he would marry Mary; they would jointly rule Scotland and Mary would be nominated Elizabeth's heir. It was Norfolk's intention to lay the idea before Elizabeth and only proceed with her permission. Unfortunately, he lacked the courage to confront the Queen. Unfortunately, also, some of his bolder allies in the north began to take up arms. Fearful and hopelessly compromised, Howard withdrew to his East-Anglian estates. He was ordered to return to court and when he did so he was conveyed to the Tower (October 1569).

His detention was an honourable one. The Queen ordered that the Duke was to be housed in 'any lodging in the Tower near joining to the Long Gallery, so it be none of the Queen's own lodgings; and to suffer the Duke to have the commodity to walk in the gallery.'[26] It was an embarrassment to have to shut up the premier peer of the realm and obviously the palace buildings were the only suitable accommodation. Meanwhile his friends at court pleaded with the Queen on his behalf and devised many methods of secretly keeping the prisoner informed of events there and in the north. They smuggled messages in bottles of wine. When that was suspected they bored a hole in the wall of his room from the adjoining chamber and poked letters through to him. Another device used was to wrap messages in black paper and throw them into the dark corner of the Duke's privy. For his part, Norfolk appealed to the Queen's mercy and assured her he had abandoned all thought of marriage with Mary. Elizabeth did not relent until the following summer when, partly because of the plague, she gave Norfolk permission to remove to his London house.

The northern rebellion had been put down very easily and had brought a fresh crop of prisoners to the Tower. This failure seemed to make Mary's friends even more determined. Now there appeared on the scene Robert Ridolfi, Florentine banker, London merchant, and papal spy. He attempted to co-ordinate the activities of Catholic malcontents and foreign sympathizers into one grand design which should sweep Elizabeth from the throne. Foolishly, Howard allowed himself to be dragged into the babbling Italian's plot. In August 1571 the government stumbled on coded letters written by Norfolk to Mary's friends. On 5 September the Duke was back in the royal prison, not this time in the palace apartments and free to take exercise in the Long Gallery, but in the Bloody Tower, a close prisoner. The Council ferreted out several other conspirators of high and low degree, the most valuable of whom was Charles Bailly, apprehended at Dover with letters from Spanish supporters preparing to back the insurrection with money and men. Bailly had been held in the Tower the previous year on suspicion and after his release he had been carefully watched. Now he was thrown into the Coldharbour, examined and racked until he had produced code keys and lists of names. Later he was moved to the Beauchamp Tower where he added to the mural decorations of his cell.

All the conspirators, save those who fled, were rounded up and placed in Coldharbour and the Salt and Beauchamp Towers. But there was no blood bath: most of the rebels, like Bailly, were eventually released. Not so the Duke of Norfolk. He was convicted of high treason in January 1572 and thereafter waited for death. But the Queen could not bring herself to kill him. Four times she signed his death warrant. Four times Howard was bidden to make himself ready for the scaffold. Four times Elizabeth sent urgent messages to cancel the execution. It was all very trying for the Duke. It was agony for the Queen's advisers. They begged her to have away with traitors, especially popular figureheads such as Norfolk. Only when parliament added its corporate voice to the clamour did Elizabeth give in. Norfolk was beheaded on Tower Hill on 2 June. It was fourteen years since anyone had been executed on that spot.

What Howard and other noblemen such as the Talbots and Stanleys really objected to was the loss of their power. The Tudors had created a thicker layer of moderately wealthy landowners between the old feudal nobility and their peasants. Central government had made serious inroads into the vast areas which had once been almost independent principalities. There was a time when large areas of the north towards the border acknowledged 'no king but a Percy' but when Thomas Percy, seventh Earl of Northumberland was executed (1572) for his part in the revolt one of the royal commanders who helped bring about his downfall was his brother, Henry. The subsequent career of Henry, the eighth Earl, indicates clearly just how acute was what has been called 'the crisis of the aristocracy'. With the title he seemed to assume the mantle of ancient patronage and power. Twice he was imprisoned in the Tower on (quite justified) suspicion of being in contact with Catholic agents. He was deprived of some of his appointments in the north but instead of taking such mild punishments as a warning he grew angrier and more resentful. He redoubled his efforts to set the Queen of Scots free and enforce religious tolerance for Catholics.

By the 1580s it was folly for any opponent of the government, especially a marked man such as Henry Percy, to pit himself against the counter-espionage system brought to such a peak of efficiency by William Cecil and Francis Walsingham. But Northumberland was incorrigible. The extent of his foolish conspiracy came out in 1584 when Francis Throckmorton and William Shelley, two of the lesser lights in the plot, were arrested and taken to the Tower. Both men were courageous and quite determined to reveal nothing. Throckmorton scribbled a note in cipher on a playing card to the effect that he would die a thousand deaths before he informed on his Catholic friends. That was before he met the Duke of Exeter's Daughter. Under torture he and Shelley confessed all – names of principals, agents and foreign supporters, plans for the despatch of a French army sent by the Duc de Guise, and proposed landing places. Northumberland was arrested again in December. He was kept a close prisoner in the Tower and subjected to frequent examination. Despite being confronted with all the facts now at the Council's disposal he persisted in declaring his innocence.

He was never to be brought to trial. On 21 June 1585 he was found on his bed shot through the heart, the weapon still in his hand. A jury brought in a verdict of suicide but this, of course, did not satisfy the Earl's co-religionists. Within months a pamphlet printed in Cologne was being circulated which accused the government of Percy's murder. It was claimed that the Lieutenant, Sir Owen Hopton, had changed Northumberland's Warder on direct orders from the Council the day before the Earl's death. The government took the rumours seriously enough to carry out an official enquiry and this upheld the findings of the coroner's court. Yet there is still room for doubt. Northumberland's remains are believed to have been interred in St Peter's but canon law forbade the burial of suicides in consecrated ground. With the foreign situation deteriorating rapidly Percy's death was very convenient to Cecil and his colleagues who may well have feared another long drawn out contest with the Queen over the Earl's execution. Despite the draconian measures urged on her, Elizabeth refused to have done with Mary, Queen of Scots or carry out a purge of her known supporters. Many of the Catholics held in the Tower were released or exiled after shorter or longer terms of imprisonment. In the end the Queen's political instinct was proved right. She avoided being dubbed a religious persecutrix and she had the satisfaction of seeing her enemies overreach themselves. The attempted Spanish invasion of 1588 united the realm as never before and religious differences proved less important for most Englishmen than national survival.

Nevertheless, anti-Catholic activity continued throughout the reign. There were some Tower prisoners who could not be released and in Elizabeth's reign more warrants for torture were issued than under any other English sovereign. Most of the Queen's Lieutenants of the Tower were men of Puritan faith, and were perhaps chosen for that reason. Sir Owen Hopton, for one, took a delight in forcing his prisoners to attend Protestant worship. Yet not all the Tower's officers were as insensitive, particularly those who had charge of men of obvious saintliness and courage.

This is borne out by the story of John Gerard, a Jesuit priest who spent several years in England preaching and conducting banned Roman Catholic rites. Throughout his stay he was sheltered by friends from vigilant government agents but at last he was captured and found himself, after a succession of imprisonments, in an upper chamber of the Salt Tower. From there he was led out, on several occasions, to the Lieutenant's Lodging to be examined by members of the Council in connection with the latest assassination plot against the Queen. When he refused to speak he was taken to the basement of the White Tower and there suspended by the wrists from iron manacles for hours on end. The manacles or gauntlets seem to have been the most popular form of torture at this time. Between bouts of inflicted pain he was returned to his cell where his Warder, one Bennett, showed him as much pity as he dared. He cut up the prisoner's food (for Gerard had lost the use of his hands), provided extra clothing with money smuggled in by the Jesuit's friends and kept a good fire burning in the cell. The interrogators gained nothing from Gerard, who was eventually allowed to remain in his chamber.

A close rapport now existed between the prisoner and his gaoler who was prevailed upon to take Gerard across the Privy Garden to the Cradle Tower to administer the Sacraments to his friend, John Arden. The Cradle Tower was in the Outer Wall and it soon appeared to the prisoners that escape might be possible. They had many friends in London and, thanks to the pliant Bennett, a means of contacting them. The Warder brought oranges which were used to make an invisible ink for messages smuggled out of the Tower by the unsuspecting Bennett. However, there was soon no need for this subterfuge: the schemers realized that the gaoler was illiterate and that he was so far involved in their plot as to be unable to betray them. One escape plan failed but that subsequently employed was as simple as it was effective. A thin cord and a lead weight were conveyed into Arden's cell. On the night appointed Gerard stayed late in his friend's apartments while confederates drew up to the Wharf opposite the Cradle Tower in a boat. The weighted line was thrown across the moat and a stout rope attached to it. The prisoners drew this up to the roof of the tower, made it fast, and then slid down it to their friends who rowed them to safety. It is not quite clear what happened to Bennett. In an account Gerard wrote later describing his clever escape he asserted first of all that the gaoler was totally ignorant of the scheme he was unwittingly aiding and, later, that his friends got Bennett away from the Tower to save him from certain death. We can only hope that the Warder did escape, but if he did it must have been immediately after the prisoner's departure and before they were missed. It is difficult to see how Bennett can have left the Tower so quickly and linked up with Catholic friends who got him away into the country, without being privy to the plans of Gerard and Arden.

While the conflict between England and Spain continued from year to year that between the Tower and the City also dragged on. It, too, was characterized by bitterness on both sides. It, too, had its moments of violence. As we have said, it was probably the land deals attendant on the confiscation of monastic property round the hill which revitalized this ancient feud. Throughout the country the intricacies of the reallocation of church lands and the disputes arising therefrom kept generations of lawyers very comfortably busy. But the issue was complicated by the other ancient rights claimed from time to time by Tower officials. Early in Elizabeth's reign the Lord Mayor complained to the Council about the Gentleman Porter, Sir William George who had been,

> compelling poor victuallers strangers, coming to London by ship or boat, with fish, fruit or such victuals, to give him such a quantity as pleased him to take, as two or three codfish from each boat,

143

etc., without payment. Such as refused he caused to be imprisoned in the Tower, whereby the victuallers were discouraged to come to the City, and their number decreased, to the great hurt of the markets and the victualling of the City.[27]

Many disagreements concerned the competence of the courts of the City and the Liberty and the rights of arrest enjoyed by officers of those courts. The citizens felt themselves to be at a distinct disadvantage in any dispute with residents of the Tower or its Liberty. The Lieutenant was in the habit of protecting his own people from arrest. If one of his men was apprehended he sometimes retaliated by locking a Londoner up in the Tower until the detainee was released. In 1585 the Queen's principal justices outlawed these practices with the proviso that royal officers 'daily attendant at the Tower' should be exempt from prosecution in the City courts (but not, of course, from prosecution at common law). The Lieutenant held his own court baron within the castle and the London authorities claimed that he had no right to cite their citizens to appear before it. It was another hundred years before these legal matters were fully resolved and then only after the question of boundaries had been settled.

The legal and territorial issues were always closely related. In 1580 the Sheriff and the Lieutenant argued about the execution of a murderer. The Tower official erected a gibbet and told the City authorities to stand aside while the malefactor was despatched. The Sheriff protested. The two men retired to discuss the matter and the outcome was that the criminal was executed at Tyburn.

The case sounds trivial enough but it is only a symptom of an intense jealous rivalry between the City and the Liberty which affected all levels of society. In 1582 the Mayor and Sheriff complained to the Council that when, in accordance with ancient custom, they had presented themselves at the Tower as part of their inauguration they had been turned away with insults. Three years later Sir Owen Hopton sent some of his men to occupy one of the gardens on the Hill to which he laid claim. Finding two rival claimants in possession, the Tower men arrested them and brought them back to the castle. The City authorities sent a lawyer to Sir Owen to persuade him to release the captives. He, too, ended up in a Tower cell. Only the intervention of the Queen's justices sufficed to set the men free. In 1595 there was a much more serious incident. Groups of Yeoman Warders and City apprentices fell to blows on Tower Hill. The Lord Mayor turned out with his officers to break up the riot, only to be ordered to leave the Liberty.

Now that the land around the Tower was no longer an open space, a considerable amount of money was involved in the territorial disputes which came to implicate not only the officials of the City and the Tower but also the Sheriff of Middlesex. In 1590 it was estimated that the Gentleman Porter was obtaining £131.14s.6d. per annum in rents from properties he and his predecessors had built within the Liberty. But were they within the Liberty? That was the question. Houses, shops, workplaces, gardens and enclosed yards had appeared on the Wharf, inside the Bulwark, outside the Bulwark, around the (long since ruined) Postern Gate and on both sides of the City wall. The situation was ripe for confusion. The Lieutenant claimed that the Postern Gate had once been part of the Tower's defences. The Lord Mayor counter-claimed that it had been attached to the City wall. Londoners affirmed that they owned the land on which the Tower Hill scaffold stood and that the handing over of condemned prisoners to the Sheriff at the Bulwark Gate proved their ownership. Nor was it only rents and rights that were at stake. It was for reasons of security that the Constable had originally been given control of the area around the Tower and his successors were still sensitive on the issue. In the late sixteenth century it was ordered that, 'no household within the Liberties of the Tower shall take any tenants to dwell within their houses, but such as have been their own servants, or else their own friends . . . it is not meet that any stranger born out of this realm should dwell within the Tower, and the Liberty of the same.' The suburbs continued to spread and become more populous. Many of the points at issue between City and castle remained unresolved and there was little peace around Tower Hill.

The final important episode of Elizabeth I's reign which involved the Tower was the rising of Robert Devereux, Earl of Essex. Born in 1566, this handsome, headstrong nobleman was the last of Gloriana's 'courtier-lovers'. To some extent Robin Devereux replaced Robin Dudley (who died in 1588) in her affections. Like Leicester, Essex was her Master of Horse and her closest companion. They danced together, hunted together, flirted, played cards far into the night. From her latest young admirer the ageing Queen sucked vitality and youthfulness. The favourite was showered with presents and honours. But, as with all Elizabeth's gallants, there was a price to be paid – ceaseless attention and unquestioning loyalty. Essex was not the first courtier to find the conditions of his privileged position irksome. And there was always the complication of rivalry – others ever ready to tear down the favourite and turn the affections of the Queen away from him. Essex's arch enemy was Sir Walter Raleigh.

For years the Earl had served Elizabeth with devotion and mounting frustration. He burned for his talents (which he undoubtedly overestimated) to be fully used. Yet time and again he found his ideas rejected in the Council Chamber, and his actions on the battlefield

145

hampered by ministerial interference. He believed there was a conspiracy at court led by Raleigh and the Queen's Secretary, Robert Cecil, working against his – and therefore England's – interests. He had many arguments with Elizabeth's other advisers and some furious quarrels with Elizabeth herself. Often he would be dismissed from the court or withdraw of his own volition in a fit of petulance. Always he was eventually restored by a forgiving Queen who could not bear to be parted for long from her Robin.

In 1599 Essex was sent to Ireland, that graveyard of English political and military reputations, with wide powers to reduce the colony to order. The campaign was a disaster, partly because the situation was highly complex and difficult, partly because Essex's qualities were inadequate, and partly because his own hands were tied by frequent orders from London. As failure followed failure Devereux grew depressed and the Queen grew angry. She told him to stay at his post and obey orders. He demanded that she stop listening to his detractors. He had, he remarked bitterly, armed himself for the expedition with a breastplate but now he saw that armour for his back would have been more useful. At the end of six months, with typical impetuosity, he disobeyed orders and rushed back to court. The Queen would have none of him. She banished him from her presence and had him placed under guard in his London house. Not until August 1600 was his liberty restored.

It was too late: Devereux's tortured mind, imagining all kinds of mischief directed against himself, was turning to the consideration of desperate remedies. Perhaps the tragic outcome might have been avoided if he had not been so fatally attractive to the wrong people. By the end of the year everyone in the capital had heard the rumours.

The Earl of Essex is now returned to London and it is much noted how his doors are set open to all comers. Sir Gerry Merrick, his steward, entertaineth at his table many captains, men of broken fortunes, discontented persons, and such as saucily use their tongues in railing against all men. Sermons are preached there daily by zealous ministers to which the citizens flock in great numbers . . . And if any showeth a dislike of these things, he is forthwith censured as an envier of my Lord's honour and liberty. Moreover now and then he letteth fall words which show his disdainful stomaching the power his adversaries have with the Queen, nor will he listen to the wiser counsels of his friends. These things are brought to the Queen's ears and alienate her affection from him more and more, and especially one speech inflameth her most of all, for he said that being now an old woman, she is no less crooked and distorted in mind than she is in body.[28]

146

At the beginning of February 1601 Essex and a few friends launched a harebrained scheme whose aim, if it had any very clear one, was to remove the Earl's enemies from the court. With a few hundred followers Devereux imagined he could gain control of the Tower, the City, and Whitehall Palace. They rampaged through London's streets while the citizens stared at them wide-eyed and not a hand was raised to help. Essex was taken prisoner that night and Elizabeth ordered him to be removed to her fortress and lodged in Robin the Devil's Tower – the choice can hardly have been a coincidence.*

On 19 February Essex and his supporter, the Earl of Southampton, were taken for their trial and condemnation at Westminster. At last Robert Devereux's pride was crushed. His last days were devoted to preparing for his end. He spent his time thinking on his Saviour, lamenting his sins and making his peace with men. He asked that his execution might be private and this the Queen granted. She had experienced her usual difficulty in signing the death warrant but on 24 February the deed was done. The next morning Essex stepped out onto Tower Green, the last state prisoner to be executed within the fortress until the despatching of spies during World War I.

Among the small group of witnesses was one who would not have missed the sight for worlds. But even he was sensitive enough to the condemned man's feelings to watch at a distance, from the 'Armoury' (perhaps the White Tower) Sir Walter Raleigh could not have realized on that cold winter's morning that he was destined to spend almost the rest of his life in the Tower of London.

In the first historical and architectural guide book of London, John Stow's *Survey of London* (first edition 1598) the author informs us

> This tower is a citadel, to defend or command the city, a royal palace for assemblies and treaties, a prison of estate for the most dangerous offenders, the only place of coinage for all England at this time, the armoury for warlike provision, the treasury of the ornaments and jewels of the crown and general conserver of the most records of the royal courts of justice at Westminster.[29]

However, a report prepared for the queen in that very same year analysed the Tower's functions differently. The building contained, wrote Sir John Peyton:

> First, your majesty's royal stores of ammunition for war, with the dangerous charge of your highness's magazine of powder.
> Secondly, your majesty's rich treasure of jewels, plate and furnitures.
> Thirdly, your highness's records.
> Fourthly, the prisoners for causes of state.[30]

---

* This tower has since been known as the Devereux Tower.

Stow's catalogue is the more comprehensive and the one likely to be of greater interest to contemporary visitors but it was the royal servant who correctly identified those activities of major interest to his sovereign. John Peyton was the newly-appointed Lieutenant of the Tower and it was in his interests to give Elizabeth the most accurate and relevant advice. Peyton's report provides us with an account as droll as it is detailed of the state of the royal fortress at the end of its first half millennium. (See Appendix.2)

Some things had not changed in all that time:

> The City of London did and doth pretend title unto your majesty's soil of Tower Hill and East Smithfield . . . To admit of this their challenge were dangerous and inconvenient unto the safety of the place.

The keepers of the Tower were overworked and underpaid (a perennial complaint):

> These 30 warders your majesty doth allow 8 pence a piece *per diem*, in respect of which small wages, regarding the dearness of these times wherein the price of all things and all men's labours are increased, they are grown to exceeding poverty, and those most poor that best attend your majesty's service.

The state of the fabric was, as usual, giving cause for concern:

> Your majesty's lodgings and many other buildings within the Tower are in decay . . .
> The Tower gates and prisoners' lodgings are in decay.
> The ancient sluices and vaults that were wont to be maintained to take in water out of the Thames (for the strengthening of the Tower ditch) are now utterly decayed.
> The Tower ditch, being the special strength of the Tower, is in great decay and in many places landed (i.e. silted or blocked) up to the Tower wall.

Other abuses had grown up in recent decades by default. Guarding of prisoners had become lax because, as a result of gaolers receiving gratuities in return for privileges, family members and servants had virtually unlimited access to them. Unofficial perks had multiplied as Tower officers milked their positions for all they were worth.

> There hath also been suffered a common brewhouse and bakehouse to be kept within the Mint and also a common hackney stable to let horses to hire, who have had their continual passage with their carriages and horses in and out of the great gates . . .

Tower residents received guests and lodgers without any reference to the Lieutenant. The development of slums was in part the fault of Tower officers who drew rents from the proliferating houses built within and without the walls many of which were occupied by 'very poor and disordered persons'. The Lieutenant's final complaint was that the Tower residents were so numerous that, 'there is not within the Tower any place sufficient for their burial.'[31] The picture Peyton conjures up is of a crumbling building complex so overcrowded and swarming with unauthorised and semi-authorised visitors that it is a wonder that any prisoner was ever kept secure for more than a few hours. It should be noted, however, that Sir John was an officious, over-zealous martinet. In 1603 he was removed from office and demoted to the governorship of Jersey in which distant little fiefdom he managed to make himself several enemies and was habitually involved in litigation.

7

On 2 May 1641 an event occurred at the Tower which, though seldom recorded in the history books, was intensely symbolic of the changes taking place in the nation. A certain Captain Billingsley rode up to the Lion Gate and demanded admission, in the name of King Charles, for himself and the troop of a hundred soldiers he had with him. The Lieutenant, Sir William Balfour, refused, leaving Billingsley no choice but to turn, clatter away through the Bulwark Gate and report his failure to his master. The Tower of London had stood for five and a half centuries. Throughout that time no one had ever disputed the fact that it was a royal fortress, a royal palace, a royal prison. Kings and queens had exercised their prerogative in sending subjects to the Tower for short or long spells of incarceration. They did not excuse such actions and they did not allow anyone else to share their privilege. This was largely why the Tower was regarded as the embodiment of royal power. But in 1641 one of the King's ministers was sent to the Tower by parliament and Charles was unable to effect his release.

Since the death of Henry VIII, England's rulers had been unable to neglect the importance of public opinion, and particularly of London opinion. More and more the crown was obliged to rely on taxation for its ordinary revenue. Taxation could only be granted by parliament and parliament demanded in return an ever greater share in the government of the realm. Within parliament, the House of Commons, representing, if not 'the people', at least the yeomen, gentlemen and burgesses, was speaking with a more confident voice. No one in England believed in democracy (except for the radical Levellers who were generally regarded as a very dangerous group) but it was towards democracy that the constitution was headed and when Charles I tried to throw it into reverse the result was civil war. Change was inevitable but it need not have been violent. Elizabeth had yielded a little and yielded gracefully. She knew how to handle parliament, and her public appearances were magnificently stage-managed. She won and she held the hearts of her people. By contrast James I completely lacked dignity and never really understood his subjects. He and, later, his son regarded parliament as an obstructive body of men setting themselves up in opposition to the King who was 'God's lieutenant upon earth'. The first Stuarts tried to return to a medieval style of government: they summoned parliament as little as possible; exploited to the full feudal sources of revenue; restored the power of the episcopate; and relied for advice on court favourites. By so doing they precipitated a constitutional crisis which for eleven years swept away the monarchy.

None of this could be foreseen in 1603 when London welcomed the King from over the border, if not with wild rejoicing, at least with relief. The anarchy which they had long feared might follow the death of childless Elizabeth had not materialized. King James made a leisurely progress southwards and arrived in the capital on 7 May. Four days later he decided to inspect his Tower.

> His Majesty set forth quietly by foot to Whitehall where he took barge. Having shot the Bridge his landing was expected at the Tower stairs, but it pleased his Highness to pass the Tower stairs towards St Katharine's, and there stayed on the water to see the ordnance on the White Tower ... being 20 pieces, and the great ordnance on Tower Wharf 100 pieces, and chambers [i.e. small cannon used to fire salutes] to the number of 130 discharged and shot off. Then he came to the stairs with the Lord Admiral, the Earls of Northumberland and Worcester, the Lord Thomas Howard and other noblemen. At his coming up the Sword was presented by Sir Thomas Coningsby, gentleman usher of the Privy Chamber, and by the King delivered to the Duke of Lennox who bore it before him into the Tower. All the prisoners of what quality soever, even Jesuits, have been set at liberty.[1]

The King did not stay at the Tower; he went on to Greenwich and remained there until the coronation in July. There was to be no grand procession through the streets this time. London had prepared its pageants and decorations but that frequent summer visitor, the plague, was in town and the government deemed it wise to deter people from crowding into the City and making the contagion worse. But the citizens were not denied their traditional spectacle. On the following 12 March the court came to the Tower and spent three days there before setting out with full pomp and ceremony for the opening of parliament. We are told that what fascinated James most about the fortress was the menagerie. He admired the lions and commented that they must be the fiercest beasts in England. One of the courtiers demurred; there was, he said, no animal to rival the English mastiff for courage and tenacity. Immediately, the King ordered three of these dogs to be brought.

> Which being done, the King, the Queen and the Prince went secretly to the Lion's tower, and caused the fiercest lion to be separated from

his mate, and one dog alone put in the lion's den, who straightway flew to the face of the lion. But the lion shook him off, and grasped him fast by the neck, drawing the dog upstairs and downstairs. So another dog was put into the den, who likewise took the lion by the face, and he began to deal with him as with the former; but whilst he held them both under his paws they bit him by the belly, whereat the lion roared so extremely that the earth shook withal . . . The third dog was then put in and likewise took the lion by the hip. The first dogs are dead but the third is like to recover, concerning which the Prince hath commanded that he shall be sent to St James' and there kept and made much of, saying that he that hath fought with the king of beasts shall never after fight with any inferior creature.[2]

Lions and mastiffs were not the only creatures that James tormented in the Tower. Even before the start of the new reign English courtiers had been manoeuvring for the favour of the King who was to come. Foremost among them was Robert Cecil. He succeeded in maintaining his position of principal advisor, and James allowed his opinions of other prominent Englishmen to be greatly influenced by Cecil. That is largely how he came to dislike Sir Walter Raleigh and his cultured circle. Even before the King reached London Sir Walter had been deprived of his post as Captain of the Guard and ordered to give up his tenancy of Durham House. That was bad enough but a few weeks later Raleigh and his friends, Lord Cobham and Lord Grey de Wilton, were arrested on treason charges. The reason for this was their fringe connection with two ill-conceived, foolish conspiracies, the Bye and Main plots, one aimed at forcing a policy of religious toleration on the King, and the other at removing him altogether in favour of his cousin, Arabella Stuart.

Together with other suspects, the three courtiers were taken from the Tower to Winchester for their trial, for the judges, like everyone else who could afford to do so, had moved well away from the plague-infested capital. They were, of course, found guilty and condemned to death. But James, unwilling to begin his reign with a spate of executions, commuted the sentences to imprisonment during his majesty's pleasure. Thus there came together in the Tower a remarkable little coterie of learned and accomplished men who passed their time in reading, writing books and poetry, conversing on every aspect of contemporary culture and politics, and conducting scientific experiments.

The distinguished prisoners were permitted considerable freedom of movement and generous allowances for food, fuel and other necessaries – Raleigh had £308 per annum and the two peers £516 each.

9 The Great Fire of London, 1666. An eye-witness view by an unknown Dutch artist

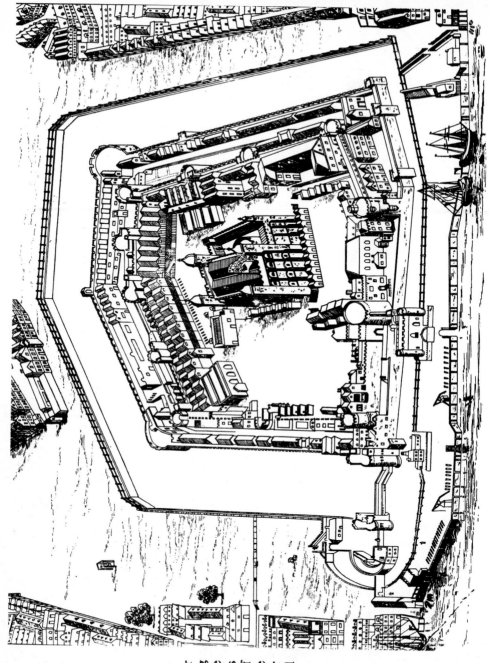

10 A view of the Tower shortly before the building of the Grand Storehouse (begun in 1688). It shows clearly the proliferation of buildings devoted to the Ordnance within the Inner Ward

11a This view of the Tower in the 1690s clearly shows the complex dominated less by the White Tower than by the splendid new Grand Storehouse behind it

11b The press room of the Tower Mint in the eighteenth century

12 The executions of the Scottish peers, the Earl of Kilmarnock and Lord Balmerino, after the 1745 Jacobite Rebellion, indicating clearly the enormous crowd which assembled to watch

13a Many strange and cruel events such as lion and bear baiting occurred in the menagerie. This contest between a lion and two tigers appears, however, to have been accidental

13b The Tower menagerie in the Lion Barbican

14a As a result of the disastrous fire of 1841 the Tower lost one of its most splendid buildings, the Grand Storehouse, and others were severely threatened

14b Until the building of new docks down river the Tower waterfront was always thronged with shipping

15a The Wellington Barracks was built on the site of the Grand
Storehouse in the prevailing Gothic Revival style

15b The moat, drained by
order of the Duke of
Wellington, served
generations of Tower
children as a playground,
but during World War II it
was commandeered for a
more essential purpose

16a A direct hit on the Victorian North Bastion in 1940 revealed the line of the original curtain wall which was restored after the war

16b The bomb damage inflicted on the Tower in World War II was not an unmitigated disaster. The destruction of the late Victorian Main Guard revealed part of the wall built by Henry III. Restoration work is seen in progress here

In addition they could furnish their rooms at their own expense and command whatever luxuries their resources permitted. Raleigh's family could stay with him, friends could visit and the prisoners could enjoy the ministrations of barbers, surgeons, chaplains and other attendants. Sir Walter's chambers in the Bloody Tower were comfortable and were especially extended in order to accommodate his wife, his young son and his three servants. In February 1605 his wife gave birth to another boy who was duly baptized with the name of Carew in St Peter's. Raleigh took exercise in the Lieutenant's garden, grew plants there and equipped a small shed in which he distilled cordials from various herbs, roots and berries.

Henry Brooke, Lord Cobham and his suite were lodged in the Beauchamp Tower and a special turret was made available to house his collection of a thousand books. There he read, translated the classics, and wrote letters to his brother-in-law, Robert Cecil. Correspondence seems to have been Thomas Grey's principal relaxation. From his extensive chambers in the King's Lodgings he wrote to friends in political and diplomatic circles in order to keep himself fully informed of current events, and especially of the war in the Netherlands.

At the end of 1605 a fourth member was added to this band of cultured prisoners. For wealth and extravagance of lifestyle he easily excelled the rest. He was Henry Percy, the 'Wizard Earl', the son of the Earl of Northumberland who had died violently in the Tower in the previous reign. He now found himself condemned for misprision of treason in connection with the Gunpowder Plot (Thomas Percy, Henry's second cousin, was one of the instigators of the plot). He was allotted rooms in the palace (vacated for him by Grey) but soon complained that they were damp and stuffy. Accommodation that was good enough for the King of England was apparently less than adequate for the Earl of Northumberland. Percy was moved to the Martin Tower where he certainly set himself up in almost regal splendour. As far as possible his household was organized independently of the normal Tower routine. His food was brought and prepared to his own specifications. He dined off silver and gold plate. His chambers were equipped with fine furniture, hangings, carpets and paintings. His wardrobe was extensive; tailors, laundresses and haberdashers were employed at the rate of about £1,000 a year to cater for his fastidious needs. Payments and presents to the Lieutenant and his staff amply recompensed them for any inconvenience and there can be little doubt that the Earl was a very popular prisoner.

He was also a prisoner who excited considerable curiosity. His interests had always been in the fields of alchemy, astrology and philosophy, and he devoted his enforced leisure to enthusiastic study.

Like Raleigh, he had a still-house built where he concocted medicines and potions. He employed three prominent mathematicians, Thomas Harriot, Walter Warner and Thomas Hughes and the alchemist Nicholas Hill. Percy and his colleagues in the Tower spent hours on end absorbed in their studies and experiments with the aid of these specialists. This was an age in which esoteric knowledge was suspect and when there was no clear distinction in most men's minds between scientific enquiry and dabbling in forbidden arts. The Northumberland–Raleigh circle were sometimes dubbed atheists, and a shocked chronicler wrote of Harriot that he

> made a philosophical theology, wherein he cast off the Old Testament, [from which it followed that] the New one would have no foundation. He was a Deist. His doctrine he taught to Sir Walter Raleigh, Henry Earl of Northumberland, and some others. The divines of those times looked on his manner of death [he died of a cancerous ulcer on his face] as a judgement upon him for 'nullifying the Scripture'.[3]

Northumberland and Raleigh both catered within the castle for their sons' education. Percy leased the Brick Tower so that his heir, Algernon, could establish his household there and be carefully tutored under his father's eye. When the time came for young Algernon to extend his knowledge by making a continental tour, Northumberland devoted several weeks to writing an *Advice to his son on his travels*.

For years these distinguished prisoners remained in confinement. They constituted yet another of the Tower's curiosities and the increasing numbers of visitors were always anxious to catch a glimpse of the Wizard Earl and his friends. The King showed no inclination whatsoever to release them. Lord Grey died in St Thomas's Tower in 1614. Five years later Cobham expired in sordid circumstances. His health had been failing for some years and in 1617 he was allowed to go to Bath for the waters. He returned to the castle but appears to have had liberty to withdraw occasionally because of his illness. It was eventually in a house in the Minories that he died, his body remaining unburied for some time while the government and his family squabbled over whose responsibility the funeral was. By then Raleigh had already been executed (we shall return to him shortly). Thus only Northumberland was left, quietly pursuing his studies and smoking tobacco. At last, in 1621, friends at court engineered his release. On 18 July the guns of the Tower saluted a remarkable man who had spent almost sixteen years within the walls. The Earl, for his part, demonstrated his wealth and unbroken pride by journeying to Bath in a magnificent carriage drawn by eight horses, thus cocking a snook at the Duke of Buckingham, James's favourite, who had taken to touring the country in a coach and six.

We must now move back in time to consider the incidents which first brought Northumberland to the Tower – incidents connected with that most notorious of all English conspiracies, the Gunpowder Plot. The conception of this bizarre and extreme undertaking probably dates from March 1604 when at a house in Lambeth Robert Catesby told his friends, John Wright and Thomas Winter, that 'he had bethought him of a way at one instant to deliver us from all our bonds and without any foreign help to replant again the Catholic religion.'[4] Eventually there were drawn into the plot Robert Winter, John and Christopher Wright, Thomas Percy, Robert Keyes, John Grant, Ambrose Rookwood, Everard Digby, Francis Tresham, Thomas Bates and, of course, Guy Fawkes. They were mostly men of good family and they were all fanatical Catholics. The plan – to blow up the King, the judges, Lords and Commons assembled for the opening of parliament in November 1605 – was exceedingly bloodthirsty and, on the face of it, quite impracticable. Yet it came within an ace of succeeding and it gave the King a very severe fright. Some of the conspirators had originally expressed misgivings at dealing out so much death but their 'holy' cause was one which seemed to justify any means for its accomplishment. England had made peace with Spain. The penal laws against Catholics were not rigidly enforced. Yet for a minority of Englishmen their country was still in schism from the true church, a situation they would do anything to change. They were egged on (or, at least, not prevented) by Jesuits and recusant priests.

After the failure of the plot its principals were rounded up, Catesby, Percy, the Wrights, Thomas Winter and Rookwood were shot down when troops stormed Holbeach House. The remainder were captured piecemeal and brought into the Tower. They were thrown into the foulest cells, tortured and examined daily in the Council Chamber of the Lieutenant's Lodging.* Their confessions implicated others including priests who were then arrested and joined the principal conspirators. Many of them seem to have been kept in the basement of the White Tower, although Fawkes is said to have spent fifty days in Little Ease. The government and the officers of the Tower exercised little restraint in their treatment of the prisoners. The crime was so odious, the men themselves so adamant of the righteousness of their actions, that few of their gaolers can have felt any sympathy for them. In addition, Cecil and other councillors now realized that they had an opportunity to undermine the insidious activities and

* This was the upper part of the old hall which had been divided by the insertion of a floor.

propaganda of the Jesuits. Most important of all, they wanted to deter the King from his proposed toleration of Catholics and *rapprochement* with the Pope. So, the prisoners were racked and manacled again and again, questioned for hour after hour and when these methods failed to produce some of the details and names the government wanted, the wretched men were put into shared cells where their conversations could be overheard.

Two men died as a result of their handling in the Tower. One was Francis Tresham who, according to Cecil, succumbed to 'a natural sickness, such as he hath been a long time subject to'. The other was the Jesuit, Nicholas Owen, who – officially – committed suicide in March 1606. Owen, or 'Little John' as he was affectionately known, is a very interesting character. He was active in England for over twenty years and his speciality was the building of priests' holes and escape passages. These ingenious chambers were concealed within cupboards, under staircases, in the thickness of walls and behind chimneys, and undoubtedly saved many recusant priests from discovery. Owen was also reputed to be a master of escapes and to have got away from many prisons, including the Tower (in 1597). Legend also attributed to 'Little John' the escape of Gerard and Arden in 1597.

The man who had charge of the Gunpowder Plot conspirators was Sir William Waad, one of the most active, if least pleasant, men ever to hold the office of Lieutenant. He was appointed in August 1605 on the death of Sir George Harvey, of whom it was sadly reported that he died 'in poor estate, the reputation of his place requiring that which the allowances of the office would not countervail'.[5] It was obviously not every man who could make a handsome profit out of the lieutenancy. Perhaps Harvey was not sufficiently hard and self-seeking; certainly the privileges he allowed Raleigh and his colleagues and the fact that he often invited them to dine with him suggest an easy-going nature. Waad was a bird of a totally different feather. He was in his sixtieth year and had behind him a long, vigorous career as diplomat, secretary to the Council, spy and persecutor of Catholics. He had been one of Walsingham's principal agents in tracking down papist plots and examining recusant priests. Cold, efficient and single-minded, he was ideally qualified to extract every drop of incriminating information from Guy Fawkes and his confederates.

Waad, apparently, had his own little band of trained inquisitors whom he brought into the Tower with him and who were more effective than the Yeoman Warders in obtaining information. Like every skilled interrogator Waad knew how to use kindness and charm as well as cruelty and terror. This is shown most clearly in his handling of Henry Garnet, the Jesuit Superior, whose arrest and conviction was the government's main triumph in the whole Gunpowder Plot affair.

Garnet, a humble, saintly man, arrived at the Tower in February 1606. He was well lodged, provided with good food and wine. He was allowed to communicate with friends. He found the Lieutenant 'very kindly in his usage and familiarity' and his gaoler became a close friend, particularly after he declared a desire for conversion to the Roman Catholic faith. The Warder offered to deliver messages secretly to Garnet's friends and also showed the prisoner a hole in the wall through which he could talk with another captive priest. Of course, all that the Jesuit wrote and said was reported to Waad and in this way the government obtained proof that Garnet had been privy to Catesby's plot. Confronted with this, Garnet confessed. He was tried and condemned to be hanged and quartered. His cause was largely discredited and the long sequence of Catholic-inspired treasons came to an end.

It was not only the perpetrators of the Gunpowder Plot who engaged Waad's attention. He was appalled by the general laxity operating in the Tower. The Yeoman Warders apparently left much to be desired.

> Anciently the Warders held their places only by a Bill of His Majesty and since His Majesty's coming to the crown, these grants are passed under the Great Seal, whereby great inconvenience doth arise for they have no care, many of them, to execute their office, but perform their waiting by a deputy, and seldom come to give attendance, being farmers in the country, others citizens, others artificers, some bankrupts, some given to drunkenness and disorder and most of them very ungovernable.
>
> Another inconvenience cometh thereby, also by selling their places to unfit persons, so that he that hath a place, for his own life, doth sell the same to another for the person's life that doth buy the same. One of the Warders is a Gentleman Server in the court, and a Warder of the Tower. Another sold his place for money, and begged the late Queen to let him have the [position] again and yet never giveth attendance. There are two other Warders that hold their places from one that sold it to them both.[6]

The martinet might complain but he had little influence in matters which involved wealthy and important men close to the King.

But in the matter of state prisoners he could act. The freedom enjoyed by Raleigh and his colleagues he found shocking. He complained that when Sir Walter was working in his little garden he was fully on view to visitors who would often stop and speak to him. Waad obtained the Council's permission to build a high wall around Raleigh's little plot. But there were worse offences: the curfew was ignored by prisoners and warders alike. Northumberland and his friends went to each others' quarters and stayed talking late into the night. Visitors, also, came and went at all hours. Waad soon put a stop to such unseemly behaviour. There was, however, little he could do about another of Raleigh's tedious habits, that of parading along the wall-walk between the Bloody Tower and the Lieutenant's Lodging and showing himself to people on the Wharf.

Waad proved to be equally vigilant on the vexed question of the Lieutenant's privileges and the bounds of his jurisdiction. He made a collection of documents on the subject to demonstrate the ancient rights enjoyed by his predecessors. But the feud was perpetuated by frequent minor aggravations. In 1605 'the Lord Mayor and aldermen, not content with voiding the town ditch into the Tower ditch, have caused a sluice to be opened which will bring all the soil from the Minories into the town ditch, and so into the Tower ditch, which stinks very vilely, and puts those in the Tower to great shifts for sweet water'.[7] Four months later the City authorities were again deliberately provocative.

> Notwithstanding a command given a fortnight ago not to renew any quarrels with the Lieutenant of the Tower, last night the Lord Mayor compassed the greater part of the Tower with the sword carried before him, accompanied with the sheriffs, and a rabble of sergeants and took possession of the Postern, and so came back again in great bravery, bidding the people bear witness of his triumph.[8]

In 1616 the Lieutenant had to send a protest to the Lord Mayor when a party of workmen appeared on Tower Hill and began to erect a small lock-up prison. It availed him nothing; his messengers were rudely dismissed and the offending building stayed.

It was Waad's zeal and uprightness that led to his downfall. The loyal Lieutenant would apply to his prisoners every restriction, every mode of torture without qualm for the sake of king and country. He would not connive at murder to satisfy the corrupt passions of a dissolute courtier. This brings us to the unsavoury Overbury scandal which did more than any other single event to discredit the Stuart court in the eyes of the people. Sir Thomas Overbury was an old and close friend of Robert Carr, Viscount Rochester, the King's favourite, and when the latter became infatuated with Frances, Countess of Essex, Overbury aided the affair. He became a less enthusiastic confidant when the Countess began proceedings to dissolve her marriage and Rochester determined to wed her. Overbury saw Frances Howard for what she was, a ruthless, ambitious, unprincipled whore as well as a dabbler in black arts, and earnestly entreated his friend to disentangle himself from her. The lady conceived an intense hatred for interfering Overbury and this was shared by her family who were angling for political power. They all knew that Overbury had information which could prejudice the success of the nullity proceedings in the archbishop's court. They used their influence with James to secure a diplomatic appointment for Sir Thomas overseas. But Overbury declined the bribe. Rochester had now turned against his friend and decided that a spell in the Tower would have a salutary effect upon him.

On 26 April 1613 Overbury was arrested suddenly at court, taken down river and delivered into Sir William Waad's hands to be kept a close prisoner. That may have been all that Carr intended: it was not enough for Frances Howard and her relatives who realized that Overbury must be silenced permanently. It soon became obvious that Waad was not the man to fall in with their foul scheme. Trumped up charges of incompetence and dishonesty were brought against him and he was dismissed. The new Lieutenant was Sir Gervase Elwes, a creature of the Howards. The next step was the introduction of Richard Weston to the Tower as Overbury's gaoler. It was Weston's task to poison Overbury with the contents of phials obtained from Lady Essex's confederates, Anne Turner, a brothel-keeper and necromancer, and the apothecary James Franklin. The dosing of the prisoner's food, which came directly from the Lieutenant's kitchen, began immediately and soon produced the most distressing symptoms:

This morning, notwithstanding my fasting till yesterday, I find a great heat continues in all my body, and the same desire of drink and loathing of meat, etc., I was let blood Wednesday 10 o'clock [yet] to [this] day, Friday, my heat slackens not [and I have] the same loathing of meat, having eaten not a bit since Thursday . . . sennight to this hour, and the same vomitting yesternight. About 8 o'clock after Mr Mayerns was gone I fainted.[9]

At the beginning Elwes probably did not realize what Weston was doing. When he discovered the truth he lacked the courage to stand up to his patrons and protest. Poor Overbury had no one to help him. Slowly he wasted away and not until it was too late did he realize why. This may seem surprising until we realize that Overbury had been in poor health when he came to the Tower. Imprisonment usually had an undermining effect on a man's constitution and even the doctors who were permitted to treat Sir Thomas attributed his deterioration to natural causes. It was, of course, vital to the plot that the physicians should be deceived which was why the poison was administered in small doses. When Overbury at last suspected the truth he threatened to expose Elwes, the Countess, Carr, everyone and even hinted that he knew things about the King which James would not want revealed. This worried his tormentors into more precipitate action. The Lieutenant moved Overbury to a damp, dark cell which had no external windows. There was now no risk that the wretched man might be able to get some message out of the castle. But still he would not die. He was little more than a skeleton covered in sores but the slow poisons administered by Weston had not done their work. It was vital to finish Overbury off before the doctors grew suspicious. A young apprentice of theirs was bribed by Mrs Turner to add mercuric chloride to his patient's enema. Thomas Overbury died after hours of violent agony about dawn on 15 September. It only remained to dispose of the evidence as rapidly as possible.

> See him interred in the Chapel within the body of the Tower instantly . . . let no man's instance move you to make stay in any case . . . Fail not a jot herein as you love your friends; nor stay one minute, but let the priest be ready; and if Lidcote [Overbury's brother-in-law] be not there, send for him speedily, pretending that the body will not tarry.[10]

Before the sunset on that same day Overbury's remains lay beneath the flagstones of St Peter's chancel.

Everything went well for the callous murderers. Lady Essex was disencumbered of her unwanted spouse; she married Carr, now elevated to the Earldom of Somerset, amidst scenes of unparalleled splendour; and the Howards were riding high. Then the rumours began slithering around the Tower and out to the narrow streets and alleys of the City. It was impossible that the chickens should not come home to roost: the Carrs had plenty of enemies ever on the lookout for damaging information; there were too many minor conspirators in the plot; and Elwes's conscience was troubling him, as well it might. Sir Ralph Winwood, Secretary of State, began ferreting out the truth. He had a willing accomplice in Waad whose knowledge of the Tower personnel and ability as an interrogator were invaluable. How the ex-Lieutenant must have relished gathering the scraps of information which would bring down those who had displaced him. Elwes soon broke down and confessed everything to Winwood. With the other minor characters in the tragedy he was arrested and imprisoned in the Tower. They were all condemned and hanged, Elwes, by his own request, being executed on Tower Hill and not at Tyburn (November 1615).

But it soon became apparent that there was one law for the poor and quite another for the rich. The Countess of Somerset, the prime mover of this hideous crime, also made a full confession. With her husband she was lodged in the Bloody Tower, recently vacated by Sir Walter Raleigh. They were not brought to trial until the following spring. They were condemned to death and returned to the Tower, where they established themselves in a splendid style suitable to their rank and wealth. And there they remained. While the populace demanded that they should pay the penalty for their abominable crime, King James pardoned first the beautiful Countess and, later, her husband. In 1622 they were permitted to leave the Tower and to live quietly in one of their country houses. All love between them had long since faded, and enforced co-habitation must have been an effective form of punishment. Frances soon had worse to endure – the cancer which shortly brought her to her grave. The Earl was already dead politically, though he continued to enjoy his rural obscurity until 1645.

Another unfortunate inmate of the Tower at this time was the Lady Arabella Stuart. Her only crime was that she aspired to the same freedom of action enjoyed by women who were not close to the succession. She was kept at court, unmarried and likely to remain so. Then at the age of thirty-five she fell in love with William Seymour, grandson of that other Seymour, the Earl of Hertford, who had married Lady Catherine Grey. Now history was to repeat itself with similar sad results. The couple were summoned before the Council early in 1610 and told that marriage was out of the question. Arabella and William declared that they had no intention of marrying without royal consent and there the matter was allowed to rest. But in July the King heard to his chagrin that the couple had been wed in secret. Seymour was immediately taken to the Tower and his wife was placed in the custody of the Bishop of Durham.

The poor woman was desperate. She appealed in vain for clemency and she made herself ill with crying and refusing food. An extant letter of hers contains the melancholy complaint of one who felt herself utterly without friends, 'every one forsakes me but those that cannot help me'. Yet help was at hand. Arabella had always been of interest to those looking for a thoroughly English alternative to James I. One such was the Countess of Shrewsbury who now devised a scheme to get the young couple abroad and there to use Arabella as a pretender to the throne. Seymour's wife was probably ignorant of the political implications of this plan but she fell in with it eagerly as the only means of being reunited with her beloved.

In May 1611 the Bishop of Durham began the long journey north to his see accompanied by his charge. At Highgate the lady feigned illness. The moment her unsuspecting guardian left her to rest, Arabella and her confederates put their scheme into operation. The melancholy lady was transformed into a young gallant with yellow riding boots, cloak and short sword. She and her attendants reached the Thames and made their way down river to freedom – and William. Seymour, meanwhile, was also donning a disguise. In his chamber in St Thomas's Tower he adopted the ragged garb of a carter's boy and shambled out of the castle in the wake of a waggon carrying faggots. One wonders what Lieutenant Waad had to say to the porters! Both the lovers got away to sea, but not together. Missing the rendezvous because of bad weather, Seymour landed at Ostend. Arabella made for Calais in a sluggish French ship. The runaways had only a few hours start. The Countess of Shrewsbury was arrested. She and her servants were questioned and, before long, the King's ships were crossing the Channel in pursuit. It was the *Adventurer* which caught up with Arabella's vessel.

She was taken to the Tower and accommodated first in the Lieutenant's Lodging and later in the Bell Tower. She was well looked after and provided with every comfort. She had the company of the Countess of Shrewsbury and access to all the other distinguished 'guests' but her recent experiences had broken her spirit. One attempt was made to rescue her. When it failed all hope was crushed and the unfortunate woman gave herself up totally to melancholy. In the end it turned her mind. Death when it came in 1615 robbed her only of an insane half life which she had no desire to keep.

One prisoner had been the constant witness of all these sad events. During his long sojourn in the Tower Sir Walter Raleigh became what he had never been before – a popular hero – and achieved in the literary sphere accomplishments of an order which had always been denied him in maritime ventures. The Tower of London may be said to have made the Raleigh legend. Arrogant, sarcastic, over-sensitive, he had always been in conflict with those around him and his weaknesses had contributed not a little to the failure of the attempt to colonize Virginia and explore the Orinoco basin. He never enjoyed the success of Drake, the popularity of Essex, or the high command of Howard of Effingham. During the latter part of Elizabeth's reign he had always walked in other men's shadows, a situation he resented bitterly. But during his imprisonment he became a living reminder of the 'good old days' and within a decade of his death he was being hailed as a symbol of opposition to Stuart oppression

James had fully intended that Raleigh should sink into obscurity, but Raleigh had no intention of doing anything of the sort. As well as intriguing visitors to the Tower with his experiments and conversation he wrote letters and pamphlets offering the King and his ministers unwanted advice on a variety of subjects. He became famous for his cordial, a distillation of pearl, musk, hartshorn, mint, borage, gentian, mace, red rose, aloes, sugar, sassafras, spirits of wine and a score of other ingredients. James's Queen and his son, Prince Henry, were among the many exalted customers who sent their servants down to the Tower for phials of cordial which they took for many ailments. Henry was quite captivated by the grave prisoner who was so well read and could speak with authority on philosophy, science, travel, politics and literature. Doubtless he recognized in this last of the 'Armada captains' a man of action and of restless intellect, one who contrasted markedly with the effeminate, easy-going sodomite who was his father. Raleigh took to writing tracts and small treatises for the heir to the throne and it was for Henry that he embarked upon his greatest work, the *History of the World*. Though unfinished, this book, first published in 1614, was to have an immense influence. It was one of the best-sellers of the century, and within a generation was profoundly influencing a new breed of political and cultural leaders – Eliot, Milton, Cromwell. It had great breadth of scholarship (Raleigh cited and quoted from over six hundred authors), and perception of human motivation. In an age when the Stuarts tried to establish the political orthodoxy of the divine right of kings Raleigh was the arch heretic, lucid and devastating in his exposure of the weaknesses of past rulers.

> Now, for King Henry VIII, if all the pictures and patterns of a merciless prince were lost in the world, they might all again be painted to the life out of the story of this king. For, how many servants did he advance in haste and with the change of his fancy ruin again, no man knowing for what offence? To how many others, of more desert, gave he abundant flowers from whence to gather honey, and in the end of harvest burned them in the hive? How many wives did he cut off, and cast off, as his fancy and affection changed? How many princes of the blood (whereof some of them for age could hardly crawl towards the block) with a world of others of all degrees did he execute?[11]

No wonder James I tried to suppress the book.

Before the publication of the *History of the World* Raleigh's young patron had died, not even the celebrated cordial saving him. His passing was a tragedy for England and for Raleigh, who would probably have been restored to favour and fortune as the Prince's influence increased. Sir Walter was, however, given one last chance to re-establish his own reputation. In 1616 he was permitted to leave the Tower, under constant guard, in order to lead another expedition to the Orinoco. In 1595 he had travelled up the river in search of El Dorado, the fabulous ruler of a kingdom richer even than the Inca empire. He had found only dense jungle and native myths but his conviction remained undimmed that in the Guinea highlands there was a golden land ripe for plunder. Now, at last, the government was prepared to take him seriously. In March 1617, fourteen years after the old Queen's death, Sir Walter Raleigh set out on the last great Elizabethan adventure.

It was a disaster. There were no gold mines to be found. Some of Raleigh's men got involved in a clash with Spanish forces, which had been strictly forbidden. In the fighting he lost his own son, Wat. On Midsummer Day 1618 he arrived back in Plymouth ready to pay the price of failure. He had done enough to justify the King in removing his head but the government was resolved on one last act by which Raleigh should compromise himself finally. A shabby 'escape plot' was rigged and Sir Walter fell into the trap. After his recapture he was lodged in the Beauchamp Tower. He only left it to go to Westminster on 28 October to hear that the sentence pronounced in 1603 was to be carried out on the morrow. During all the times of sorrow and stress in the Tower poetry had been Raleigh's greatest consolation. He wrote many verses, most of them melancholy or angry reflections on the cruelty of fate. This little poem seems to sum up much of his thinking:

> What is our life? a play of passion,
> Our mirth the music of division,
> Our mothers' wombs the tyring houses be
> Where we are dressed for this short comedy,
> Heaven the judicious, sharp spectator is,
> That sits and marks still who doth act amiss,
> Our graves that hide us from the searching sun
> Are like drawn curtains when the play is done.
> Thus march we playing to our latest rest.
> Only we die in earnest; that's no jest.

From this time onwards the struggle of parliament and the common law judges to limit the exercise of royal prerogative increasingly dominates English history. In 1621–2 the country's leading legal expert, Sir Edward Coke, spent an uncomfortable spell in the Tower for persistently upholding the independence of the judiciary. The government recognized Coke's immense talent and tried by preferment to win his support for the crown but Sir Edward refused to submit to pressure. In 1610 he laid it down that the King could not change or make law by proclamation. He was appointed Chief Justice of the King's Bench but still refused to submit to political pressures. In 1616 he was suddenly dismissed from office after challenging the crown's right to quash common law proceedings by issuing a writ. Gradually he was restored to favour, though not to high legal office. Parliament now became his principal arena and there he became the most outspoken opponent of the government's pro-Spanish policy and especially of the proposed marriage alliance between the two nations. James's patience now snapped: he told the Speaker to stop the house debating 'anything concerning our government or matters of state' and he warned that he would punish any member who defied him. Coke and his supporters drew up a 'Protestation' asserting their ancient privileges concerning debate and freedom from arrest. James responded by apprehending Coke and other leaders and throwing them into the Tower. Then he sent for the Commons journal and tore out with his own hand the page containing the Protestation. Coke stayed in the Tower for nine months – that was a triumph for the prerogative. He was released because no charges could be proved against him – a triumph for the law.

With the accession of Charles I in 1625 monarchy regained dignity but became more private and withdrawn. Plague again prevented the traditional coronation procession but the King had no stomach for public display and did not give the City the gratification of welcoming him with sumptuous pageantry on a subsequent occasion. In fact, Charles I became the first reigning English monarch who never visited the Tower of London. From the closed world of the court he attempted to rule his kingdom through favourites and ministers of his own choosing, foremost among whom was George Villiers, Duke of Buckingham. Such men were, inevitably, disliked and mistrusted, as they were associated with unpopular and usually disastrous royal policies. Thousands of loyal Englishmen still supported the idea of legitimate monarchy and would fight for it on the battlefields of the Civil War but thousands more felt at best indifference and at worst contempt for a King they did not know. Charles's unpopularity was increased by the ill-feeling aroused over constitutional and religious issues. Anti-Catholic sentiment was very strong throughout the country but Charles was married to a Catholic wife who deliberately flaunted her religion (she refused, for example, to attend the coronation because it was performed by a Protestant archbishop) and he attempted to enforce ritual unity on the Church of England in the shade of high church ceremonial which, for most people, was indistinguishable from 'popery'. The King tried for four years to work with a recalcitrant parliament and then ruled for eleven years without one. His attempts to raise revenue, enforce law and pursue policy without the consent of the people could only multiply discontent. It became inevitable that increasing support would rally behind political extremists and religious extremists (Puritans) and that these forces would unite in an uneasy alliance to challenge and, if necessary, pull down the monarchy.

The opposition was soon provided with martyrs. The first was the assassin, John Felton. Felton was a soldier who had lost the use of his left arm in the wars, had been subsequently refused further employment by the Duke of Buckingham and, as a result, been reduced to a state of penury. As well as his personal grievance against

Villiers, Felton shared the common belief that most of the country's ills could be laid at the Duke's door. He read reports of Buckingham's censure in parliament and the pamphlets put about by enemies of the government. After long brooding he concluded that it was his responsibility to play the avenging angel. The cast of his thought is indicated by words from a contemporary book which he copied and pinned inside his hat: 'That man is cowardly and base and deserveth not the name of a gentleman or soldier that is not willing to sacrifice his life for the honour of his God, his King, and his country.'

On 19 August 1628 Felton went to a cutler on Tower Hill and bought a tenpenny dagger, which he fitted into a special compartment in his coat so that he could draw it quickly with his good hand. He walked most of the way to Portsmouth where Buckingham was getting together a naval expedition to fight against France. He entered the Duke's lodgings which were crowded with men seeking appointments on the coming campaign. There, in the press, John Felton struck down the most unpopular man in England. He was immediately arrested but it was a fortnight before he was conveyed to the Tower to await trial. By then everyone knew about his crime and his journey to London became more of a triumphal progress, people pressing round him with such cries as 'God bless thee, little David'. During the ensuing days visitors crowded into the Tower hoping to catch a glimpse of their saviour. King Charles was heartbroken and angrily demanded that the assassin should be racked and so forced to reveal the names of his confederates. Interestingly, the idea was dropped when Charles's advisers told him that torture was against the law; so far had the royal prerogative been weakened. While Felton sat in his cell, no doubt enduring the taunts of his gaolers, his name was being toasted by gentlemen all over England and a plethora of pamphlets and poems praising his action circulated among the common people. He was condemned on 27 November and executed at Tyburn the next day.

The only violence of which the other martyr was guilty was of the verbal kind. Sir John Eliot was a Cornish gentleman who sat as a member of parliament for the first time in 1624. He was a friend of the Duke of Buckingham and was not originally an opponent of the court. But he became increasingly angry at the government's bungled foreign policy and at the large sums of public money being used to sustain it. At the same time his natural gift for oratory made him the leader of the commons. In 1626 Eliot was loud in his complaints against Buckingham over his policies towards Spain and France. At last he persuaded the Commons to impeach the Duke (i.e. to cite him to appear before the House of Lords as a court of law to answer charges of offences against the state). This was, in effect, a claim that ministers of the crown were accountable to parliament. There was no legal way that King or favourite could avoid compliance with this demand. Angrily, Charles struck at his enemies. On 11 May Eliot and a colleague were thrown into the Tower. The Commons protested and told the King they would not proceed to any business (including the grant of taxation) until their members were released. Eliot was set free on the 19th. Charles had to dissolve parliament in order to save his friend from being tried.

In 1628 Eliot was instrumental in forcing the King to grant a Petition of Right which safeguarded citizens from the exercise of certain prerogative functions including 'imprisonment without cause shown'. Thanks largely to Eliot's fiery oratory the dispute between King and Commons grew rapidly more bitter and both sides took up entrenched positions. Matters came to a head on 2 March 1629 when the Speaker was held in his chair to prevent the adjournment of the House while Eliot read out three resolutions on which he wished the Commons to vote. Two days later he found himself in the Tower 'for notable contempt by him committed against ourself and our government, and for stirring up sedition against us.'

Eliot's accommodation and conditions of imprisonment were changed frequently but for the first few weeks he was strictly confined and permitted no visitors or writing materials. The Lieutenant, Sir Allan Apsley, had to use considerable vigilance to see that these orders were complied with, for many people came to see the prisoner, including some who, because of their rank, it was not easy to turn away. The Earl of Lincoln, Lord Rochford and the Earl of Bolingbroke were among those caught, 'going obscurely by themselves directly to Sir John Eliot's lodging, and being stopped by a warder I set of purpose over his lodging. Then, they desired to speak with Sir John's keeper, and would have had his keeper to have brought them to him, which he refused.'[12]

In the following January sentence was passed against Eliot that he should be detained during the King's pleasure. Charles's pleasure was that his enemy should never be set at liberty again. He hated Sir John as the man who more than any other had hounded Buckingham and was as guilty of his friend's death as if his hand had been on the fatal dagger. Sir John was also ordered to pay a fine of £2,000, to which he responded that 'he had two cloaks, two suits, two pairs of boots and goloshes, and a few books; that was his present substance, and if they could pick £2,000 out of that much good might it do them.'[13]

Eliot rapidly composed himself to face a long imprisonment. He wrote to the Lieutenant expressing the desire 'that convenient lodging might be provided for him, and that he might be permitted to send his upholsterer to trim it up, for he had no prospect of quitting it speedily.'[14] He devoted himself to setting down his political

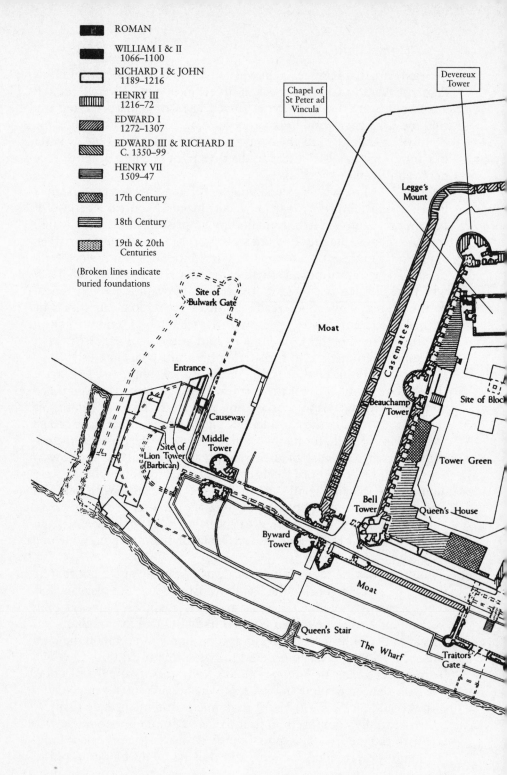

ROMAN

WILLIAM I & II
1066–1100

RICHARD I & JOHN
1189–1216

HENRY III
1216–72

EDWARD I
1272–1307

EDWARD III & RICHARD II
C. 1350–99

HENRY VII
1509–47

17th Century

18th Century

19th & 20th
Centuries

(Broken lines indicate
buried foundations

Site of
Bulwark Gate

Chapel of
St Peter ad
Vincula

Devereux
Tower

Moat

Legge's
Mount

Casemates

Entrance

Causeway

Beauchamp
Tower

Site of Bloc

Middle
Tower

Site of
Lion Tower
(Barbican)

Tower Green

Bell
Tower

Queen's House

Byward
Tower

Moat

Queen's Stair

The Wharf

Traitors'
Gate

25   0   100   200

SCALE OF FEET

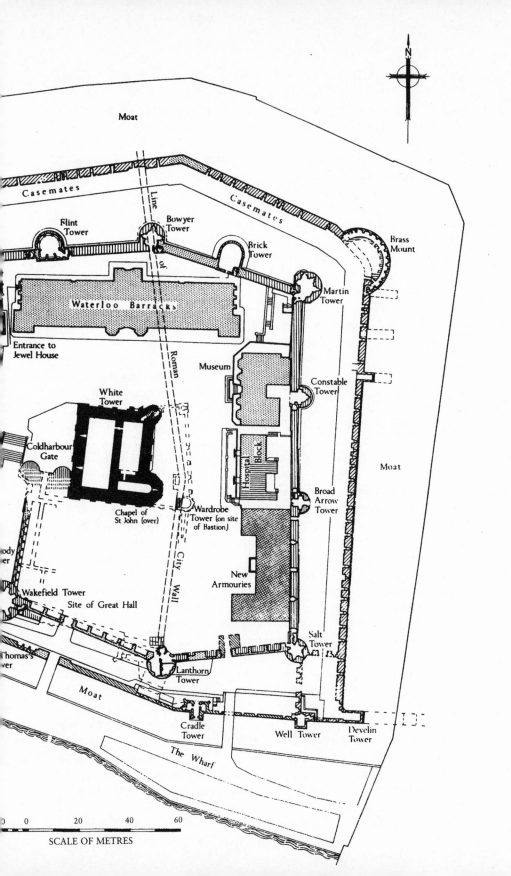

Moat

N

Casemates

Casemates

Flint
Tower

Bowyer
Tower

Brass
Mount

Brick
Tower

Line

of

Martin
Tower

Waterloo Barracks

Roman

Entrance to
Jewel House

Museum

Constable
Tower

White
Tower

Coldharbour
Gate

Hospital Block

Moat

Wardrobe
Tower (on site
of Bastion)

Chapel of
St John (over)

Broad
Arrow
Tower

ody
er

City Wall

New
Armouries

Wakefield Tower

Site of Great Hall

Salt
Tower

homas's
ver

Lanthorn
Tower

Moat

Cradle
Tower

Well Tower

Develin
Tower

The Wharf

0   0   20   40   60

SCALE OF METRES

philosophy in such books as *The Monarchy of Man* and *De Jure Maiestatis: A Political Treatise of Government*. He was now allowed reading and writing materials and he had the freedom of the Tower. He wrote many letters, some of them displaying considerable charm, courtesy and wit and had much business to attend to regarding the care of his family and estate. For some reason he was closely confined again at the end of 1631. 'My lodgings are removed. I am now where candlelight may be suffered, but scarce fire. None but my servant, hardly my sons, may have admittance to me; my friends I must desire for their own sakes to forbear coming to the Tower.'[15]

His health was already deteriorating. His appeals to the King for more lenient treatment were met with cold refusal. Sir John Eliot died of tuberculosis in November 1632. His family petitioned for permission to take the body back to Cornwall. Charles's reply was succinct: 'Let Sir John Eliot's body be buried in the church of the parish where he died.' The pioneer of parliamentary liberty was, accordingly, interred in an unmarked grave in St Peter's.

Within a decade parliament was to demonstrate that it, too, could use the Tower for the restraint of its enemies. Indeed, the fortress was to feature prominently in the political life of the nation as King and parliament drifted towards civil war. In 1637 Bishop Williams of Lincoln was detained there on a charge of betraying royal confidences and two years later the Earl of Loudon came within an ace of losing his head on Tower Hill. John Campbell, Lord Loudon, was a representative of the popular party in Scotland which opposed the religious changes being forced upon the land. In 1640 he was in London as an ambassador from the Scottish assembly when a letter of his was produced, allegedly seeking the aid of the French King. Charles angrily ordered that the 'traitor' be taken to the Tower and executed on the sole authority of a royal writ. The King was at the end of his tether. Opposition to his rule was widespread and he was facing the unwelcome prospect of having to recall parliament as the only means of raising revenue. His high-handed treatment of Campbell was the desperate act of a man driven into a corner and determined to strike back against his adversaries. It was, of course, very foolish: apart from condemning Loudon without trial, which would undoubtedly cause a storm of protest on both sides of the border, it ignored the immunity due to him as an ambassador.

The Lieutenant of the Tower, Sir William Balfour, was in a quandary: he was the King's officer but he was being asked to associate himself with an act of dubious legality at a time when tension in the City was at a peak. Being himself a Scot, he also knew something of the situation north of the border. He discussed the situation with Loudon to see if there was some way out of the dilemma. Loudon bethought himself of his friend, the Marquess of Hamilton and Balfour hurried to the nobleman's London lodging. Hamilton immediately agreed to go to the King and the two men rode to Whitehall. But it was late. Charles had already gone to bed. Very few men had the right to disturb him, but one of the few was the Lieutenant of the Tower of London. He took Hamilton into the bedchamber. Charles was adamant: Campbell must die. When all persuasion had failed, the Marquess turned to leave. 'If Your Majesty be so determined,' he said 'I'll . . . ride post for Scotland tomorrow morning, for I am sure before night the whole City will be in an uproar and they will come and pull Your Majesty out of your palace. I will get as far as I can, and declare to my countrymen that I had no hand in it.' The King, at last, gave way but Loudon had to spend several months in the Tower.

The two men on whom Charles relied most heavily during the 'eleven years' tyranny' (1629–40) were Thomas Wentworth, Earl of Strafford, and William Laud, Archbishop of Canterbury. Both were able men who, in happier circumstances, might have served their country well. As it was, they became the arrogant and intractable agents of an arrogant and intractable King, who was determined to impose his own political and religious beliefs on the people. Strafford was away from the centre of affairs for most of the period, being first President of the Council of the North and then Lord Deputy of Ireland but he was widely known to be the adviser who most resolutely urged the King to firm uncompromising action. He advocated a war against Scotland financed by 'loans' forced from Charles's wealthier subjects and prosecuted with an army he would personally bring over from Ireland and which, it was widely believed, he would use against the English if necessary. Laud rigorously enforced the beliefs and practices of the high church minority on the English church. He persecuted Puritans, forcing many of them to flee abroad (this was the period of the establishment of the first American colonies, which were set up by bands of emigrants seeking religious freedom) and his name was execrated because of the punishments meted out through the courts of High Commission and Star Chamber.* Probably life was no more harsh during the years of Charles I's personal rule than at earlier periods. If the King had been able to finance his government indefinitely he might have been permitted to do so. But the groups of Englishmen he was alienating had found in parliament a powerful weapon and as soon as Charles was forced to summon Lords and Commons again they used that weapon against him.

* One Puritan propagandist, Alexander Leighton, was fined £10,000, and was sentenced to have both nostrils slit, both ears cut off and his face branded. That done, he was whipped, pilloried and imprisoned for life.

In May 1640 Charles called another parliament. It proved to be no more co-operative than its predecessors and was dissolved after only three weeks. But independent monarchy had reached the end of the road. The Scottish war fizzled out when the enemy occupied Newcastle. Bankrupt morally as well as financially, Charles issued writs summoning what would go down in history as the Long Parliament. There was no doubt that the Commons' first action would be to remove the King's 'evil counsellors'. Strafford made one last, bold effort to fend off the inevitable. It was arranged that Charles would review his troops in the Tower. The leaders of the Commons would be among those present and they would be instantly arrested. The scheme was transparent. It only served to precipitate the action Strafford's enemies took. On 10 November they impeached 'Black Tom' Wentworth of treason. He was taken from Westminster to the Tower in a closed carriage and the route was lined with jeering crowds. Four months later Archbishop Laud joined him.

The Commons eventually decided to proceed against Strafford by bill of attainder. It went slowly through its various stages. The Lords were concerned about the wisdom of so momentous an action. The King, who had given his faithful servant a solemn promise – 'upon the word of a king, you shall not suffer in life, honour or fortune' – delayed proceedings by making counter proposals. He offered concessions in exchange for Wentworth's life. Unfortunately for the success of these negotiations, Charles was at the same time laying complex plots to rescue Wentworth and make a new bid for independence backed by military power. The Irish army remained in its barracks; ships hired by Strafford's secretary stood ready off Tower Wharf. Messages were sent to the governor of Portsmouth to put the town in a state of defence. Money was brought across from the Netherlands. On 1 May Captain Billingsley made his appearance at the gate of the Tower, demanding admittance. It was another dilemma for poor Lieutenant Balfour. Yet, in all probability, he had already chosen sides. He had received Strafford in the name of parliament and he would only release him on the same authority. It seems likely that royal agents had already approached him with a plan to release Wentworth and that he had refused. Now, he sent Billingsley away empty handed. He was deprived of his office a few months later. His subsequent career shows that he had definitely thrown in his lot with parliament. He served with conspicuous courage and skill in many Civil War engagements and in 1645 the Commons voted a considerable sum as 'a fit recompense and acknowledgement of the faithful services done by him to the public'. When the Lords heard of Charles's machinations they delayed no longer in passing the attainder. It only remained for the King to add his signature.

Charles hesitated. He consulted his judges on the legality of the proceedings. He asked his bishops to find a loophole for his conscience. The London mob thronged Westminster screaming for justice on 'Black Tom' but still the King stayed his hand. It was the Constable of the Tower who finally forced him to act. The Earl of Newport owed everything to the Stuarts. A bastard son of the Earl of Devonshire, he had commended himself to King James and Buckingham and had rapidly accumulated titles and lucrative posts. In 1634 Charles had appointed him Master of the Ordnance, a position from which Newport made vast profits by selling gunpowder at exorbitant prices. Early in 1641 the Earl was made Constable of the Tower in the hope that he would help save Strafford and, indeed, secure the Tower against parliamentary opposition should the need arise. But Newport was already changing sides. He was a member of the minority in the Lords who were in favour of constitutional reform. He now told Charles that if he received no royal warrant to hand Wentworth over for execution he would attend to the matter on his own authority. With that the King broke down and signed away his friend's life.

On 12 May the Earl of Strafford, sombrely dressed, walked calm and dignified from his prison lodging. He had earlier asked for permission to spend some time with Laud before his death but when Balfour had told him he would have to make his request to parliament, Wentworth refused to demean himself. But the old Archbishop was at his window in the Bloody Tower when the condemned man passed through the archway below. Strafford stopped and bowed his head. Laud pronounced his blessing, and then fainted. A tumultuous crowd of over 100,000 had gathered on the Hill and special stands had been erected to afford a better view to those who cared to pay for the privilege. The walls of the Tower itself were lined with the families of the castle's personnel and any who could through friendship or bribery procure an invitation. Sir William Balfour was anxious about conducting his charge through the press and offered Strafford his coach. The Earl declined. 'I dare look death in the face, and I hope the people, too. I care not how I die, whether by the hand of the executioner or by the madness and fury of the people: if that may give them better content, it is all one to me.'[16]

Those who have left a record of the event seem agreed that Strafford died with cheerfulness and nobility of bearing. Among those whom curiosity had brought out to Tower Hill was the young John Evelyn. The entry in his diary makes it quite clear where his sympathies lay:

May 7th. I went again to Lond. with my bro. and on the 12th following beheld on Tower Hill the fatal stroke which severed the

173

wisest head in England from the shoulders of the Earl of Strafford, whose crime, coming under the cognizance of no human law, a new one was made, not to be a precedent, but [to bring about] his destruction, to such exorbitancy were things arrived.[17]

Evelyn was in a minority: all over London that night bonfires were lit.

It seemed that there was no stopping parliament. Throughout the summer they passed bill after bill restricting the royal prerogative and enhancing their own power. As one member remarked, 'reformation goes on as hot as a toast.' But by the autumn there were signs of anxiety. Some of the Lords and Commons believed that matters had gone far enough. Rifts were becoming evident between radicals and moderates. The King, when he realized this, allowed himself once more to hope – and to scheme. In August parliament had instructed the Earl of Newport to take up his residence in the Tower in order to secure it. Apparently he was somewhat dilatory in complying, for the order had to be repeated in December. The King was determined to maintain control of the fortress and on 22 December he dismissed the turncoat Balfour and installed Sir Thomas Lunsford, a young adventurer of ill-repute who had, in a brief, eventful career been both a murderer and an outlaw. Newport protested and threatened to take personal control of the Tower. He was immediately deprived of the constableship. However, the Commons also expressed their disapproval in very strong terms. Once again the King gave way. Lunsford was removed from office after the shortest tenancy in the Tower's history – four days. Charles now installed another of his supporters, John Byron, but he proved as little to the taste of parliament as his predecessor. The garrison had been reinforced by trained bands from the Liberty and the surrounding parishes – those men that the Lieutenant had always been able to call upon in times of need. Charles did not trust these citizen-soldiers and he instructed Byron to replace them with royal troops. The result was a scuffle during which the trained bands of the City rushed to the aid of their comrades. Byron's men were repulsed and, the next day, parliament sent for the Lieutenant to demand an explanation. The unfortunate man told his interrogators everything and they demanded his dismissal. The King resisted but Byron himself had no desire to continue in what must have been an extremely difficult appointment. He petitioned the King to set him free 'from the vexation and agony of that place'. On 11 February Sir John Conyers took over command.

A hundred and fifty, even a hundred, years earlier the monarch's first action on detecting incipient revolt would have been to move into the Tower with his court and summon all loyal magnates to muster there with their forces. Charles did not do so. In 1642 he travelled to the north and the Midlands seeking support from the people of those parts. Parliament thankfully occupied the power vacuum left in the capital and that included taking control of the Tower. Nothing could indicate more clearly the change that had come over this ancient building within three or four generations. No longer was it seen as a viable royal refuge, a place from which the King could carry on his government and which he could defend against rebellious subjects. The courts and the departments of state had established permanent headquarters elsewhere. There could be no return to household administration as Charles discovered during the Civil War. Nor was warfare any longer a relatively simple combat between baronial levies. The gentlemen and merchants of the land now commanded between them more wealth and patronage than the nobility. Influence was fragmented. Royalist and parliamentary forces in the coming conflict would be composed of individual recruits, town militias and small detachments from the estates of hundreds of greater and smaller landowners. The King and his enemies had to go out and win support; they could not rely on stone walls. Parliament held the Tower because they were the dominant party in the City and south-east England.

There were, of course, royalists in London. Sir Richard Gurney, who became Lord Mayor in 1641 was one of them. The election was hotly contested and while the aldermen solemnly voted in the Guildhall partisan mobs gathered outside, each group in battle array. For nine months Gurney tried to keep London loyal to the King's cause, resisting not only parliamentary pressure but also the wilder demands of the sovereign. He had to tell Charles that he could not guarantee the peace of the City if Lunsford remained as Lieutenant of the Tower and later on he declined to proclaim as traitors five M.P.s for whom the King was searching. But in every way possible he tried, against mounting opposition, to hold the capital to its allegiance. In August 1642 he was impeached by the Commons, deprived of his office and sentenced to be detained in the Tower during parliament's pleasure. He remained there until shortly before his death in 1647.

His place was taken by Sir Isaac Penington, a Puritan, a member of the House of Commons, and a man well trusted by parliament. So well trusted, in fact, that they appointed him also to be Lieutenant of the Tower. Penington held the office for three years, during which and after he served the parliamentary and Commonwealth regimes too faithfully for his ultimate benefit. At the Restoration of the Monarchy he returned to the Tower, this time as a prisoner. He died there at the end of 1660.

The history of the years 1642–60 followed a pattern which has become all too familiar to us in recent years if we have observed the fate of various states in Africa and South America. The first stage was a political revolution carried through by parliament with the help of the army (1642–8). This gave way to a military coup which set up a 'Commonwealth' dominated by soldiers (1649–53). Finally, the squabblings of various factions within the government were terminated when Oliver Cromwell established a dictatorship (the Protectorate, 1653–58). When death had removed his firm hand from the helm a brief period of chaos intervened before Charles I's son was invited to return as King. During this period of violently clashing ideologies and rapid reversals of fortune the Tower, like every other prison in the land, was kept full. There was no clearcut division throughout the country into two camps, Roundheads and Cavaliers or Royalists and Parliamentarians. Men displayed a rich variety of political and religious allegiances: there were Presbyterians, Independents, Anglicans, Baptists, Republicans, Monarchists and dangerous extremist groups such as the Levellers and the Fifth Monarchy Men. Political and military activists changed sides, following the dictates of conscience or self-interest. In this situation, and whatever regime was in power, the country was always full of opponents, potential opponents and suspected opponents of the government.

Hundreds of prisoners passed through the Tower portals during these troubled years. Many of them were doomed to die for the crime of being on the wrong side at the wrong time. The problems of guarding this enormous influx of prisoners must have been immense; it is certainly no surprise to discover that there were a large number of escapes and attempted escapes during this period. Every chamber that could be used for prison lodgings was used. A surviving document indicates that the White Tower was now commandeered by the Ordnance Office and detainees were housed in the Cradle, Well, Salt, Broad Arrow, Constable, Martin, Beauchamp, Bell, Bloody, Wakefield and Lanthorn towers and in the Nun's Bower, a group of cells over the Coldharbour Gate. One interesting and welcome discovery is that the use of the rack seems to have ceased. The Duke of Exeter's Daughter 'died' as a result of the collapse of royal prerogative power, her last known employment being in 1640. There is a reference to the rack being prepared for prisoners in 1673 but there is no indication that it was actually used and three years later it had been moved out of the White Tower and was merely one of the items listed in the Ordnance stores inventory.

William Laud went to his death on Tower Hill in January 1645 at the age of seventy-one. The charges originally urged against him had been incapable of proof, so the Commons decided to proceed by the simpler process of attainder. Even so, they had difficulty in getting the Lords to pass the bill. After he had been condemned Laud produced a pardon from the King. This was swept aside with the assertion that the crown had no right of pardon when conviction had been by process of attainder – a clear indication that the high-minded parliamentarians who had removed the iniquities of royal prerogative had merely replaced it with a prerogative of their own. The Commons even refused the old man's request that the usual barbarous punishment for treason be commuted to beheading – so intense was their hatred of the quondam persecutor. Later, however, they relented. Thus, on a bitter winter's morning, Laud ascended the scaffold and laid his neck on the block after asserting that he had done nothing 'which deserves death by the known laws of the kingdom' and that he had only laboured 'to keep a uniformity in the external service of God according to the doctrine and discipline of the church'.

Inevitably, it was not only extremist partisans and fanatics who fell foul of their enemies. One of the most level-headed men to suffer was Arthur, Lord Capel of Hadham. He came to parliament in 1640 an ardent reformer determined that the crown should be shorn of some of its powers but the violent language and equally violent policies advocated by the Commons leaders caused him to desert to the royalist camp. He fought for the King in many places and was finally captured at the siege of Colchester in 1648. He was brought to the Tower, tried and condemned, despite the pleas of many of his opponents who recognized in him a man of rare qualities. He was lodged in one of the towers in the outer wall and his friends managed to smuggle a rope in to him. With this he let himself down to the moat under cover of darkness. Unfortunately, he could not swim but friends indicated to him a place where the ditch was shallow and he began to wade across. Comparatively shallow it may have been, but the bottom was very muddy. The water came up to Capel's chin – and he was a tall man. More than once he was tempted to call for help, the block being preferable to death by drowning. At last he reached the far side and was hurried away by his friends who hid him in a house near the Temple while soldiers scoured the City for him. A few days later he was taken across the river in disguise to another refuge at Lambeth. But the boatman's suspicions were aroused. Sensing an opportunity to make some money he betrayed Capel to the authorities and the unfortunate man was brought back to the Tower, from which there was no second escape.

This means of getting away from the Tower seems to have been the most popular (although most people who attempted it could swim). A surprising number of prisoners managed to obtain ropes and this suggests that some of the Warders were not as devoted to the parliamentary cause as their superiors may have wished. A different technique was employed by another royalist Captain Daniel O'Neill. He escaped dressed as a woman. Such exploits must have made life very difficult for the principal officers of the Tower. Every time a prisoner made a successful or near-successful escape bid there were awkward explanations to be made to the higher authorities. The atmosphere inside the fortress must have been not unlike that at Colditz Castle in World War II, with intelligent, high spirited prisoners showing open contempt for their guards and always plotting something. Nor were the royalist captives only concerned with their own plight. They managed to keep themselves well informed about what was happening throughout the country. The most successful of the succession of Lieutenants who served under Commonwealth and Protectorate was, if Cromwell's opinion is to be accepted, Sir John Barkstead who held office from 1652 to 1659. According to the Protector, he became expert at sensing the mood of his charges: 'There was never any design on foot but we could hear [about] it out of the Tower. He who commanded there would give us account that within a fortnight or such a [time] there would be some stirrings; for a great concourse of people were coming to [the prisoners] and they had very great elevation of spirit.'[18] Yet, for all his devotion to duty, Barkstead appears to have been a rogue who took every opportunity his office provided to line his own pocket. His Lieutenancy and his other military appointments brought him £2,000 a year and he added to this by extorting money from prisoners in a variety of unpleasant ways.

Among all the comings and goings of important and potentially troublesome men, the short stay of a young female prisoner – 'a brown, beautiful, bold, but insipid creature'[19] – probably excited little interest. Her name was Lucy Walter and she had with her her seven-year-old illegitimate son, James. She had recently arrived from the Continent and she was kept in the Tower for about six months during 1656. She had committed no crime and Cromwell eventually concluded that there was no reason to detain her. But it would be as well to keep an eye on her and her little boy, for the lad's father was the man royalists called Charles II. Young James would one day be raised to the peerage as the Duke of Monmouth.

When Oliver Cromwell died in 1658, borne down by the burden he had assumed, the Tower was full of prisoners – a sure sign that after sixteen years new forms of government had still not been accepted by the people. The men who occupied that varied accommodation were those who had been detected in royalist plots or in attempts to assassinate the Protector. Despite all that he had done for England his situation was still insecure and he must have known that what he built up would probably not long survive him. It is little wonder that he ordered men and women to prison and to death on the merest suspicion of disloyalty. Yet he could be generous. Sir William Davenant, the poet, spent several years as a royalist captain and an agent travelling between England and France, where the heir to the throne was living. In 1650 he was captured, tried and sentenced to death by hanging. But he was reprieved. Perhaps it was that other poet, John Milton, Cromwell's Latin secretary, who was the agent of his deliverance. Davenant spent two years in the Tower, during which he wrote some of his finest verses, verses which give us fresh insights into the minds of the men who were caught up in the turmoil of those terrible years.

> Preserve thy sighs, unthrifty girl,
> To purify the air;
> Thy tears to thread instead of pearl,
> On bracelets of thy hair.
>
> The trumpet makes the echo hoarse
> And wakes the louder drum.
> Expense of grief gains no remorse
> When sorrow should be dumb
>
> For I must go where lazy Peace
> Will hide her drowsy head;
> And, for the sport of kings, increase
> The number of the dead . . .

After Cromwell's death, few of the leading men accepted the rule of his son, Richard. Soon parliamentary and military factions were once again fighting for control. This inevitably meant changes at the Tower, although the fate of Lieutenant Barkstead seems to have been the result of his own cruelty and avarice rather than of political manoeuvring. There was a steadily increasing volume of complaints against his behaviour and, early in 1659, he was called to give an account of himself before the Committee of Grievances. According to legend, Barkstead panicked and, before leaving the Tower, buried the evidence of his extortion – the large fortune he had amassed. The Committee reprimanded him, dismissed him from office and installed in his place Colonel Thomas Fitch. In December a group of parliamentarians obtained control of the Tower, at the second attempt, and it was entrusted to a committee of four headed by Anthony Ashley Cooper.

The Long Parliament which now reconvened was divided between those totally opposed to the re-introduction of monarchy and those prepared to consider overtures to the King in exile. Colonel Herbert Morley, who was appointed Lieutenant of the Tower on 7 January, belonged to the latter group. The royalists, prominent among whom was Morley's old friend John Evelyn, tried to persuade him to seize the Tower for the King. But the Lieutenant hesitated and thus, if

Evelyn is to be believed, missed the greatest opportunity of his life. Later, the diarist records, Morley,

> saw his horrible error and neglect of the counsel I gave him, by which he [would have] certainly done the great work, with the same ease that Monck did it [later], who was then in Scotland and Morley in a post to have done what he pleased, by which he [would have] made himself the greatest person in England next the King; but his jealousy and fear kept him from that blessing and honour.[20]

General George Monck was soon on his way southwards at the head of a sizeable army. He proved to be the *deus ex machina* who overawed the contending parties, enforced the election of the Convention Parliament, and invited Charles II to return. During the early months of 1660 there were alarms as anti-monarchists tried to divert the obvious direction affairs were taking. It was in part due to Morley's support at the Tower that these attempts came to nothing.

Little change came over the fabric or institutions of the Tower in the first half of the seventeenth century or perhaps it would be truer to say that such changes as did occur were the result of neglect rather than of positive policy. We have already seen that there was much to be desired in the discipline and efficiency of the Yeoman Warders. Offices were bought and sold. Duties were often performed by deputy. In such matters the guardians of the Tower took their examples from their superiors. Just as the Constableship had ceased to be a resident occupation but rather an honour conferred upon some great officer of state so, now, other positions were tending in the same direction. Lieutenants were men who had other court or military functions. Their duties were sometimes performed by deputies or subordinates (usually the Gentleman Porter). Much the same was true of the Master of the Ordnance.

No new buildings appeared in this period though the existing ones sometimes changed their functions. The principal reason was the ever increasing space occupied by the Ordnance and the Records. By the end of the fourteenth century the Tower of London had become the principal depository for the records of most of the courts and state offices. In various chests and presses were housed charters and rolls going back to the time of Edward the Confessor. These vitally important documents covering virtually every aspect of home affairs and foreign policy with which the kings and queens of England had been involved were considered a part of the royal treasure. They were housed originally in the White Tower but by the mid-sixteenth century most of them had been removed to the Wakefield Tower, which was, in fact, commonly known as the Record Tower. The two problems which had always concerned the keepers of these parchments and papers were preservation and accessibility. It was important to keep the records intact and safe not only from decay, worm and rodent, but also from human intruders who might have reasons for removing or altering certain documents. The muniment cupboards and coffers housing the records were equipped with stout locks whose keys were held by trusted royal servants. Accessibility was a greater problem and one which became worse as, inexorably, the bundles of deeds and charters, the rolls recording proceedings in King's Bench, Common Pleas and Exchequer, the statutes of old parliaments, the rolls of Chancery, and the documents relating to other aspects of government increased. It had always been understood that the records should be available to the public yet little attempt had ever been made to catalogue the collection or put it in order. It was Elizabeth I's custodian of the records, William Bowyer, who took the Herculean task in hand. He devoted eight years of his life to sorting, arranging and listing the more valuable muniments. Unfortunately, his immediate successors did not build upon Bowyer's foundation and a measure of chaos returned. The troubled years of the mid-seventeenth century and the attendant pre-occupation of Tower staff with a great influx of prisoners were not conducive to painstaking work on the records. It was left to a more peaceful era to take in hand once more this arduous but necessary work.

Under the first two Stuarts the Tower continued to be a showplace, an important part of the intinerary of every visitor to London, especially a state visitor such as King Christian of Denmark:

> Thence they proceeded by Cornhill, Gracechurch Street and Fenchurch Street to the Tower, where King James himself met his highness, and in his own person conducted him to the Jewel House where the most rare jewels and beautiful plate were shown him, and likewise in the Wardrobe the richest robes, hangings, clothes of estate, and furniture were displayed. Then they passed on to the office of the Ordnance, where he viewed the warlike provision of the great ordnance, which at an hour is ready for any service, over every piece being the ladles and sponges, and the traces and collars for the horses to draw them away; and after that to the armoury where all manner of arms are kept in readiness. Then King James led him up to the Mint, which they viewed, and thence to the lions. When their pleasures had been well delighted with these shows, the tide serving to shoot the Bridge, they took their barges and were rowed to Whitehall.[21]

This function largely ceased after 1642. During the Commonwealth the Crown Jewels and many other 'baubles' of monarchy were broken up or diverted to other uses. The new regime had no use for the Tower as a royal museum.

In 1552 the last of the other mints had been closed and the Tower Mint became the only issuer of coin for England and Dublin. After the union of the crowns in 1603 Edinburgh continued to make money for Scotland. In 1560 there was a further expansion when new premises (the 'upper mint' or Irish Mint) were built in the eastern part of the Outer Ward. The Mint continued its invaluable work year after year with few crises (except for 1626 when many workers died of plague) until 1642, when parliament seized the Mint. Several craftsmen left and some of them took tools and dies with them. These were taken to the King who was, therefore, able to continue producing coins at emergency mints set up at Shrewsbury, Oxford, Exeter, York, Bristol and Weymouth, using silver and gold plate donated by his supporters. After Charles's execution in 1649 the Commonwealth, of course, had to strike new coins without the King's head. The new designs were not much liked. One displayed two shields side by side which a wit described as:

> A silver pair of breeches neatly wrought
> Such as you see upon an old Rump* groat.

* i.e. Rump Parliament 1648–53.

8

Charles II, like England, had been the victim of war, a war between opposed political ideologies and he had no intention of letting such a situation re-occur. He sometimes told intimates that he was resolved never to go on his travels again and behind the sardonic self-interest of that remark there was an astute political realism. The monarch who was welcomed home with such unfeigned relief and joy established a government that was both pragmatic and popular. In public he tried to be what his people wanted him to be. His political and religious beliefs he kept to himself. Parliament he treated with respect and courtesy, deluding its members sometimes into thinking they had more power than, in fact, they had. Extremists he overcame, as far as possible, with toleration.

At the outset of his reign he made two important decisions: he would re-introduce the customary coronation procession from the Tower to Westminster; and he would not indulge in a retributive blood bath. The coronation had to wait for over a year, for the regalia had to be replaced at a cost of £31,000.9s.11d. The date most appropriately chosen for the event was 23 April – St George's Day – 1661. On the day before, Charles II came by water to the Tower to assemble all the worthies of the land for the great cavalcade. This took place on the afternoon of the same day. The King, therefore, did not sleep in the Tower nor did he carry out there any of the other ancient customs such as the making of knights of the Bath (this had already taken place at Whitehall). The procession, however, which was destined to be the last of its kind, did not fall short of its predecessors in magnificence. Samuel Pepys witnessed it from an upper window of 'Mr Young's, the flagmaker in Cornhill' and was suitably impressed.

> . . . it is impossible to relate the glory of the day, expressed in the clothes of them that rode, and their horses and horse-clothes, among others my Lord Sandwich's embroidery and diamonds were ordinary among them. The Knights of the Bath was a brave show of itself; and their esquires . . . Remarkable were the two men that represented the two dukes of Normandy and Aquitaine. The bishops came next after barons, which is the higher place; which makes me think that the next parliament they will be called to the House

of Lords. My Lord Monck rode bare [headed] after the King, and led in his hand a spare horse, as being the Master of the Horse. The King, in a most rich and embroidered suit and cloak, looked most noble. Wadlow, the vintner at the Devil in Fleet Street, did lead a fine company of soldiers, all young, comely men in white doublets. Then followed the Vice-Chamberlain, Sir G. Carteret [with] a company of men all like Turks; but I know not yet what they are for. The streets all gravelled and the houses hung with carpets before them made brave show, and the ladies out of the windows, one of which over against us I took much notice of, and spoke to her, which made good sport among us [So] glorious was the show with gold and silver, that we were not able to look at it, our eyes at last being so much overcome with it. Both the King and the Duke of York took notice of us, as they saw us at the window.[1]

The procession stopped to hear loyal addresses at the various triumphal arches erected in the City – 'some of which, though temporary and to stand but one year, were of good invention and architecture with inscriptions'.[2] The fountains ran wine, the church bells rang and there were bonfires at night.

Long before this, the necessary executions had begun. For most active parliamentarians and Cromwellians there was an amnesty but no clemency could be extended to the regicides (those who had participated in the trial and death of Charles I). One of the more remarkable men now humbled by the new regime was Hugh Peters. He was a Puritan preacher who had emigrated to Massachusetts in the 1630s. At the beginning of the Civil War he returned to England and found his vocation as a preacher with Cromwell's New Model Army. His sermons were possessed of rough eloquence and ready humour and they were extremely effective. Before a battle he would put heart into the men. After the capture of a town he would persuade hundreds of defenders of the justice of the parliamentary cause. He preached on social and political evils and on the need for reform. His enemies later accused him of being the prime mover in the execution of the King. This was not true; he frequently denounced royal misgovernment but he was never in a position to dictate policy to the leaders of the revolution. Peters was not a political activist; he *was* the voice of the anti-monarchist party. He was the man who could most easily be identified by enemies and who thus became a principal target for their hatred while some more powerful opponents of Charles I escaped punishment. During the Commonwealth and Protectorate Peters was very busy. Though largely ignorant of matters of policy he frequently pontificated upon them, seeking to

184

apply Christian principles as he understood them to every aspect of government business. He even advocated that a completely new code of law be drawn up and that, then, all the old records in the Tower, being 'mere monuments of tyranny', should be destroyed. Peters was arrested on 2 September 1660 and confined in the Tower. He was tried and condemned on 13 October. While in detention he was allowed to preach to his fellow prisoners and his powers in that medium seem to have been undiminished to the end. On 14 October he delivered his last sermon on the text 'Why art thou cast down, O my soul, and why art thou disquieted within me? Hope thou in God, for I shall yet praise him, who is the health of my countenance and my God' (Psalm 42, 11). His words were undoubtedly a source of consolation and strength to himself as well as to those who were about to suffer in the same cause. He was executed two days later.

Among the regicides were three ex-Lieutenants of the Tower, Sir Isaac Penington, as we have already seen, died in the castle in 1660. Robert Tichborne was tried in October of that year. He could not deny his part in the death of Charles I but sought to excuse himself by his youth and inexperience: 'It was my unhappiness to be called to so sad a work when I had so few years over my head; a person neither bred up in the laws, nor in parliament where laws are made . . . Had I known that then which I do now, I would have chosen a red hot oven to have gone into as soon as that meeting.'[3] He was sentenced to death but in his favour it was urged that he had shown many kindnesses to royalist prisoners in his charge. The sentence was, therefore, commuted to imprisonment and Tichborne died in the Tower twenty-two years later. Barkstead escaped to Germany but afterwards visited the Netherlands and, while there, was arrested in 1661. He was brought back and locked in the Tower. All the regicides had by then been condemned, some, like Barkstead, *in absentia,* so it only required positive identification for sentence to be carried out. On 19 April 1662 he was hanged, drawn and quartered at Tyburn. His head was mounted on a pole and displayed over St Thomas's Tower.

The passing of this not very attractive man was to have a most bizarre sequel. Some six months later a certain Mr Wade went to the home of the Earl of Sandwich and reported that Colonel Barkstead had concealed £7,000 (the figure later rose to £20,000) in butter ferkins before he had been deprived of his office. Sandwich obtained the King's permission to search for this hidden treasure, the arrangement being that Wade and his partners were to have £2,000, Sandwich £2,000 and King Charles the remainder. The Earl, of course, had no intention of handling pick and shovel himself so he employed one of his protégés. Fortunately for posterity that protégé was Samuel

Pepys. In the pages of the famous diary we can read the whole funny, sweating, frustrating story of the great Tower treasure hunt.

It began that very day (30 October) with Pepys excitedly collecting his warrant and presenting his compliments to Sir John Robinson, Lieutenant of the Tower (he was also Constable of the Tower and Lord Mayor of London). Robinson gave his permission for work to start immediately and that afternoon Pepys went to the Tower with a colleague, Mr Lee, Wade, Captain Evett (a collaborator of Wade), William Griffin (an employee of Pepys in the Navy Office), and a porter laden with tools. It soon became obvious that Wade and Evett did not know the exact location of the cache. They were acting on behalf of a third party, the real informant, about whose identity they were very mysterious. Evett cast about for some time, then armed with a candle, he led the party to a cellar with an arched vault – probably the basement of the Bell Tower. They then discussed whether they should begin excavations straight away or wait until morning. There was no real question; the lure of gold was too strong. Off came the men's coats and they set to work on the earthen floor with picks and spades. After four or five hours of back-breaking work they had had enough and had found nothing.

> . . . however, our guides did not at all seem discouraged; for that they being confident that the money is there [that] they look for, but having never been in the cellars, they could not be positive to the place and therefore will inform themselves more fully, now they have been there, of the party that do advise them.[4]

With the insatiable optimism of the gambler Pepys accepted this assurance, locked the cellar

> . . . and up to the Deputy Governor (my Lord Mayor . . . being gone an hour before); and he doth undertake to keep the key of the cellar, that none shall go down without his privity. But Lord, to see what a young, simple, fantastic coxcomb is made Deputy Governor would make one mad; and how he called out for his nightgown of silk, only to make a show to us; and yet for half an hour I did not think he was the Deputy Governor, and so spoke not to him about the business but waited for another man. At last I broke our business to him; and he promising his care, we parted and Mr Lee and I by coach to Whitehall . . .[5]

It is interesting to digress briefly at this point. Whatever Pepys may have thought of Robinson's deputy, the passage above does illustrate some trends concerning the appointments of senior Tower officers. Firstly we notice that the terminology was becoming imprecise. During the Commonwealth the man in charge of the day-to-day running of the Tower was sometimes called the Governor, instead of the Lieutenant: the terms seem to have been interchangeable. We see, also, that the Lieutenant did not reside in the Tower. Such an important person as Sir John Robinson could not, of course, be expected to spend all his time within the castle but, in fact, the resident Lieutenant became the effective governor of the Tower prison while another officer, the Major of the Tower, assumed responsibility for the military functions of the fortress and its 'bricks and mortar'.

Thoughts of Barkstead's treasure filled Pepys's mind and he was back again in the cellar with his companions two days later. Wade and Evett claimed to have received more precise information, so much so that Pepys was convinced that success was only a few shovelfuls of earth away. But after two or three hours of digging without discovering anything remotely resembling a butter ferkin, 'we went away the second time like fools'. The little diarist now began to suspect that he was involved in a wild goose chase. He took Wade and Evett to the Dolphin tavern and questioned them closely. They protested that their informant was someone who had been very close to Barkstead in his last days at the Tower. Pepys told his informants to gather more precise information and to come to his Tower Hill office the following Monday morning (3 November).

At that meeting he once again allowed his hopes to be raised. Wade and Evett told him that they had once again consulted with,

> their prime intelligencer, a woman, I perceive, and though we have missed twice, yet they bring such an account of the probability of the truth of the thing, though we are not certain of the place, that we shall set upon it once more, and I am willing and hopeful in it. So we are resolved to set upon it again on Wednesday morning and the woman herself will be there in a disguise, and confirm us in the place.[6]

The Wednesday excavation was, in fact, postponed and it was on the morning of Friday 7 November that the party reconvened. This time the 'prime intelligencer', who was, or purported to be, Barkstead's mistress, put in a brief appearance and confirmed that this was, indeed, the cellar where the Lieutenant told her he had buried his fortune. Clearly, Pepys and his companions wanted to be convinced and they set to work again with enthusiasm. They were at it all day, pausing only for a light meal – 'upon the head of a barrel dined very merrily'. It was lost labour. By the end of the day they had dug over the entire floor and could confidently say that nothing was concealed there, 'we were forced to give over our expectations, though I do believe there must be money hid somewhere by him, or else he did delude this woman in hopes to oblige her to further serving him, which I am apt to believe.'[7]

But the matter was not over. Wade and Evett sought another meeting with Pepys the following week. Their earnestness and sincerity impressed him. 'I have great confidence,' he wrote, 'that there is no cheat in these people, but that they go upon good grounds.' Even so, the Clerk of the King's Ships was no longer prepared to neglect his many important duties in the search for nebulous treasure. It was not until 17 December the searchers reconvened in the Tower. It was a dismal day of drenching rain and when Evett reported that his information was now that the money was buried in the open, in front of the Garden House (between the Lieutenant's Lodging and the Bloody Tower) they all decided to wait for better weather.

Two days later they returned. It was a cold Friday morning. This and their earlier fruitless efforts dissuaded Pepys and Lee from personally taking part in the excavations. Thus, while the others dug up the north-west corner of the Lieutenant's walled garden, they 'did sit all day till three o'clock by the fire in the Governor's house; I reading a play of Fletcher's, being *A Wife for a Month*, wherein no great wit or language.' As the winter light began to fade the two men went out to survey the progress of the workmen. They found four sweating and ill-tempered labourers, standing around a hole, wide, deep – and empty, whereupon, 'having wrought below the bottom of the foundation of the wall, I bade them give over, and so all our hopes ended.' Samuel Pepys returned to his newly-refurbished house in Seething Lane a sadder, wiser – and apparently grumpier – man; 'and so home and to bed, a little displeased with my wife, who, poor wretch, is troubled with her lonely life.'[8]

The sad feature of this entertaining tale is that it raises more questions than it solves. Was there ever a treasure? If so did Barkstead succeed in getting it away before disgrace banished him from the Tower? Or did some other inmate secretly unearth it and disappear to a remote part of the realm to live in wealthy obscurity? Perhaps – most fascinating speculation of all – Barkstead's horde is still in the Tower. If so it is no thanks to the scores of other hopeful searchers who have sought in vain since the time of Samuel Pepys.

In September 1666 very different circumstances brought Pepys to the Tower. In the small hours of Sunday 2nd his servants woke him with news of a fire in the City. Putting on his nightgown he went to the window and saw a glow in the sky around Mark Lane. It was a matter of small interest; fire among the crowded, timber-framed tenements near the river was common enough. In the morning, however, his household was buzzing with fresh news: the blaze was still raging and was said to have engulfed three hundred homes already. He decided to walk down to the Tower where he got Sir John Robinson's young son to take him to the best vantage point. There were others there already and through the shifting obscurity of the smoke they could see the conflagration reaching from the Bridge westwards along Thames Street. Already, men and women were emerging onto the open ground of Tower Hill with carts and pack animals laden with belongings. Horrified and still incredulous, the watchers realized that the capital of England was burning.

The Lieutenant told Pepys how the fire had started accidentally in Pudding Lane. That, at least, was a relief; both men knew that only six months before a group of fanatics had been executed for plotting to kill Robinson and other prominent figures and fire the City. Later that day the goldsmiths brought their entire stock and reserves of money and plate – some £1,200,000 worth – into the Tower for safety. The gates were also opened to the homeless and injured, while Yeoman Warders and other inhabitants went out into the stricken City to offer what assistance they could. Throughout Sunday and Monday the fire raged unhindered. Fanned by a brisk easterly wind, it leaped from street to street, house to house. Blowing up buildings in its path availed nothing; sparks and flaming debris flew across the open spaces. As the holocaust spread northwards and westwards the Tower became a refuge for more and more of the dispossessed.

On Tuesday the wind dropped and it seemed the worst was passed. But this was only the beginning of the second phase of the conflagration, the phase that was to place the Tower itself in jeopardy. Until now all the efforts of the firefighters had gone into a vain attempt to stop the flames moving westwards. No thought had been taken for the buildings lying immediately behind the blaze. The slackening wind now enabled the fire to change direction. It began to creep eastwards along Tower Street and Thames Street. It took little imagination to guess what might happen if sparks started fires within the fortress. Evelyn almost certainly exaggerated the danger but it was a real danger and one which frightened many people. Had the neighbouring houses taken fire, he suggests, and spread the blaze to 'the White Tower where the magazines of powder lay, [the resulting explosion] would undoubtedly have not only beaten down and destroyed all the Bridge, but sunk and torn all the vessels in the river and rendered the demolition beyond all expression for several miles even about the country at many miles distance.'[9]

The goldsmiths were now in as great a hurry to get their treasure out of the Tower as they had been to convey it thither two days before. They soon had it stowed in barges and moving upriver to Westminster. But Robinson was not idle; he had the greater part of the gunpowder trundled out onto the Wharf and conveyed out of the danger zone by ship. Other barrels were used to blow up houses

189

beyond the Bulwark and in the surrounding streets, and this stopped the eastwards spread of the blaze.

By Friday it was all over. Apart from smouldering embers and isolated blazes, the Great Fire of London had been and gone. And of all the ancient monuments the Tower of London was almost the only one left standing amid the blackened landscape. St Paul's, eighty-four London churches, Baynard's Castle, forty-four livery company halls – all had been destroyed. The great Guildhall was gutted, though fortunately the City records stored in the vaults beneath survived. Devastation had reached to its very gates but the Tower had survived the greatest crisis in its history.

Edward I's walls looked down upon the creation of the new City which rose from the ashes of the old. They also witnessed a considerable rebuilding programme within the Tower. Basically what happened was that the Palace was swept away and new structures appeared to the north, east and south of the White Tower. These edifices, proliferating over the next two and a half centuries, were almost entirely devoted to the needs of the Ordnance Office and the military establishment. In 1663–4 the building known as the Horse Armoury (now the New Armouries) was constructed in what had been the King's Garden, as an additional Ordnance storehouse. It is interesting to notice that the Traitor's Gate entrance had apparently fallen into disuse: a specific order was issued that it should be opened up to allow building materials to be brought in. In the 1670s, the Royal Lodgings, dilapidated and long since abandoned by the sovereign were abolished along with the Coldharbour, the Jewel House and the other accretions along the south side of the White Tower. Yet another Ordnance storehouse and office appeared on the site. All the Ordnance staff now had rooms suitable to their rank and the new complex included an impressive wainscotted board room (known originally as the Great Room).

The Ordnance buildings, however, were not devoted entirely to the practical purpose of keeping the materials of war. They still had a large collection of ancient armour and weapons and, in the 1680s, it was decided to mount what may be termed the first museum display in the Tower's history. This was the 'Line of Kings', a splendid collection of mounted figures clad in armour of various periods and purporting to represent some of the Stuarts' great ancestors on the English throne. The exhibition, located on the first floor of the Horse Armoury, was opened to the public and immediately became a major attraction. So successful was it that a new gallery was soon fitted out in the Coldharbour complex to display Spanish weapons allegedly captured at the time of the Armada. The historical basis of all these exhibits was extremely suspect, none more so than a gruesome array of torture implements which, it was claimed, were being especially conveyed to England in Philip II's great galleons to help in the work of reconverting the people to Catholicism.

The function of the Tower as a museum was now well established. Yeoman Warders regularly augmented their income by showing visitors around. No other place could offer such a variety of attractions – weapons and old armour, wild animals, instruments of torture, a fabulous collection of plate and jewels and, if the visitor was lucky, a glimpse of some celebrated prisoner behind a barred window on one of the wall walks. Pepys was frequently at the Tower both as a guest of the Lieutenant and on navy business but it was also one of his favourite spots for pleasure outings. In 1668 while his wife was out of town he carried on a mild flirtation with Mrs Knepp, a pretty actress. As well as singing with her in the rural grottoes of Kensington, and regaling her with lobster and wine at the Cock, he took her to see the lions at the Tower. Later in the same year he was back with a party of friends, seeing everything that was to be seen, especially 'the crown and sceptres and rich plate, which I myself never saw before and, indeed, [it] is noble and I mightily pleased with it.'[10] The regalia was now kept in a locked cupboard on the ground floor of the Martin Tower beneath the apartments of the Deputy Keeper of the Jewel House. The office of Keeper was, as we have seen, an honour bestowed on prominent royal servants. In the 1660s, for example, the incumbent was Sir Gilbert Talbot who spent most of his time abroad on diplomatic duties.

This brings us to the celebrated attempt to steal the Crown Jewels in 1671. It is yet another of the events in the history of the Tower over which a large question mark stands. Let us start at what is both the end and the beginning:

> Here lies the man who boldly had run through
> More villainies than ever England knew;
> And ne'er to any friend he had was true.
> Here let him then by all unpitied lie,
> And let's rejoice his time was come to die.[11]

This is part of a scurrilous contemporary ballad written after the death of Thomas Blood, alias Allen, alias Ayliffe, an Irish adventurer who became so much of a legend in his own time that men refused to believe he was dead and his body had to be exhumed in order to dispel the rumours. He was one of the many bold and reckless spirits thrown up by the years of revolution and civil war, a Cromwellian soldier possessed of startling audacity and a touch of the blarney. He accumulated rich estates as a result of his services to the Protector and lost all at the Restoration. Blood then became an outlaw and was destined to remain one for most of the rest of his life. In 1663 he led an insurrection against the Lord Lieutenant of Ireland, the Duke of Ormonde. The central act was to be the capture of Ormonde himself at Dublin Castle. The plot was elaborate and displayed Blood's love of disguise. He and his men gained access to the fortress dressed as blacksmiths, carpenters and tradesmen. The scheme miscarried, many of Blood's confederates, including his brother-in-law, were caught and executed, and a price was put upon his head. For years he avoided discovery, often using disguise (his favourite aliases seem to have been priests and ministers) and sheer effrontery to evade his pursuers. His later adventures took him to Holland, England and Scotland where he was closely involved with various dissident groups. But was Thomas Blood just a desperate 'loner' all this time or had he, in fact, become a double agent? If at some time his enemies had successfully apprehended him, a secret deal might well have been preferable to a summary execution for both parties. A man with Blood's reputation was eagerly welcomed into the ranks of republicans, Fifth Monarchy Men and Covenanters and could easily betray their plans to the government. The adventurer was certainly known to the Duke of Buckingham, a member of Charles II's 'Cabal' of intimate advisers and was later accused by some of being in the pay of that nobleman. Any such arrangement was then and has remained since by its very nature unverifiable but it seems almost certain that Blood was a denizen of the shadowy world of espionage and counter espionage.

In 1667 'Colonel' Blood, as he liked to be called, carried out a bold rescue of his colleague, Captain Mason, who was on his way to York for trial. Shortly afterwards one of the Colonel's enemies, William Levings, was poisoned in York jail at a time when Buckingham was Lord Lieutenant of the county. In 1670 a group of desperadoes, led by Blood, held up the Duke of Ormonde's coach in St James's Street in broad daylight, abducted the occupant and galloped with him towards Tyburn where it was their declared intention to hang him. They were thwarted in this but Blood escaped. Blood was, as we have seen, a bitter enemy of Ormonde – but so was the Duke of Buckingham.

So far from fleeing the capital after this escapade, Blood was within months or even weeks planning the most audacious *coup* of his life. It was worked out with the skilled precision of a military manoeuvre. First came a reconnaissance expedition. One evening in April Blood and an accomplice presented themselves at the Martin Tower in the guise of a clergyman and his wife anxious to see the royal treasures. The 77-year-old Deputy Keeper, Talbot Edwards, willingly obliged, unlocking the cupboard and watching the looks of incredulous admiration on the faces of his visitors. Unfortunately, the lady was so overcome that a restorative had to be administered and Mrs Edwards' hospitality prevailed upon so that she might rest and recover. This enabled the thieves to discover all they wanted about the building and the arrangements for securing the jewels. It also opened up a relationship with the Edwards which subsequent visits transformed into a trusting friendship (Blood was, as Evelyn said, 'very well spoken and dangerously insinuating'). On one of these social occasions the 'clergyman' took a fancy to a brace of pistols belonging to the Deputy Keeper and ended up buying them at a handsome price. Having thus simply disarmed the old man everything was ready for the crime to be committed.

On 9 May, at seven o'clock in the morning, Thomas Blood returned with three accomplices. They all had daggers and pistols which they had concealed beneath their cloaks in order to smuggle them past the porter (for no weapons were allowed into the Tower) and they carried sword-sticks. Ostensibly they had come to arrange a marriage between Miss Edwards and the clergyman's nephew. Blood suggested that his friends might like to see the jewels before they all proceeded to business. They entered the Jewel House and, as Edwards stooped to lock the door behind them a cloak was thrown over his head and a wooden plug pushed into his mouth. The old man must have been terrified but he made as much commotion as he could despite the threats of his assailants. They hit him over the head and, when that failed to quiet him, thrust a dagger into his stomach. He fell to the ground, dead for all the thieves knew, while his assailants prised open the jewel cupboard and began helping themselves to the objects they had come for.

From all the treasures on view, many of which were easily portable, Blood deliberately chose St Edward's Crown, which he had to crush in order to conceal, the Sceptre, which had to be filed in two, and the Orb, which one of the thieves stuffed into his breeches. While all this was going on the criminals' luck ran out. The Edwards's son arrived home suddenly and unexpectedly after years abroad in the army. Blood's lookout gave the warning. They dropped the Sceptre and hurried away across the Inner Ward. But the Deputy Keeper, amazingly, was able to remove his gag, drag himself to the doorway and raise the alarm. The thieves were now at the Byward Tower. Hearing the hue and cry they started to run. The porter barred their way – and was shot down. Blood and his men crossed the small drawbridge onto the Wharf and rushed towards the St Katharine's end. But the waterfront was thronged with people and the runaways were slowed down. Their pursuers were closing on them. They caught up. There was a brief but fierce struggle. Only one of the gang reached the waiting horses and escaped. The rest were taken and the Crown Jewels were recovered.

The sequel is more incredible than the robbery itself. The three villains were taken back into the Tower, locked up and examined by Sir Gilbert Talbot, Sir William Waller and Dr Chamberlain. As Keeper of the Jewel House Talbot had an obvious interest in the attempted theft but who were the others? Waller was a Middlesex justice and a government informer, later employed to some effect in winkling out Roman Catholics at the time of the Popish Plot. Chamberlain appears to have been one of a London family of physicians who enjoyed considerable court patronage. According to the records these comparative nonentities were the only men to interrogate Thomas Blood, who had just committed a unique crime, all but murdering an old and faithful royal servant in the process. There is no suggestion that the scoundrel was badly treated in the Tower or subjected to vigorous questioning. Indeed, he told his captors that he would only speak to the King and he was taken to Whitehall for this purpose two days later. But before that we read of a quite staggering social event. On the afternoon of the day following the crime John Evelyn went to dine with Lord Clifford, Charles's Treasurer and a member of the Cabal. His fellow guests were: 'Monsieur de Gramont and several French noblemen and one Blood, that impudent, bold fellow, who had not long before attempted to steal the imperial Crown itself out of the Tower . . .'[12] The wording of the diary entry suggests that Evelyn had got his dates wrong and that the dinnertime encounter with Blood occurred a little later. This may or may not be the case; the important point is that Thomas Blood was not punished for his crime and that he was on terms of some intimacy with the most powerful men in the land. This also astonished Evelyn:

> How he came to be pardoned and even received to favour, not only after this, but several other exploits almost as daring, both in Ireland and here, I could never come to understand. Some believed he became a spy of several parties, being well [esteemed among] the sectaries and enthusiasts and did his Majesty service that way, which none alive could [do] as well as he. But it was certainly as the boldest attempt, so the only treason of this nature that was ever pardoned. The man had not only a daring, but a villainous, unmerciful look, a false countenance, but very well spoken and dangerously insinuating.[13]

On 12 May Blood was taken to Whitehall and was interviewed there by Charles, his brother James, Duke of York and other members of the court. The King had from him (if he knew them not already) all the details of Blood's earlier life and crimes and then sent him back to the Tower. The adventurer remained under lock and key for just over two months and only once in that time does his confidence seem to have worn thin. That was when, on 19 May, he wrote a letter to the King accusing the joint Treasurers of the Navy, Osborne and Littleton, of being the prime movers behind the attempt on the Crown Jewels. These two officials were both Buckingham's protégés but they seem to have been respectable enough gentlemen and no one appears to have paid any attention to Blood's accusation. On 18 July he was released. On 1 August he was pardoned. The lands he had lost in 1660 were restored to him and he was granted a pension of £500. Much of the remaining nine years of Blood's life was spent earning that allowance as a government agent.

Clearly, the attempt on the regalia was no ordinary theft. Its full explanation lies somewhere in the involved politics of clashing factions and personalities in Charles II's court and government. It was a demonstration aimed at convincing someone, presumably the King, of Blood's abilities as a conspirator and we shall not be far wrong if we see Buckingham and, perhaps, one or two other members of the Cabal as the instigators of the plot. Only some such situation explains the choice of objects taken from the Martin Tower, Blood's lack of anxiety about his fate, and his ultimate reward by the King. His momentary panic on 19 May may be explained by a sudden apprehension that his superiors were about to 'drop' him and allow him to take the full blame. As a demonstration of Blood's talents the escapade was not an unqualified success but it had enough redeeming features and the man himself was sufficiently impressive for Charles to be satisfied that this one-time Cromwellian could be useful to him. With religious and political factions severely threatening his independence of action and with groups of malcontents stirring up trouble throughout the realm, the King certainly had need of devious, unscrupulous and unprincipled men.

Charles himself was more devious, unscrupulous and unprincipled than most. He made secret treaties with France to gain money and so to become less dependent on parliament. He became a concealed Catholic having pledged himself to uphold the Protestant succession. While agreeing with the people's representatives that the disastrous war with Holland should be brought to an end he was assuring Louis XIV of his continued support. Most members of parliament placed no trust whatever in the King but there were very few who were prepared to push their opposition as far as their predecessors had in 1642. What happened instead was the emergence of the party system. By about 1680 the political groups who fought their battles on the floors of the House of Commons and the House of Lords had become identified as the Whigs (staunchly Protestant and pledged to further restricting royal power) and the Tories (the King's party drawing much support from high-churchmen and those who favoured toleration for Roman Catholics). They were led by two men we have met before: Anthony Ashley Cooper, now Earl of Shaftesbury, was the principal opponent of the court whose spokesman was Thomas Osborne, raised to the peerage as the Earl of Danby.

No holds were barred in the conflict between these parties and from time to time Shaftesbury and Danby found themselves conducting their campaigns from within the Tower of London. In 1677 the opposition lords charged the King with illegally proroguing parliament. This enabled the Tories to bring Shaftesbury and three of his supporters to book on a technicality and they were sent to the Tower during the pleasure of the King and parliament. The others were released after a few months but Shaftesbury remained in prison for almost a year. At first he carried on a vigorous campaign of attacks upon his opponents and demanded release but when he realized that this was a tactical error he relaxed his efforts and used his stay in the Tower to recruit his health. He read books, enjoyed the visits of friends and studied closely the maps of the European war.

Within months of his release Shaftesbury began to enjoy his revenge. The government's foreign policy was in shreds. There was widespread anxiety about the growing power of France. And there was considerable agitation at the prospect of childless Charles being succeeded by his brother James, a declared Roman Catholic. These misgivings were fanned into a public panic in the autumn of 1678 by the revelation of the Popish Plot. This was a fabricated conspiracy 'unearthed' by two troublemakers, Titus Oates and Israel Tonge. They claimed that leading Catholics were planning to murder the King, place James on the throne and force their religion on the country. In the ensuing persecution hundreds of Catholics were imprisoned, thirty-five were executed and fresh legal restrictions were placed on non-Anglicans. All this played into Shaftesbury's hands. He carried through a bill which debarred Roman Catholics from sitting in either house and he acquiesced in the despatching of five Catholic peers to the Tower.

For over two years the lords were detained without trial. During this time a new Habeas Corpus Act (1679) clarified the law on illegal detention but when the prisoners sought to take advantage of this the judges decided that the new legislation did not apply to people impeached by parliament. All they achieved by their complaints was a worsening of their prison conditions. They were more confined; the number of their visitors was restricted; and they were limited to six servants each – who had to be Protestants. Furthermore they were subjected to frequent visits from Anglican bishops and theologians intent on converting them.

Only one of their number was eventually brought to trial, in November 1680. This was William Howard, Viscount Stafford, who was chosen, according to one contemporary chronicler because he was 'deemed to be weaker than the other lords in the Tower for the same crime, and less able to labour his defence'. However, in that opinion his opponents were wrong for, according to the writer, Stafford's eloquence at the bar of the House of Lords was little short of miraculous.[14] It availed him nothing; convicted on the perjured evidence of Oates and his confederates, Stafford was sentenced to be executed on Tower Hill. He went to his death on 29 December still protesting his innocence. His last letter from the Tower was to his daughter, Ursula:

Good Daughter,
I know you will bear what happens to me with patience and resignation. I thank God that I know myself in every kind innocent, and that I have confidence in God's mercies, and doubt not but through the mercy and passion of our Saviour to obtain everlasting happiness. I pray God to bless you.
I am your affectionate father,
William[15]

Not long afterwards the Popish Plot fraud was unmasked.
But not before its wide net had caught the largest fish of all. In April 1679 Lord Danby was attainted by parliament and sent to the Tower. His parliamentary opponents, with no regard for truth whatsoever, had accused the minister of complicity and stirred the London mob against him. The King had dissolved parliament in order to prevent a bill of attainder being brought in but the assembly which replaced it proved no less hostile. Danby was impeached and committed to prison while his enemies howled for his conviction and death. However, parliament was again dissolved and proceedings against Danby stopped. Yet, the Earl remained in the Tower. From his fairly comfortable lodgings Danby continued his work in a stream of pamphlets and letters and in messages to the King urging him to stand firm against Whig pressure. Access to him seems to have been largely unrestricted; his wife stayed with him and he was able to entertain friends, including John Evelyn. 'I went to the Tower and (after four years imprisonment) gave a visit to the Earl of Danby, late Lord Treasurer, who received me with great kindness. I dined with him and stayed with him till night. We had discourse of many things, his lady railing sufficiently at the keeping [of] her husband so long in prison.'[16]

But Shaftesbury and his men had the main battlefield almost to themselves. They campaigned for further controls over royal policy and for the exclusion of the Duke of York from the succession. In the midst of this they had time to devise fresh conspiracies against their arch enemy. One, which happened to involve the Tower, shows just how miry were the paths of political power. Edward Fitzharris, an odious Catholic conspirator, really had been involved in some mild 'popish plotting' in court circles. In 1681 he attempted to lay a false treason trail to the door of some prominent Whig. He was betrayed and clapped in the Marshalsea. Then, Shaftesbury's colleagues decided that his talents might be put to better use in the Tower. There they set him to ferreting out or concocting damaging information against Danby. The idea was that the informer would be impeached by parliament and that at his trial he would produce his devastating evidence. The plan misfired because of a legal conflict between the Court of King's Bench (in which criminal charges against Fitzharris had already been lodged) and the House of Commons. The common law judges won. Fitzharris was tried by them, without damaging revelations being made, and condemned to death. The Whigs bungled that little sortie but their retreat was turned into a rout by the Chaplain of the Tower, Francis Hawkins. This zealous servant of the crown decided to take a leaf from the opposition's book. He went to Fitzharris and promised a royal pardon in return for a signed confession from the prisoner involving a leading Whig politician in his original conspiracy. Once the document was written the wretched informant was executed and his 'confession' made public. The Tories triumphed and Hawkins was promoted to be Dean of Chichester.

The collapse of Titus Oates's conspiracy and some bad errors of political judgement brought Shaftesbury down again. In 1681 he was once more taken to the Tower where his rival was still incarcerated. When he appealed to the common law judges for release or trial according to the Habeas Corpus Act he was refused on the interesting grounds that the Tower was outside the jurisdiction of the court. So, despite the whittling away of the royal prerogative since 1640 and the supremacy achieved by statute law, the Tower of London remained a prison where men might be detained without trial. But no longer was the King's writ the only authority for committal: now the Tower had become a security prison peopled by those who had fallen foul of one or other political faction and who had been locked up in the name of crown or parliament.

The court party was now riding high. Charles was ruling without parliament and the Whigs were totally discredited. Shaftesbury was ill and despondent. In the hot summer of 1681 he suffered from fits and had to be removed by the Lieutenant to cooler lodgings. He had now been charged with treason and he knew that the government was compiling a case against him. Convinced of the outcome, he began putting his affairs in order and disposing of some of his goods. But when it came to the trial the Earl's supporters packed the jury and their leader was acquitted amidst scenes of great rejoicing. The Whigs even caused a medal to be struck with a bust of Shaftesbury on one side and a picture of the Tower on the other, with the sun emerging from clouds. But the fortunate politician still had powerful enemies and considered it wise to flee to Holland. Danby remained in the Tower until 1684, still too unpopular for the King to risk releasing him.

Before we have done with this seamy period in our national life we must record one more mysterious tragedy which took place in the Tower in 1683. In June of that year another 'conspiracy', the Rye House Plot, was uncovered. This time the murderous conceivers (for the deaths of Charles and James were part of the plot) were supposed to be Whig peers. A clutch of noblemen were therefore arrested and taken to the Tower, including Arthur Capel, Earl of Essex, an emotionally unstable man given to fits of black depression and raging outbursts of self-justification. Among the mish-mash of invention and half-truth concocted by the paid informers there were gobbets of fact, for Essex and his colleagues had certainly discussed diverting the succession from the Duke of York even though they could not agree on a suitable alternative. The Earl, therefore, had much to fear and it is no wonder that he sleeplessly paced the floor of his room in the Lieutenant's lodging on the night of his arrest (10 July). When on the following morning he was moved to the apartments in which his wife's grandfather, the Earl of Northumberland, had died and from which his own father had been taken out to execution, he may well have felt himself doomed. On the 12th he desired to speak with the King's friend, Lord Clarendon, and after this interview he seemed to be much easier in his mind. The next day one of his colleagues was led out of the Tower to his trial and at the same time the royal brothers came to the castle, ostensibly to inspect the Ordnance Office but really, in the opinion of some, to gloat over their enemies. As Charles and James were re-embarking in their barge a cry went up behind them that Lord Capel was slain. His servant had found him in his closet with his throat cut.

Suicide was the official and probably the true verdict but, inevitably there were many who suspected foul play and there were certainly odd circumstances about the death.

It was wondered yet by some how it was possible he should do it, for the wound was so deep and wide, as being cut through the gullet, windpipe and both the jugulars, it reached to the very vertebrae of the neck, so as the head held to it by a very little skin as it were, which [prevented] it from being quite [off]. The gripping, too, of the razor and cutting his own fingers was a little strange, but more, that having passed the jugulars, he should have strength to proceed so far, as an executioner could hardly have done more with an axe, and there were odd reflections upon it.[17]

Two thirteen-year-old children, playing outside at the time of Capel's death claimed to have heard cries coming from his room and to have seen a bloody razor flung from the window. Under examination, the boy's testimony wavered but Jane Lodeman stuck firmly to her story. Yet another incident in the Tower's history upon which it is not possible to stamp the words 'case closed'.

Charles II died in 1685. He was succeeded by his brother who was opposed by an increasing volume of Protestant–Whig opinion. James II was cast in the stubborn Stuart mould of his father and grandfather and quickly squandered such goodwill as existed at the beginning of the reign. He should have been warned by Monmouth's Rebellion, which broke out within weeks of his coronation. Instead, he interpreted its easy suppression as proof that he had the support of the people. James, Duke of Monmouth, the late King's natural son, was a romantic, soldierly young man. He had been honoured by his father with great titles, lands and court appointments. He was 'extraordinarily handsome and adroit, an excellent soldier and dancer, a favourite of the people, of an easy nature [but] debauched by lust [and] seduced by crafty knaves'.[18] His was the last West Country revolt, the heir to a long line of insurrections in which the independent-minded men of the far counties severely shook the English throne. Recent research has demonstrated that Monmouth's army was no peasant rabble armed with scythes and that it came very close to victory at the Battle of Sedgemoor. The facts are, however, that it lost and that Monmouth was brought, a prisoner, to London. He threw himself on the King's mercy but on 13 July he was conveyed to the Tower in James's own barge, his fate already decided by the passing of an Act of attainder. He was allowed one servant, visits from his wife and officially approved friends but otherwise he was kept a close prisoner.

James II had decided that his nephew's death should be soon and public, in order to put a speedy end to any other revolutionary plans discontents might be hatching. On 15 July Monmouth was escorted from the Tower by the Lieutenant and handed over to the sheriff's men at the 'bars', the traditional place for such transactions. He was marched to the scaffold through a crowd largely sympathetic to the condemned man. There was no heroic end for the popular hero; rather the opposite. He quickly completed his devotions and made no speech.

He was more concerned about the skill of his executioner, the notorious Jack Ketch*. A contemporary pamphlet gives the gruesome details of Monmouth's last moments.

> . . . the axe he took in his hand and tried it with his nail to see whether it was sharp enough and, giving the executioner six guineas, said 'Pray do your business well: do not serve me as you did my Lord Russell. I have heard you struck him three or four times. If you strike me twice I cannot promise you not to stir.' He also told his servant to give the executioner six more guineas if he did his work well. He then took off his coat and threw off his peruke and, having prayed, laid himself down and fitted his neck to the block with great composure of mind. But soon after he raised himself upon his elbow and said to the executioner, 'Prithee, let me feel the axe,' and, feeling the edge, added, 'I fear it is not sharp enough.' 'It is sharp and heavy enough,' was the reply. Then the executioner proceeded to do his office. The Duke would have no cap, nor be bound, nor have anything on his face. And yet, 'for all this,' writes an eye-witness, 'the botcherly dog did so barbarously act his part, that he could not at five strokes of the axe sever the head from the body.' After the third stroke the executioner threw away the axe and offered forty guineas to anyone who would finish the work. The bystanders threatened to kill him unless he took the axe again, and he completed his task. If there had been no guard he would have been torn to pieces by the crowd.[19]

James now pursued an uncompromising policy of Catholicising his kingdom. He appointed his co-religionists to all major offices, he refused to attend worship in the church of which he was head, and he published two declarations of indulgence which set aside existing statute laws in the interests of religious toleration. In the spring of 1688 Archbishop Sacroft and six of his fellow bishops questioned the legality of the second declaration and asked to be excused from ordering its promulgation in churches. Stupidly, James decided to put the harmless ecclesiastics on a boat and have them rowed to the Tower, where they awaited their trial on a charge of seditious libel (the 'libellous' document being the petition they had presented to the King). Their journey became a triumphal procession. The banks were crowded and many Londoners went out in small boats to cheer their Protestant champions. At Tower Wharf the scenes were even more enthusiastic and the treatment accorded them in prison was more like that of honoured guests than criminals awaiting trial.

* Ketch's name was soon to be linked with that of Judge Jeffreys in the popular annals of butchery. A popular rhyme of the times ran:
> While Jeffreys on the bench
> Ketch on the gibbet sits.

The lenient treatment extended to the prisoners by the officers in the Tower ran clean contrary to the orders issued by Sir Edward Hales, the Lieutenant. This Roman Catholic soldier was a close friend and supporter of the King and held a number of significant appointments including Deputy Warder of the Cinque Ports, Lieutenant of Dover Castle and Master of the Ordnance. He was not much liked by his subordinates especially when it was known – or rumoured – that he planned to build another chapel in the Tower for 'popish' services. On the Sunday after their committal the seven bishops attended communion in St Peter's where the Chaplain refused to read the declaration of indulgence as he had been instructed, for which disobedience he was deprived of his office. That same day the Tower ordnance boomed out the tidings that a son and heir had been born to the King. The bishops were much encouraged by the displays of sympathy and support. They declared that they were unlawfully detained and, on those grounds, they refused to pay the fees demanded of them for their upkeep. By prayer and mutual study they prepared themselves for the ordeal of their trial. On 15 June they were arraigned in Westminster Hall and – to the unrestrained delight of the populace – acquitted.

James II's siring of a son was his last folly. Many Englishmen who naturally shrank from rebellion against the throne were sufficiently appalled at the prospect of a Catholic succession to throw in their lot with the Whig and Tory noblemen who offered the crown to William of Orange, husband of James's older daughter, Mary. The King realized that he had gone too far and, while William and his Dutchmen hesitated, he tried by making concessions to regain popularity. One of his actions was to remove Sir Edward Hales. He was replaced by a man who, a matter of weeks before, had been a prisoner in the Tower. This odd appointment, which speaks eloquently of confusion in high places, put Sir Bevil Skelton in command of the fortress. This weak, haughty man had been until recently a diplomat, first in Holland, then France. He had done his best to serve James's interests in a delicately balanced situation only to be recalled and imprisoned for exceeding his instructions. When the King realized that Skelton's appreciation of diplomatic events had been substantially correct, he released him, then appointed him Lieutenant of his former prison.

But time was running out. William of Orange had already landed at Torbay. James joined his army at Salisbury, then changed his mind and decided to flee. On 11 December he left London with a small party of friends, including Sir Edward Hales, disguised as Hales's servant. They got as far as Faversham, where Hales was recognized and arrested. The ex-Lieutenant was brought back to the Tower where he remained for eighteen months. His master was more fortunate: he escaped at the second attempt. On the day of the King's flight parliament took over effective government. One of its first acts was to remove Skelton from his post. It was thus Skelton and not Hales who accompanied James on his journey to France. Tuesday 11 December was an eventful day: as well as the events already recorded, it witnessed the attempted escape of the most hated man in England, Judge George Jeffreys.

In 1677, as an aspiring young lawyer, Jeffreys had attached himself to the court party and for eleven years he had been its mainstay on the judicial bench. Administrators and politicians came and went but not once did Jeffreys falter in his loyalty to the crown or lose royal favour. He harried juries, twisted the rules, ranted at witnesses, and brought the full severity of the law to bear on all enemies or supposed enemies of the crown. He is chiefly remembered for the ruthlessness with which he filled the gibbets and gallows of the West Country after Monmouth's Rebellion but for years before that he had been using the same tactics in other courts and it was ever his aim to make the judiciary the servant of the crown rather than the servant of the law. He had been handsomely rewarded by the grateful Stuarts: Privy Councillor, Lord Chief Justice, Baron Jeffreys of Wem, Lord Chancellor – those and other honours came his way. So did a considerable fortune, much of it extracted from the unfortunate victims of his 'bloody assize'. He was at his post until the end and only when James fled did Jeffreys take thought for his own safety. He disguised himself as a sailor and hid on a ship moored at Wapping together with over £37,000 in cash. But he was recognized, arrested and committed to Lord Lucas, the new Lieutenant of the Tower, under a warrant from the provisional government:

> We, the peers of this realm, being assembled with some of the Privy Council, do hereby will and require you to take into your custody the body of George, Lord Jeffreys (herewith sent to you), and to keep him safe prisoner until further order; for which this shall be your sufficient warrant.[20]

This document was technically invalid, for there was no king, no sitting parliament, and the great seal which should have been used to authorize it had been flung into the Thames by the departing monarch. Had the London mob had its way there would have been no need for a warrant. When he was discovered Jeffreys was only saved by some of the local militia from a public lynching. Even the next day when the carriage conveying him through London was escorted by two regiments of train bands its progress was severely impeded by crowds howling for blood.

Perhaps some of the citizens, as they saw the procession pass safely within the portals of the Tower, consoled themselves with the thought that soon Jeffreys would be brought out for public execution. In the event, the mob was cheated of this satisfaction. Though only forty years old, the ex-Chancellor was a sick man. Ambition had taken its toll of his body and mind. For years he had driven himself hard and, when the pressure had become too great he had taken refuge in alcohol. This mode of life combined with mental depression to undermine his health. He had grown hardened to unpopularity: in the days of his wealth and power he had been able to ignore it, even laugh at it. Now, lonely and friendless, he brooded. He seldom left the chambers in Yeoman Warder Bull's house where he was confined. He even forbore attending chapel services because of the hostile stares of the congregation. But in his prison the hatred of the people reached him. One day a barrel of his favourite Colchester oysters arrived. 'Thank God, I still have some friends left,' he said, as the gift was opened. Out fell a heap of empty shells and a rope halter. Doctors were unable to arrest his steady decline:

> ... there has not been any help wanting that skill or art could invent for the continuation of his life, but it has all been as ineffectual and vain as the supplications of the distressed were sometimes to him, in the time of his power. For about this month last past, he has been in a very languishing condition, still wasting away more and more, in which time he has hardly been in a capacity to take anything to sustain nature, unless a little sack to revive it . . . So he continued decaying till the 19th of this instant, April, 1689, when about half an hour after four in the morning he died in the forty-first year of his age.[21]

Even Jeffreys' body was unwanted: permission was given for his family to remove it and give it private burial. The option was not taken up and the Judge was interred in St Peter's.*

During these disturbed years there were developments of a positive nature at the Tower. In 1686 the age-old dispute over the boundaries of the Liberty was resolved. The King ordered a commission under Lord Dartmouth, Master-General of the Ordnance, to decide on the vexed question. The old demarcation line round the castle and the hill was now finally confirmed. In addition three other areas in which the Ordnance had an interest were brought within the Liberty. Known as the Little Minories, the Old Artillery Ground and the Wellclose, the three plots had been crown property since the Dissolution of the Monasteries. We have already seen how the site of the Abbey of the Poor Clares (Minories) had been occupied by Ordnance storehouses and offices. Much the same was true of the

---

* Some years later Jeffrey's body was, in fact, removed and buried by the family.

Wellclose, anciently a part of St Mary Graces Abbey, which was apparently used as a saltpetre store. The Old Artillery Ground was land originally belonging to the Priory of St Mary Spital. It had for many decades been used as a firing range by the Tower Ordnance, train bands and the Honourable Artillery Company. In recent years these three sites had been abandoned and when in 1671 the Ordnance Office acquired Tower Place, Woolwich, they were sold as development land. It must have been this that caused the inhabitants, concerned at the possible loss of ancient rights and privileges, to petition for a recognition of their special status. Accordingly the three areas were incorporated into the Tower Liberty, exempt from the jurisdiction of the City and the county of Middlesex. The Constable of the Tower exercised the office of sheriff and the Liberty had its own court and judicial officers. One of the more thorny points of dispute with the London authorities was now decided in the Tower's favour. The commission found that the court of record 'now and of ancient time holden within the said Liberty' had full powers to hold pleas, including those involving outsiders.

There was another area, not altogether easy to define but comprising most of the modern London boroughs of Tower Hamlets and Hackney (formerly Hackney, Stepney, Shoreditch, Poplar and Bethnal Green), which from early times had a special connection with the Tower. Originally it consisted of those villages and settlements outside the City wall which were closest to the fortress. As we have seen, these communities could be called upon by the Constable or Lieutenant to provide guards for prisoners and other duties for which their own staff might, from time to time, prove inadequate. The connection became closer when Sir William Waad obtained the right to muster the militias in these places. James II's commissioners confirmed the right of these Tower Hamlets, as they came to be called, to their own magistrates and sessions of the peace. But they were not part of the Tower Liberty, probably because their connection with the Tower was one of customary service and not territorial ownership.

Within the Tower the Ordnance Office was still expanding. The 1680s saw the destruction of the Elizabethan premises on 'the hill' (i.e. the area of the Inner Ward north of the White Tower) and their replacement by the Grand Storehouse. To judge from old prints the building was aptly named. It was a long, two-storey, red-bricked edifice in the prevailing Classical style, with an impressive portico and central lantern towering over all. It stood high above the castle walls and dominated the entire complex. With carved wooden mouldings and ingenious decorative motifs made up of skilful arrangements of weapons, the storehouse was scarcely less impressive from within. It is no surprise to learn that, on its completion in

1692, William and Mary were entertained there at a lavish banquet. In 1680, the old eastern Iron Gate entrance was demolished, largely because it was impeding the flow of water in the moat. At about the same time some of the walls and towers were strengthened to permit extra cannon to be mounted on them. Accommodation also had to be found in this period for a permanent garrison. The professional army had its genesis in Cromwell's New Model Army. In the half century following the Civil War, despite the hostility of freedom-loving Englishmen to the idea of a standing army, the need for a permanent, trained soldiery was obvious. Various foot and mounted regiments were founded and there is no doubt that, if he had had time, James II would have built up a large royal army as the basis of his power. After 1660 soldiers were garrisoned permanently in the Tower. Barracks were made for them in buildings previously occupied by the Mint. To make further space stables and coach houses were moved onto the Wharf and the Ordnance transferred its carriage stores to nearby Goodman's Fields.

The bringing of a new category of residents into the Tower raised problems. The garrison had its own officers and its functions were military, as basically were the Yeoman Warders'. There was thus room for demarcation disputes over spheres of responsibility. However, the basic function of the Yeoman Warder as guardian of the Tower, controlling access at the gates, was never infringed. There was a serious attempt by James II to tighten the regulations governing the Tower staff. All Warders who had acquired grants of their office for life were obliged to surrender them. In future all such appointments were held during the sovereign's pleasure. Other customs such as living out, subletting Tower lodgings, and taking paying guests were discouraged but not, it would seem, effectively stopped. There were obviously limits beyond which the government, especially James's insecure government, could not go. The Lieutenant's perquisite of selling offices was, however, brought to an end.

During the reign of William and Mary a series of renovations and 'improvements' were carried out by the Surveyor General of His Majesty's Works. This was none other than the architect of the new London, Sir Christopher Wren. He put the Bloody and Beauchamp Towers in a good state of repair and carried out necessary alterations to the Inner Wall and some of its towers. Unfortunately he also enlarged almost all the Norman windows of the White Tower into the wide windows which remain to this day.

The steady expansion of the Ordnance Office, the growing need for staff accommodation, the establishment of the garrison, and the provision of fresh attractions for the visiting public apparently restricted the accommodation available for prisoners. The Tower was now reserved almost exclusively for state detainees whose social standing entitled them to expect a reasonable standard of comfort. In 1695 Sir Christopher Wren was asked to report on the prison accommodation in the Beauchamp and Bloody Towers and to estimate the cost of erecting a new prison building behind the Chapel. His reply is interesting for the light it casts on the sort of lodgings considered appropriate to prisoners of rank.

In obedience to Your Lordships' order of the 15th instant, that I should view the several places in the Tower therein mentioned – viz. Beauchamp Tower and ye Bloody Tower and report what expense will put them in condition to hold prisoners of state and what number they will hold, I have accordingly viewed the same and peport that both the said places were put the last summer in better repair than they have been in many years, being whited, mended and made strong, but to make them fit for prisoners of state, if by that expression it be intended that they should be wainscotted and made fit for hangings and furniture it may cost £200 or much more but with such walls and winding stairs they never can be made proper with any cost without rebuilding. I have also in pursuance of Your Lordships' order viewed the place behind the Chapel and considered and do approve the annexed draught proposed to be built which I take to be as large as ye place will afford containing 15 square and if it be well build in 3 storeys, cellars and garrets it will cost £600. As to the number of prisoners the place may hold, I can only report what number of rooms each place contains. Beauchamp Tower hath a large kitchen, two large rooms, and two small servants rooms. Bloody Tower hath a large kitchen, two large rooms, and one closet. The new building may contain nine single rooms, besides cellars and garrets and a kitchen . . .[22]

This was a very important period in the history of the Mint. Charles II brought back with him from exile John Roettier, an engraver of incomparable skill who was to serve at the Tower until his death in 1703. He was assisted in earlier years by his brothers and later by his sons, and he produced a succession of excellent coins and medals. In 1667 he struck a medal for the King with a representation on the reverse of the Duchess of Richmond, a royal mistress, as Britannia. It was the first appearance of a device which has been used on British coins until the present day. There were many visitors to the Mint and the officers made an admission charge to those who came to admire their work. Few were disappointed.

My Lord Brouncker and I to the Tower, to see the famous engraver Roettier, to get him to grave a seal for the (Navy) Office. And did see some of the finest pieces of work, in embossed work, that ever I did see in my life for fineness and smallness of the images thereon, and I will carry my wife thither to show them to her. Here I also did see bars of gold melting, which was fine sight.[23]

Mechanization came to the Mint at the Restoration. Its craftsmen had resisted the innovation for decades but now £1,000 was invested in machines and £400 in converting and extending buildings. In recent years soldiers and other Tower staff had encroached on Mint Street. Now there was a clean sweep; beer houses, shops and blacksmiths' establishments were moved, so were tenants who had taken up residence in houses reserved for Mint personnel. Some of them resisted and had to be forcibly ejected with the aid of troops. Soon the new presses, edge markers, blank cutting machines, flatters and horse-driven rolling mills were rumbling, creaking and thumping from dawn till dusk.

In the 1690s a completely new silver coinage was issued and this necessitated a further expansion of the space allocated to the Mint. The old Irish Mint (in the eastern part of the Outer Ward) which had been commandeered by the garrison, was reclaimed and more premises were taken over for machinery and horse stables. Now it was the turn of the garrison to be put under pressure and the commanding officer complained that his men were having to sleep three to a bed. In the last days of the seventeenth century one of the most remarkable Englishmen of the age became Master of the Mint. Isaac Newton, the great mathematician and scientist, held the office from 1699 until his death in 1727. Despite continuing his researches and writing his great work on optics, Newton found time to be an energetic administrator during a period when a new coinage was being established and (as a result of the Union of 1707) the Tower Mint was taking over the work of the Edinburgh Mint.

Another man who worked in the Tower and filled his office faithfully was William Prynne. This rather unpleasant Puritan pamphleteer had had a chequered career but in 1662 he was appointed to a post which admirably suited his antiquarian predilections. He was made Keeper of the Records at the Tower with a handsome salary of £500 a year. For the remaining seven years of his life he applied himself to the task of sorting and recataloguing the growing volume of documents. He built upon the work of previous incumbents and was continually pestering the government to make more space available for the records in the Tower. He was in many ways the prototype archivist, always anxious to help people who wished to consult the documents in his charge and devoting all his energies to ensuring that these treasures of the past were fully available to the public.

For a short while in 1675 one of Isaac Newton's great rivals, John Flamsteed, was associated with the Tower and the fortress was able to add to its long list of functions that of astronomical observatory. The second half of the seventeenth century was a golden age of British science. Graced by the names of Newton, Boyle, Hobbes and a host of others, it witnessed the foundation of the Royal Society, the Greenwich Observatory and new chairs at the universities. There was virtually no distinction between amateur and professional. A man of inquisitive mind and determination could aspire to make important discoveries and there were many wealthy patrons from the King downwards only too anxious to encourage talent. The universe was the scientists' oyster and not one of them would have quarrelled with Newton's comment, 'I seem to have been only a boy playing on the sea shore, and diverting myself in now and then finding a smoother pebble or a prettier shell than ordinary, whilst the great ocean of truth lay all undiscovered before me.'

The train of events which placed John Flamsteed among the leading British scholars of the age indicates clearly the widespread fascination for scientific study even among men whose daily lives were bound up with such mundane matters as supervising the manufacture and storage of ordnance in the Tower of London. Around the middle of the century Jonas Moore was a mathematician earning scarcely enough as a tutor to keep body and soul together. At last he succeeded in commending himself to some influential parliamentarians and was appointed to supervise the drainage of the Fens. He achieved considerable success as an engineer, served both Cromwellian and Stuart regimes in a variety of posts, was knighted and eventually became Surveyor to the Ordnance. He kept up his theoretical studies and his quarters in the Tower were littered with books, telescopes and mathematical instruments. In 1670 he was introduced to a young man called John Flamsteed, the largely self-taught son of a Derbyshire maltster. Moore was fascinated to hear of Flamsteed's observations of heavenly bodies and the calculations he had based on them. He encouraged the young man and presented him with a micrometer to aid his studies. Flamsteed went to Cambridge to take a degree and to begin drawing himself to the attention of the scientific establishment with a succession of papers based on his astronomical studies. In 1674 he was back in London as Moore's guest and the older man now commended him to the King and Flamsteed sent to Whitehall a tide table, a thermometer and a barometer made to his own specification. This led to court patronage and when Flamsteed pointed out to the King the importance for navigation of accurate knowledge of the movements of heavenly bodies Charles nominated him his official 'astronomical observator' (in effect the first Astronomer Royal) and ordered him, 'forthwith to apply himself with the most exact care and diligence to the rectifying the tables of the motions of the heavens and the places of the fixed stars, so as to find out the so much desired longitude of places for the perfecting the art of navigation.'[24]

Flamsteed could rely on the help of his old friend. Moore gave him a seven-foot sextant and two timepieces by the contemporary master Thomas Tompion. He also provided the astronomer with a temporary observatory while more splendid accommodation was being built at Greenwich. This was in the north-east turret of the White Tower. It was from there that the first official observation was made in April 1675. Even when, after a few months, Flamsteed moved his telescopes and equipment down river Moore was instrumental in helping him get established at Greenwich. Ordnance workmen erected the new building, its roof was made from lead from the old Coldharbour Gate, and part of the money for its construction came from the sale of unserviceable gunpowder.

The procession of distinguished prisoners to pass through the portals of the Tower continued and we shall mention some of them shortly. In the intense personal and factional rivalries which marked the early days of the British party political system it was, one might imagine from the impressive list of names, virtually impossible to succeed in public life without spending some time in the Tower. This very fact, coupled with the comfort and privileges these detainees enjoyed, served to rob the fortress of some of its ancient terrors. Princess Anne might remark that 'it is a dismal thing to have one's friends sent to that place' but Horace Walpole, the eighteenth-century wit, could view the possibility of incarceration there much more lightly:

> There are a thousand pretty things to amuse you: the lions, the Armoury, the Crown, King Harry's cod-piece, and the axe that beheaded Anne Boleyn. I design to make interest for the rooms where the two princes were smothered: in the long winter evenings when one wants company, one may sit and scribble verses against Crouch-back Richard and dirges on the sweet babes.[25]

For a few decades the Tower was rather less closely associated than usual with the mainstream of national events. The exiled James II and his family inspired many plots against the government of William and Mary and Queen Anne but the Protestant succession was firmly established and when in 1714 Anne died without heir the crown was offered to George, Elector of Hanover, a distant cousin descended from James I. This was the signal for a more concerted effort by the supporters of James Edward Stuart, the Old Pretender (son of James II). The Jacobite Rebellion of 1715 drew some support from English

210

Tories who resented the Whig ascendancy and had little regard for the German King who spoke no English. In Scotland the Union of 1707 was widely resented for, though a majority had voted for it in the Scottish assembly, it had subsequently been enforced with some brutality on the more reluctant sections of the community. In September some Scottish peers and some northern English Catholics raised the standard of revolt. It was a half-hearted affair and neither side could extract much honour from the few engagements which took place. By the time the Pretender arrived, three days before Christmas, it was all over.

The government decided that clemency was the best policy but some examples had to be made. A group of Scottish and northern noblemen were brought to the Tower where they joined the leading members of the parliamentary Tory party who had already been lodged there. In February 1716 the Jacobite lords actually involved in the rising were tried and, with one exception, condemned to death. A strong appeal on their behalf was made in parliament and was defeated by only seven votes. In the event the King and his Whig advisers pursued a middle course; three peers were reprieved and three ordered to the block. Like most compromises, it pleased no one. There was a great deal of popular feeling against the proposed executions, though this did not prevent the mob displaying its usual macabre curiosity and flocking out to Tower Hill to watch Earl Derwentwater and Viscount Kenmure go to their deaths on 24 February. Two weeks later a violent display of the aurora borealis was seen in London and was widely interpreted as a sign of divine displeasure at the recent executions. The government was badly shaken. The sanguine Robert Walpole wrote to his brother, 'I don't well know what account to give you of our situation here. There are storms in the air, but I doubt not they will all be blown over.'[26] The King was certainly relieved when one of the condemned men, William Maxwell, Earl of Nithsdale, solved the government's problem by escaping on the eve of his execution.

This escape is the most celebrated in the history of the Tower. Others have been more difficult and more audacious but they lack the romantic elements which have commended Nithsdale's to generations of visitors. The architect of the plan was the resourceful Lady Nithsdale who travelled all the way from Scotland through atrocious winter weather. Having unsuccessfully petitioned George I for her husband's release she immediately made preparations for the scheme which must have been maturing in her mind for some time. She went to visit her husband in the Lieutenant's Lodgings, taking her maid and two female companions who had come to say their sad farewells. The ladies were appropriately lachrymose and flustered and no suspicion was aroused by their agitated comings and goings. So often did

211

the gaoler open the door to let one or two of the visitors in or out that he soon lost track of how many had come and gone. One of the 'ladies' had, of course, been the Earl, got up in a dress and hood, with rouge on his cheeks and a tear-stained kerchief held to his face to hide his beard. The last to leave was Lady Nithsdale who held a long conversation with herself in two voices, then said goodbye to her 'husband' from the half open doorway of the chamber. As she left she told the Earl's servant not to disturb him because he was at his prayers. By this time Nithsdale was already concealed in the house of London friends. A few days later he left the country in the livery of a servant to the Venetian ambassador.

The mood of Englishmen was very different a generation later when Charles Edward Stuart, the Young Pretender, made his bid to unseat the Hanoverians. The '45 Rebellion was a much more serious affair than its predecessor. The Scottish rebels, with French money and support, defeated an English force at Prestonpans and advanced as far south as Derby. 'The confusion in the City of London would not have been to be described, and the King's crown, I will venture to say, in the utmost danger', so wrote one observer. Regiments and citizen militia were mustered for the defence of the capital, arrangements made for the guns of the Tower to signal the approach of danger. On the Continent British arms had suffered a serious reverse at Fontenoy and a French invasion in support of the Pretender was widely feared. The news of the rebels' rout at Culloden in April 1746 accordingly unleashed the wildest expressions of relief and joy. The Tower guns were now fired, not as a warning, but as a signal of victory. There was dancing in the streets and bonfires all night long. The Duke of Cumberland, the British general at Culloden, was welcomed as a national hero and the Scottish prisoners when they were conveyed through the City to the Tower were protected with difficulty from the mob.

Six rebel lords were lodged in the Tower. One of them, the Earl of Tullibardine, died shortly after his arrival. The remainder were sentenced to death, although the Earl of Cromarty was subsequently pardoned, apparently as a result of the earnest pleadings of his wife who petitioned in turn the King and every member of the Privy Council. A full account appeared in the *Gentleman's Magazine* of the execution of the Earl of Kilmarnock and Lord Balmerino on 18 August 1746. It is worth quoting at some length because of the detail it gives us of the traditional ceremonial of such sombre occasions.

At six o'clock a troop of lifeguards, and 1,000 of the footguards – being fifteen men out of each company, marched from the parade in St James's park through the City to Tower Hill, to attend the

212

execution of the Earl of Kilmarnock and the Lord Balmerino, and being arrived there were posted in lines from the Tower to the scaffold, and all around it. About 8 o'clock the Sheriffs of London, and their under sheriffs and their officers, viz. six sergeants at mace, six yeomen, and the executioner, met at the Mitre Tavern in Fenchurch Street, where they breakfasted, and went from thence to the house, lately the Transport Office, on Tower Hill near Catherine's Court, hired by them for the reception of the said lords, before they should be conducted to the scaffold which was erected about thirty yards from the said house.

At ten o'clock the block was fixed on the stage and covered with black cloth, and several sacks of sawdust up to strew on it; soon after their coffins were brought, covered with black cloth, ornamented with gilt nails, etc. On the Earl of Kilmarnock's was a plate with this inscription, 'Guliemus Come de Kilmarnock decollatur 18 Augusti 1746. Etat suae 42,' with an Earl's coronet over it, and six coronets over the six handles; and on Lord Balmerino's, was a plate with this inscription, 'Arthurus Dominus de Balmerino decollatur 18 Augusti 1746. Etat suae 58, with a baron's coronet over it, and six others over the six handles. At a quarter after ten the Sheriffs went in procession to the outward gate of the Tower, and after knocking at it some time, a warder within asked, 'Who's there?' The officer without replied, 'The sheriffs of London and Middlesex.' The warder then asked, 'What do they want?' The officer answered, 'The bodies of William, Earl of Kilmarnock, and Arthur, Lord Balmerino,' upon which the warder within said, 'I will go and inform the Lieutenant of the Tower,' and in about ten minutes the Lieutenant of the Tower with the Earl of Kilmarnock, and Major White with Lord Balmerino, guarded by several of the warders, came to the gate; the prisoners were then delivered to the Sheriffs who gave proper receipt for their bodies to the Lieutenant, who as usual said, 'God bless King George!' to which the Earl of Kilmarnock assented by a bow, and the Lord Balmerino said, 'God bless King James' . . . Soon after the procession, moving in a slow and solemn manner, appeared in the following order:
1. The Constable of the Tower.
2. The Knight Marshal's men and Tipsters.
3. The Sheriff's Officers.
4. The Sheriffs, the prisoners, and their chaplains. Mr Sheriff Blachford walking with the Earl of Kilmarnock, and Mr Sheriff Cockayne with the Lord Balmerino.
5. The Tower Warders.
6. A guard of musqueteers.
7. The two hearses and a mourning coach.

When the procession had passed through the lines within the area of the circle formed by the guards, the passage was closed, and the troops of horse who were in the rear of the foot in the lines wheeled off, and drew five feet deep behind the foot, on the south side of the hill facing the scaffold.[27]

In December Charles Radcliffe was executed on the same spot and in the following April the eighty-year-old Lord Lovat also perished on Tower Hill. This extremely unprepossessing Jacobite (his portrait was painted by Hogarth) gained by his death an undying fame which his life certainly did not merit. For Simon Fraser, Lord Lovat was the last man ever to be beheaded on Tower Hill, or, indeed, in Britain. This gross, ugly, old man was led out to the scaffold on the morning of 9 April 1747. Perhaps the people of London and the surrounding areas knew that this would be their last opportunity to witness such an event. Certainly they turned out in unprecedented numbers. Stands had been built all round the Hill; they, the Tower battlements, every window and roof were crammed with spectators. One of the largest stands over against the 'Ship' in Barking Lane collapsed, spilling upwards of a thousand people in a squirming heap into the street and killing about twenty of them. Even Lovat, not a modest man, was surprised at the turnout – 'God save us!' he exclaimed as he clambered with difficulty up to the scaffold between two warders, 'Why should there be such a bustle about taking off an old grey head, that cannot go up three steps without three bodies to support it.' He made a good end and did not disappoint the crowds who had come out to witness it. Thus closed a long chapter in the history of the Tower, a chapter which had started with the impromptu beheading of an archbishop 366 years before.

Customs change and by the mid-eighteenth century hanging had come to be considered a more humane way of despatching capital offenders, though a certain symbolism continued to attach itself to decapitation and until well into the next century it was the practice with particularly odious offenders to remove their heads after hanging. Not that there were by then many such offenders lodged in the Tower. Apart from the serious insurrections of 1715 and 1745 few events provided the government with need to execute important traitors. Criminals in other categories were adequately dealt with by the prisons associated with the common law courts. But as we mentioned earlier several eminent men did find themselves locked up in the Tower for various reasons between 1660 and 1745. We will briefly consider some of them.

The Popish Plot provided an opportunity for jealous enemies to attempt the downfall of that engaging recorder of the Restoration scene,

Samuel Pepys. On 22 May 1679 he was accused in parliament of maladministration at the Navy Office and was committed to the Tower. The restriction was not onerous: he received visitors, including the other great diarist, John Evelyn, and among his well-wishers was the King who sent for his dinner a buck from Enfield Chase. But Pepys could see his carefully constructed career in ruins and he worked ceaselessly to clear himself. He was determined to be tried at common law and acquitted. On 20 June he was successful in a petition to be removed from the Tower to the Marshalsea. The latter prison was much less comfortable; there was even the risk of gaol fever, a disease never prevalent in the Tower; but the move took him out of the jurisdiction of parliament. A few days later Pepys was granted bail and was able to use his liberty to gather evidence against his accusers. Even so, it was another year before he was finally able to clear his name.

William Penn, the celebrated Quaker and founder of Pennsylvania found himself in the Tower for a spell in his youth. He was, in fact, born within the Tower Liberty (1644) to a family of some substance. He might have chosen a brilliant career in the army, the law or politics but his conversion to Quakerism barred him from all preferment and turned many of his fashionable friends against him. In 1668 he published without licence a pamphlet attacking certain orthodox doctrines and it was for this offence that he was committed to the Tower. The bishops ensured that he was kept a close prisoner and sent theologians to argue him out of his heresies. That is not the way to shake a man who is convinced he knows the truth. 'The Tower is to me the worst argument in the world,' he told his opponents. 'My prison will be my grave before I will budge a jot.' Fortunately for England and America the situation did not become that acute. His father engineered young William's release after seven months.

Among those who were brought to the Tower as a result of temporarily unsuccessful political manoeuvrings were the Duke of Marlborough and Sir Robert Walpole. In 1692 Marlborough – then still plain John Churchill – had already begun to prove his abilities as a soldier. He and his wife were on intimate terms with the Queen and with Princess Anne but Churchill did not enjoy the full confidence of William III and this irked him. He corresponded with James II with the object of seeing if the return of the old king could not be engineered on mutually satisfactory terms. The plot was discovered by rivals and revealed to the King. Churchill was stripped of all his offices and sent to the Tower with his wife. Fortunately for him (and, indeed, for his country) his enemies overreached themselves in their efforts to destroy him. They produced a forged document against him and when this was exposed the Churchills were released after an imprisonment lasting six weeks.

Walpole's incarceration occurred during a severe reversal suffered by the Whig party in 1712. He was charged with corruption and mishandling funds assigned to him as Secretary-at-War. By a small majority the Commons found him guilty and committed him to the Tower. During the debate the Speaker (an enemy of Walpole) spoke these words:

> There are confident tempers in the world that, instead of standing corrected, can glory in their punishments be they of what sort they will . . . I expect to see such a parade made, and such a countenance showed him in prison, by some sort of persons who would be glad for their own sakes to screen the foulness of the crime as well as the person convicted of it, that I am afraid that part of your judgment will not sit so heavy upon him as it ought to do.[28]

He was absolutely right. Whig noblemen rode through the City in their bright carriages to visit the prisoner and Walpole entertained lavishly. Outside, pamphlets and ballads, with such titles as *The Jewel in the Tower*, were circulated in his support while, at the ensuing by-election his Lynn constituents returned him unopposed. For himself, Walpole, denied his usual platform, turned his eloquent oratory into eloquent prose producing pamphlets such as *A Short History of Parliament* which his colleagues used to good effect in their conflict with the Tories. When, after six months, Walpole left the Tower he did so with an increased reputation and at once resumed his leading place in the politics of the day.

9

In the century after 1750 the edifice of British industrial capitalism began to be built while at the same time its foundations were being undermined by men and women who challenged the religious, moral and political assumptions on which they rested. The army and navy gave Britain a world supremacy which her commercial leaders were quick to exploit. The gap between rich and poor widened as merchants and industrialists prospered from the spoils of colonial trade while their fellow countrymen huddled together in rural and industrial slums. The position of the self-assured aristocracy who built sumptuous country houses, indulged their pleasures at Bath and Newmarket and ruled parliament seemed unassailable to all but the most penetrating observation. But political radicals, taking fire from the revolutionary movements of France and the American colonies, clamouring for change, won popular support, and set Britain on the long road of constitutional reform. Whitefield and the Wesleys brought a religious revival which challenged greed and self-interest. Their disciples swept away slavery and enforced humanitarian reforms in factory, prison and the penal system. The Tower was no longer at the centre of national life but changes and events within its walls could not but reflect the complexity and vigour of the age.

The year 1760 brought to the Tower a murderous rakehell and an earnest, evangelical lady of unimpeachable virtue. Laurence Shirley, Earl Ferrars, was rich, exotic and not a little eccentric. His young wife endured for six years the Earl's sadistic cruelty and his flaunting of his relationship with a Mrs Clifford, by whom he had four children. His extravagance and neglect put a strain not only on his marriage but also upon his finances. At length trustees had to be appointed to administer the family estates and responsibility was vested in the Shirleys' steward, John Johnson. This affront made Ferrars furious and drove him to the edge of (or perhaps beyond) sanity. He tried to turn Johnson out of his farm and when that failed he summoned the steward to his mansion at Staunton Harrold (Leicestershire), locked the door of the study as soon as they were alone there, and shot the poor man down in cold blood. He was arrested and brought by easy stages to London. Through the lively, squalid City, so well known to us from the paintings and engravings of Hogarth, he rode in his open carriage dressed like a jockey in a close fitting riding frock and jacket with spurred boots. And so he came to the Tower on St Valentine's Day, 1760.

It was Ferrars' nobility which entitled him to this most prestigious of prisons but he was not brought within the fortress to any of the traditional cells; he was lodged in the Middle Tower. One of the visitors allowed him was his aunt, Selina Hastings, Countess of Huntingdon. This saintly lady was a friend of the Wesleys and George Whitefield and the great patroness of Methodists and Evangelicals. It was she who built chapels for ministers who could gain no Anglican benefice because of the hostility of the bishops. She hoped and prayed for the conversion of her ne'er-do-well nephew, the more so after his condemnation by the House of Lords on 21 April. Her earnest exhortations wrought no change of heart in the half-crazed Earl who, eventually, almost threw her out of his cell. The Countess then sent Whitefield to the prisoner, to try on him the eloquence which had moved crowds of drink-hardened miners to repentance. It was useless; Ferrars was determined to enter death with the haughty self-assurance he had cultivated in life. He dismissed the unwanted philanthropists with their professed concern for his soul and asked instead for his mistress to come and minister to the immediate needs of his body. The request was refused and the noble prisoner had to content himself with writing poetry and listening to his gaoler read Shakespeare to him. On 5 May Ferrars donned an immaculate light-coloured coat edged in silver, black silk breeches with silver knee buckles and white stockings and set out for the noose at Tyburn in one of the most bizarre processions ever to leave the Tower of London. His open carriage and six proceeded at walking pace between columns of foot and mounted soldiers and was followed by a magnificent hearse pulled by black-plumed horses. Behind came family and friends in their coaches attended by liveried servants. The whole cavalcade took two and three-quarter hours to reach the place of execution through the crowded streets.

Within six months a new reign had begun, the long and momentous reign of King George III. This sovereign, the first thoroughly English Hanoverian, was determined to exercise more political power than his two predecessors who had been largely reliant upon, and therefore, to some extent manipulated by politicians. But if he saw himself as an absolute monarch on the French pattern he was very soon to be disillusioned. George III hated opposition, especially when it was coupled with heavy and popular satire. He thus had abundant cause to detest John Wilkes. Wilkes was a member of parliament and a journalist. In both capacities he regularly attacked the King and his ministers with a cutting and all too effective wit. Especially influential was Wilkes's paper, the *North Briton*. In the celebrated issue No. 45 in April

1763 Wilkes wrote an anonymous article about the speech from the throne which had closed the recent session of parliament. The report described it as 'the most abandoned instance of ministerial effrontery ever attempted to be imposed on mankind'. The government leaders, and by implication the King, were accused of dishonesty. George fumed. He determined to have Wilkes's scalp and a writ of seditious libel was immediately issued by the Secretaries of State, Lords Egremont and Halifax, against the author and publisher. Wilkes was apprehended on 30 April and, after a brief examination by the two earls, he was bundled off to the Tower, where the Deputy-Lieutenant was ordered to keep him a close prisoner. Meanwhile his house was searched and all his papers ransacked.

Had England been France that would have been the end of the matter. The government in Paris could have undesirables immured by *lettres de cachet* and once in the Bastille the unfortunates might never again emerge into the free air. In England the law provided the citizen with safeguards and Wilkes's confinement was illegal on at least two counts: it was an abrogation of parliamentary privilege and the warrant was inadequate in that it did not bear Wilkes's name (because the offending article was anonymous). A write of habeas corpus was applied for and granted and on 6 May Wilkes was discharged from prison on the ground of privilege. But there was a more important issue at stake. Many contemporary political observers were alarmed at the inference that the government could legally shut up its critics in the Tower. Even Wilkes's enlargement was not reassuring, resulting as it did purely from the privilege Wilkes enjoyed as a member of parliament. It indicated that the government could issue general writs against private citizens. Wilkes immediately brought actions against his persecutors, actions which were in every particular successful. His examples were followed by others who had been harassed by the King's ministers. Most of these cases were tried before Charles Pratt, Chief Justice of the Common Pleas, and it was he who was largely responsible for establishing the law that arrest and detention without reason for cause shown by ministers of the crown under general warrant was contrary to the constitution. Pratt was hailed as scarcely less a champion of liberty than Wilkes. As far as the Tower of London was concerned this clarification of the law removed the last vestiges of royal prerogative and was, perhaps, a more significant event than the final execution on Tower Hill or the death of Lord Ferrars, the last nobleman to be sent forth to his death from the Tower.

In 1780 the Gordon Riots burst upon London, proving that the spirit of sectarian bitterness was still very much alive. Lord George Gordon was the youngest son of a peer and a member of parliament of whom no one took much notice. But he was determined to be noticed. His political and religious ideas were confused but he had undoubted oratorical gifts and the dangerous ability of making prejudice appear not only respectable but righteous. The passing of the Catholic Relief Act in 1778 provided him with a cause. This modest legislation which lifted some of the restrictions on Roman Catholics inevitably raised opposition from more extreme Protestants. Gordon put himself at their head and became President of the Protestant Association. He spoke in parliament, addressed meetings and issued propaganda. The climax of the campaign came on 2 June 1780 when, after a rally in St George's Fields, Gordon marched at the head of an unruly crowd shouting 'No Popery!' to present a petition to parliament. That done, the mob got completely out of hand. For days they went on the rampage, killing, burning, looting and raping. It began as an attack on Roman churches and the property and persons of known Catholics but rapidly degenerated into an orgy of unrestrained violence. Shops, beer houses and distilleries were broken into, the prisons were opened, several attacks were made on the Bank of England. Many gunsmiths took their stock to the Tower for safe keeping and the drawbridges were kept raised. Martial law was declared and there were hundreds of deaths in clashes between rioters and troops. Soon the streets were littered with bodies. If we include those who were executed for their part in the riots the total death toll was probably in excess of 850 people.

In the midst of all this Gordon was arrested and conveyed to the Tower in a closed hackney carriage with two officers by his side and two guardsmen on the roof. He was attended by a company of infantry, a regiment of dragoons, a detachment of Horse Guards and three ranks of militiamen. He was closely confined in a 'dark, dirty little apartment', was allowed no books, pens or paper and very few visitors. Soon he was informed that he had been charged with treason. After that his prison conditions were somewhat relaxed, probably in order to enable him to receive help in preparing his defence. Among those who came to succour him was John Wesley who recorded the visit in his journal:

> I spent an hour with him at his apartment in the Tower. Our conversation turned upon popery and religion. He seemed to be well acquainted with the Bible and had abundance of other books, enough to furnish a study. I was agreeably surprised to find he did not complain of any person or thing, and cannot but hope his confinement will take a right turn and prove a lasting blessing to him.[1]

Alas for the preacher's pious hopes; George Gordon died a convert to Judaism. But that was far in the future. He was brought to trial in the following February and his conviction seemed a foregone conclusion but, thanks largely to the brilliant pleading of his counsel, the jury brought in a verdict of not guilty. He left the Tower after a stay of eight months. By that time the impact of the horrors of that appalling week in June had begun to fade. People were even beginning to reflect that perhaps the riots had been valuable in that they had released the pressure of incipient rebellion which many felt was widespread among the lower orders.

One reason for discontent was a sympathy with the American colonists with whom Britain had gone to war in 1770. The War of American Independence brought one important prisoner to the Tower. Henry Laurens was Vice-President of South Carolina and President of the Continental Congress (the body that had drawn up the Declaration of Independence). In August 1780 he set out for Holland in the hope of gaining support for the colonists' cause. His ship was intercepted and before the year was out he found himself in the Tower of London. As he was a declared rebel there needed no special warrant for his detention, especially when his papers were found to include a draft treaty with Holland. Laurens was kept in the Tower for a year and his experience can have done nothing to weaken his ardour for the revolutionary cause. He found his accommodation cramped and he did not appreciate being constantly guarded by soldiers with fixed bayonets. Most of all he objected to being charged for his board and lodging. In fact he refused to pay. After a year he was released on parole and, in 1782, he was exchanged for Lord Cornwallis, the English general who had surrendered to the colonists at Yorktown (and who was also Constable of the Tower of London). Yet for all his complaints Laurens's confinement cannot have been too arduous. He was allowed many visitors, including men sympathetic to his cause. From them he received gifts of food and comforts and he was able to see his son, currently being educated in England. On his return to America the ex-prisoner was known as 'Tower' Laurens, a nickname he took some pride in. He, in fact, wrote an account of his confinement, a document which does not show the fortress and its personnel in a very favourable light.

For most of the period 1776–1815 Britain was engaged in a warfare different from the conflict of territorial ambitions of the era dominated by Louis XIV, William III and Marlborough. It was at root a conflict of political beliefs and ideals and just as the government of Elizabeth I had regarded with alarm the potential fifth column of English Catholics, so George III's ministers feared the influence of radicals like Wilkes and Tom Paine. When discontented Luddites smashed mill machinery and when sailors at Spithead and the Nore mutinied, the aristocratic rulers of British society heard in the air the rumble

221

of the tumbrils and the rattle of the guillotine. The outbreak of the French Revolution in 1789 fired the imagination of a generation of intellectuals, as the poet Wordsworth wrote:

> Bliss was it in that dawn to be alive
> But to be young was very heaven! – Oh! times,
> In which the meagre, stale, forbidding ways
> Of custom, law and statute took at once
> The attraction of a country in Romance!
> When Reason seemed the most to assert her rights
> When most intent in making of herself
> A prime enchantress to assist the work,
> Which then was going forward in her name!
> Not favoured spots alone, but *the whole earth*,*
> The beauty wore of promise . . .

Some of these political idealists formed themselves into 'corresponding societies' which met to debate the burning issues of the day and to communicate with the French revolutionary leaders. The organizing genius behind these groups was Thomas Hardy, a London bookseller. Another prominent member was the Reverend John Horne Tooke, a strange man full of contradictions. He had been an ardent supporter of Wilkes but had subsequently fallen out with him. He was ordained but left his parish to a curate and spent all his time studying politics, philology and law. He was caught up in most of the stirring public events of the time and had something to say, in pulpit and pamphlet, about the majority of them, consistency rarely being his strong suit. During the American War of Independence he and some friends took up a collection for the relatives of the colonial martyrs, 'our beloved American fellow subjects who preferred death to slavery and were for that reason only inhumanly murdered by the king's troops.' In September 1792 the corresponding societies who now defined their aims as 'obtaining by legal and constitutional means a reform in the Commons' House of Parliament', sent a congratulatory address to the National Convention in Paris. The following year the societies held a convention in Edinburgh. This was dispersed by government order. Thomas Hardy and his colleagues determined to hold another gathering.

All this in itself was very alarming to George III and his ministers but Tooke's behaviour was even more aggravating. He decided that the cause would be helped if the government could be made to look foolish by embarking on an unsuccessful action for treason against the radicals. He, therefore, deliberately laid a false trail to deceive the authorities into believing that he was in secret communication

* Author's italics

with the French. On 16 May 1794 he was arrested and taken to the Tower. A few days later he was joined by Hardy and several of their colleagues. They were charged with high treason and the trials began in October. On 5 November the jury brought in a verdict of not guilty on Hardy and the bookseller was drawn in triumph through the cheering crowds of the City. Foolishly, the administration decided to press ahead with the charges against Tooke. All the prosecution's 'proof' collapsed, as the prisoner had intended that it should and he was acquitted.

It might have been embarrassing for the government but their vigilance was vindicated a few years later. Not all radicals were harmless. In 1798 Arthur O'Connor and a group of his friends were arrested by Bow Street Runners at Margate just as they were preparing to cross to France. They were brought to the Tower and lodged there awaiting trial as traitors. O'Connor was the editor of an Irish nationalist newspaper and his colleagues were all devotees of the cause of Irish emancipation. Their mission was to enlist the aid of French revolutionaries in setting up a similar regime in Ireland. They were taken back to Margate for their trial and one of their number, James O'Coighley, who seems to have been made a scapegoat, was sentenced to be hanged. O'Connor was acquitted of treason but as there were other charges against him he was kept in custody. However, he decided to make a run for it. Leaping out of the dock, he rushed through the crowded court room. The lights were extinguished. Fighting broke out. There was pandemonium. Only after several confused minutes was order restored and the prisoner securely handcuffed. But it became evident that some of the public had tried to help O'Connor escape. Suspicion fell primarily on Sackville Tufton, Earl of Thanet, who was known to sympathize with the captive and his cause. He was sent to the Tower as the place most befitting his rank. Tufton was the second member of his family to be held prisoner in the fortress; a seventeenth-century royalist Earl of Thanet had been confined there by Oliver Cromwell. It was almost a year before he came to trial and then he was found guilty of riot and assault. His sentence was another year in the Tower and a £1,000 fine. When he finally left in the early months of a new century he became a part of history; for he was the last peer of the realm ever to be imprisoned in the Tower of London.

The war against Napoleon became increasingly a war for survival in which invasion was a real possibility and a growing amount of the nation's resources was involved. This obviously placed great pressure on the Ordnance Office which had to expand and modernize to meet the challenge. Though the Tower had now ceased to be a major arms manufactory, the Ordnance staff there still ordered guns, powder and components from sub-contractors, carried out research and experiments into improved designs, and issued military and naval ordnance for use in current campaigns. The major workshops in the Tower were the towers along the north Inner Wall, which were used for various processes concerned with the manufacture of handguns, and St Thomas's Tower (including the watergate area beneath) which housed machinery for boring small gun barrels. Traitors' Gate had long since ceased to be used as an entrance. Throughout the eighteenth century it housed a huge water-wheel (which could also be operated by horse power) for driving the machinery in the chamber above. The machine was also used for pumping water and was part of the Tower's, woefully inadequate, fire-fighting system. The overcrowding in the fortress had become acute by the end of the century: as well as the boring machinery St Thomas's Tower included accommodation for the operator and some warders, and also the infirmary. In 1806 the water-wheel was replaced by a steam engine – the Industrial Revolution had reached the Tower.

The advent of steam and the exigencies of war led to another major change. The enormous expansion of trade in the eighteenth century brought greater pressure to bear upon the Mint. There was mounting criticism of both the quantity and quality of coins being produced and the need to modernize became obvious. The Mint officers wished to install steam-powered machines and in 1804 they approached the Tower authorities to ask whether the new boiler fires would be considered dangerous. It was the opportunity the garrison commander and the Master of the Ordnance had been waiting for. They had already re-encroached on the Irish Mint, which was now a forge for the Ordnance and they claimed that the war effort demanded that they be given all the coin makers' premises. Accordingly, the Mint and the Tower now parted company. But the former did not remove to any great distance. In fact, it remained within the Liberty, acquiring a tobacco warehouse and adjoining property on Little Tower Hill, land which had anciently belonged to Mary Graces Abbey. All this had to be demolished to make way for the New Mint, which was completed in 1810. With as much order and dignity as possible the officers moved their equipment, their staff and themselves over the next few months, though they were constantly harried by the military who were anxious to make use of the premises. The keys were formally handed over to the Constable in August 1812 by which time most of the old Mint buildings were occupied as garrison quarters and as a hospital for sick and wounded soldiers.

The Ordnance had continued to build and rebuild. In 1788 the Coldharbour office was destroyed by fire. Its replacement was a two-storey brick edifice to accommodate which the Lanthorn Tower and part of the adjoining wall were demolished. One area where the Ordnance found it easier to expand was Tower Wharf. By 1800 they already had on the quay a foundry, carpenters' and wheelwrights' workshops, a proof yard and a dung yard. There were also the warehouses of the Naval Victualling Wharf. Now an extra small arms 'manufactory' was set up to provide 50,000 guns a year for the armies fighting on the Continent.

While the war continued so did agitation for reform at home. Most movements have their lunatic fringe and there were certainly men who advocated and even practised violent measures. It was for this reason that the government had taken emergency powers including the suspension of habeas corpus and had imprisoned several people they considered dangerous. But responsible radicals were now better organized and their influence was growing. Some of them belonged to the Constitutional Association for Promoting a Reform in Parliament. A leading light of this association was the member for Boroughbridge, Sir Francis Burdett. He challenged the administration and demanded reform on every conceivable issue from corporal punishment in the army to the continuance of the war, which, he claimed, was merely an attack on the liberty of the French people. But his main concern was the reform of parliament, dominated by wealthy landowners able to buy voters and control 'pocket' boroughs. Burdett was as detested within parliament as he was popular without and the government were determined to silence him. Following the election of 1802 when Burdett was returned for Middlesex there was a great deal of chicanery which resulted in the member being deprived of his seat in 1806. The following year he was back again, this time as member for the constituency of Westminster itself.

The government were prepared to go to almost any lengths to shake off this indefatigable terrier who was snapping at their heels so persistently and this led to the farcical sequence of events which brought Burdett to the Tower in 1810. The member for Westminster published in pamphlet form a speech he had made in parliament. This, his enemies claimed, was a breach of privilege and the Speaker was induced to issue a warrant for Burdett's arrest. Burdett shut himself in his house and refused to yield. Soldiers marched to the area. So did a pro-Burdett mob. Neither side could back down now. The troops were ordered to force their way in and execute the warrant. Burdett was taken and marched under a guard several thousand strong to the Tower. Even these precautions only just prevented a conflict with a large mob which had gathered on Tower Hill. When Burdett's escort left the castle to return to the barracks there was, in fact, a clash and several people were killed. He stayed there without any further action being taken against him for several weeks until parliament was prorogued and the warrant lapsed. His radical friends had devised a triumphant procession for him through the City but Burdett, presumably deeming it unwise to risk provoking mob violence, left the fortress quietly by water and his supporters, when they later arrived to collect him, were made to look rather foolish. Sir Francis still had a long parliamentary career before him and lived to see the accomplishment of much that he had fought for in the Reform Act of 1832.

The Tower also had its 'revolutionaries' as an event in 1796 indicates. On 18 January the royal standard was flown from the White Tower in honour of Queen Charlotte's birthday. Suddenly, onlookers realized that another flag was flying beside it; the tricolour of Jacobin France. When the Major of the Tower, Matthew Smith, was informed he stormed in person to the top of the keep to haul the offending pennant down. He emerged breathless onto the roof only to find that the flag was gone. Minutes later it appeared again, waving from another part of the Tower. Arrived at that spot, the Major again missed the culprit. This cat and mouse game went on for some time until the offending flag was finally run to earth, stuffed under the bed of the deputy-chaplain's fifteen-year-old son.

At about this time there was considerable improvement in the appearance of the Tower's environs. For decades, centuries even, Tower Hill and adjacent areas had been untidy open spaces encroached upon by buildings and yards in a piecemeal fashion. Early nineteenth-century prints, however, reveal pleasant grassed areas fringed by trees, elegant buildings, walls and hedges, traversed by paved ways and lit by street lamps. The transformation began with an Act of 1797, whose preamble stated:

> . . . Great Tower Hill, lying partly within the county of Middlesex and partly within the City of London, is and for some time past hath been, in a neglected state and the roads and ways over the same are very inconvenient and in bad condition, and it would be to the benefit and advantage of the owners, leasees and occupiers of the houses and buildings in or near the said Hill and to all persons having occasion to resort to His Majesty's Tower and Ordnance, and all persons resident in the Tower and to the public in general if the said Hill were properly paved, lighted, watched, cleansed, watered, improved and kept in repair and all nuisances and annoyances within the same removed and prevented.

The Act made provision for 'walls, railings, gates, lamp irons, grass plots, walks and other ornaments' and their maintenance out of public funds.

With the end of the Napoleonic Wars in 1815 popular unrest and agitation for reform at home increased. The conflict had stimulated industrial activity and peace brought an inevitable slump. The ranks of the unemployed were swelled by discharged soldiers and seamen as well as craftsmen displaced by the new machines. In many towns there were public meetings and minor riots. Agitators like Henry Hunt and William Cobbett were popular with the crowds. The former attended meetings with an escort carrying the tricolour and wearing revolutionary caps. After one such gathering in Spa Fields a section of the mob broke away and raised the cry 'To the Tower', doubtless thinking to emulate the storming of the Bastille. They approached the fortress brandishing flags and weapons but the garrison soldiers simply laughed at them and the mob dispersed in smaller riotous bands.

But there was little to laugh at in the situation. Meetings were proliferating. An army of petitioners marched from Manchester to London. On numerous occasions troops had to be called out. People were killed. Someone threw a stone at the Prince Regent as he drove to Westminster. There were rumours of plots to seize the Tower and the Bank of England. The government decided on firm action. An embargo was placed on meetings. Habeas corpus was suspended again. *Agents provocateurs* were widely used and political activists were arrested. Among the latter was Arthur Thistlewood, a London agitator who tried to escape to America but was arrested on board his ship before it sailed. He and four colleagues were lodged in the Tower to await trial on treason charges. In the event they were acquitted, apparently because the government preferred a show of leniency to the making of popular martyrs. Clemency was wasted on fanatics like Thistlewood. Despite the fact that his schemes had once already been betrayed by paid informers, he returned to them. He now devised a plan to murder the Cabinet and seize control of the City. In 1820, he and his confederates were arrested in their headquarters in Cato Street (off the Edgware Road). Back went Thistlewood to the Tower with seven of his companions. The leader was lodged in the Bloody Tower and the others in the Byward, Middle, Salt and St Thomas's towers. From these apartments Thistlewood and four of his associates were taken to Tyburn to be hanged on 1 May. The leader died unrepentant: 'Albion is still in the chains of slavery. I quit it without regret. My only sorrow is that the soil should be a theatre for slaves, for cowards, for despots.' They were noble, if mistaken words and they virtually close the story of the Tower of London as a state prison. It would be almost a hundred years before another prominent traitor would be lodged within its walls and a hundred and twenty-one years before the last prisoner of all came to the Tower.

Peace, prosperity and commercial expansion settled on the land, and the Tower of London had to keep pace with the changing times. After the war the Tower Wharf small arms workshop was dismantled and all Ordnance manufacture henceforth took place in other depots. As its military and prison functions diminished people were able to take more interest in it as a unique historical monument. Even as the Cato Street conspirators were hatching their diabolical plot, John Bayley, a gentleman of the Inner Temple and a sub-commissioner on the pubic records, was completing the first account of the building's long, eventful history. His *History and Antiquities of the Tower of London* (1821–5) contained in two large volumes the fruit of years of painstaking research in pubic archives. More thought was taken to attract visitors. The displays of arms and armour were changed and new buildings erected to house them. The storehouses along the south front of the White Tower were pulled down and replaced by the New Horse Armoury, a Gothic edifice constructed in the conviction that new buildings in the Tower should imitate the predominant medieval style of the rest of the complex. The Line of Kings was still exhibited but was completely redesigned and, though more historically accurate, became less spectacular. The Spanish Armoury disappeared when the Coldharbour storehouses running northwards from the Wakefield Tower were completely rebuilt in the 1820s. The new display, on the first floor, was designated Queen Elizabeth's Armoury and was, again, more accurately catalogued. Also on view were trophies from the battles of Blenheim and Waterloo as well as such strangely out-of-place curiosities as a wooden diving bell used by Sicilian coral hunters. The popularity of the exhibition is proved by the numbers of people who paid (6d. a head in 1840) to see it. Between 1837 and 1841 annual attendance increased from 11,104 to 95,231.

The stocking and facilities of the menagerie were also improved at this time. The royal collection of exotic animals passed through many vicissitudes over the years. In the mid-eighteenth century it included several lions (some bred in the Tower), tigers, leopards, panthers, lynxes, monkeys, an ostrich, bears, eagles and vultures. In the 1790s an Indian elephant was presented by one of Britain's client princes, the Nabob of Arcot and in 1804 there was a polar bear in the menagerie. The collection seems to have been rather neglected during the war. In 1822 a new keeper, Alfred Cops, was appointed and within seven years he had so transformed the menagerie that the official guide could boast:

> . . . the empty dens have been filled and new ones have been constructed; and the whole of them being now constantly tenanted, the menagerie affords a really interesting and attractive spectacle to the numerous visitors who are drawn thither either from motives of curiosity of by a love of science.

The guide listed fifty-eight species of mammals, birds and reptiles.

In 1826 an event of considerable importance occurred: Arthur Wellesley, Duke of Wellington, was appointed Constable of the Tower. The hero of Waterloo was the most popular and influential man in England and it was appropriate that he should be given an honour traditionally reserved for prominent servants of the crown. He was not the sort of man to regard his new office as a largely ceremonial one and he was destined to make more changes to the Tower of London than most of his predecessors. Wellington brought to the problems of the Tower in a changing world the clear mind of a brilliant military strategist. One of his first tasks was to regulate the system of recruiting and remunerating Yeoman Warders. He swept away the last vestiges of patronage and the confusion over terms of service. The Tower staff in future were to be recruited from senior army non-commissioned officers and paid a fixed salary. In 1843 the Tower became a more salubrious if less picturesque place when the Constable ordered the unsanitary moat to be drained. After levelling and turfing it became the garrison parade ground.

Wellington called a halt to the unplanned expansion of the various departments which had their homes within the Tower. When in 1846 the Keeper of the Records sought permission to house some of his documents in the Bloody Tower the Duke refused to relinquish useful prison quarters or to dismantle the machinery of one of the few remaining medieval portcullises in working order. The same commonsense approach had already been brought to bear on the problems of the menagerie. This was doomed by its own success. Cops's excellent collection of animals was straining the existing accommodation and there was nowhere within the Tower complex for it to expand. Wellington, who regarded the fortress as possessing a dual, military/museum function, decided that the menagerie must go. The King (William IV) granted permission in 1831 but there was considerable opposition from the Keeper and the Major and it was not until 1835 that the Constable issued the peremptory order, 'The King is determined that wild beasts shall not be kept there'. The collection was dispersed, some animals going to the recently-established London Zoological Society Gardens in fashionable Regent's Park. The cages were sold and the Lion Barbican was taken over by the Ordnance Office. What became of the devoted Alfred Cops we do not know. The ordnance was made necessary by the decision to open the White Tower to the public. As more and more visitors came to the fortress it grew obvious that there was an interest in the oldest part of the Tower. Queen Elizabeth's Armoury was, accordingly, moved to the crypt of St John's Chapel in 1837, displacing the Ordnance equipment which had been stored there. 1837 was, of course, important for a very different reason: it was the year which saw the accession of Queen Victoria.

Early in the reign there occurred one of the greatest tragedies in the architectural history of the Tower. About ten o'clock on the night of 30 October 1841 a fire broke out in the Bowyer Tower, caused probably by the overheating of a stove flue. The alarm was given quite quickly and soon the Major of the Tower, Major Elrington, had the garrison troops out and manning the castle's nine hand-operated fire engines. The machines proved almost totally useless, there being only enough water available to keep one of them going. The Bowyer Tower was by now engulfed in flames. Crowds were gathering on Tower Hill, and the Major gave orders that no one whatsoever was to be admitted to the fortress. He also sent for assistance from the London Fire Engine Establishment. Unfortunately, the order and the appeal created some confusion at the main gate, as the *Punch* reporter scathingly recorded:

In the first place, by way of ensuring the safety of the property, precautions were taken to shut out everyone from the building; and as military rule knows no exceptions, the orders given were executed to the letter by preventing the ingress of the firemen with their countermand. This of course took time, leaving the fire to devour at its leisure the enormous meal that fate had prepared for it.

The Bowyer Tower was by now lost and sparks had started smaller fires on the roof of the Grand Storehouse. All efforts were now concentrated on saving this splendid building with its irreplaceable collection of ancient and modern weapons. Soldiers and firemen played their hoses onto the roof from without and within the building but nineteenth-century fire engines simply could not build up sufficient pressure to throw water far enough or with sufficient force. For half and hour or more gangs of soldiers rushed in and out of the building carrying, dragging and pushing valuable pieces to safety. At 11.20 the entire roof collapsed. Within minutes the Grand Storehouse was ablaze from end to end. Thousands of spectators had now converged on Tower Hill to watch the conflagration with horrified fascination. One observer recorded:

So intense was the heat sent forth that the multitude could scarcely remain even outside the moat, and many sank from exhaustion and pressure; the cracking of the yielding timbers was distinctly audible even on the Surrey side of the River Thames. It was a majestic sight and many around us observed, 'I shall not forget this fire even on my death-bed'.

Now there was very real fear that sparks and the intense heat would engender fresh outbreaks. Groping pinnacles of flame were reaching high into the night sky and arching over other buildings as the wind caught them. The most urgent task was to have all ammunition removed from its storehouse in the keep, then Major Elrington sent troops to the top of the White Tower to douse or remove falling debris and to cover the sky lights with dampened blankets. He ordered fire engines to play their hoses over the walls. Even those measures could not prevent wooden window frames bursting into flame and lead drain pipes melting. The next object of major concern was the royal regalia in the Martin Tower. Here again elaborate security measures hampered the work of rescue, for, though the Keeper of the Jewel House had the keys to the chamber, those to the display cases themselves were held by the Lord Chamberlain. Precious time was lost searching for crowbars. Then a group of strong guardsmen applied themselves to prising the bars wide enough apart for a man to slip through and begin handing out the Crown Jewels. By now the heat within the chamber was intense and the safety of the regalia was only ensured by a brave policeman who refused to leave until he had passed almost every item through the bars. Only a silver font proved too large to rescue. When the policeman at last hurried from the Martin Tower his clothes were smouldering but the regalia were safe and under guard in the Queen's House.

By this time there was little anyone could do but watch the blaze burn itself out. Firemen and troops continued to play their hoses on the Chapel, White Tower and Martin Tower. Policemen and warders at the gate assured clamouring relatives that all the castle residents were safe. Indeed, the only good news concerning the whole sad incident was that, with one exception, no one sustained serious injury. The exception was Richard Wivel, a fireman, killed instantly when a piece of dislodged coping stone fell on him.

By dawn the flames had died down and the Grand Storehouse, at whose birth 150 years before William and Mary had been so sumptuously entertained, was no more than a hollow brick shell. A couple of days later when the embers had cooled sufficiently to permit inspection the extent of the loss could be assessed. Some cannon and larger iron pieces had, incredibly, survived the immense heat. Others were consumed entirely, damaged beyond repair or fused with their neighbours into twisted, ungainly pieces of impromptu sculpture. One impressed observer described the scene with a verbal exuberance typical of the age: 'Above was the sky of a November morn, and below, covering the immense sweep of the floor, heaps of fused metal, of dimensions scarce to be credited, with bayonet points bristling up everywhere, close-set and countless, like long blades of grass.'[2] The 280,000 stands of arms and other contemporary ordnance destroyed could be valued: they were said to have been worth £250,000. But no price could be put upon the many unique historical pieces that had been lost.

Almost immediately the government was inviting architects to submit plans for a new building. But it was to be a barracks and not an ordnance storehouse. The fire had dealt the death blow to the Tower of London as the nation's principal weapons store. Most of the functions of the Board of Ordnance were now performed in other depots. In 1845 Ordnance clerks ceased to reside in the Tower (the major officers had long since departed). In 1855 the Board of Ordnance was abolished and its functions taken over by the War Office. In 1904 the last connection between the ordnance and museum functions of the Tower was broken when responsibility for the Armouries was handed over to the Office of Works (and more recently to the Department of the Environment).

I O

The dominant theme in the history of the Tower over the last hundred years or so has been the changes attendant on making the fortress what it is today, Britain's principal tourist attraction. The millions of visitors who walk around the castle every year are confronted by what seems at first sight to be a complex of medieval buildings. This is, of course, not the case but that it should appear to be so is largely due to those people so warmly applauded in some circles and so roundly execrated in others – the Victorian restorers.

The man responsible for the early stages of the work was Anthony Salvin. By 1840 this London architect had established a reputation as one of the foremost exponents of building in the Gothic taste. He had recently submitted designs for the new Westminster Palace and had been chagrined when the commission went to his rival Charles Barry (assisted by the more famous Augustus Pugin). But parliament's loss was the Tower's gain; Salvin's plan for the new Waterloo Barracks was accepted and in 1845, the Iron Duke himself opened the crenelated Gothic structure which remains to this day. At the same time the towers along the nearby Inner Wall had to be repaired. The Bowyer Tower was completely rebuilt while the Brick and Martin Towers required extensive restoration. (The present Flint Tower dates from 1796 when it was built to replace its dilapidated predecessor, the building which had probably housed the Tower's most notorious prison quarters.) These structures were largely rebuilt to the original pattern. The restoration work of the upper part of the Salt Tower in 1876 was also Salvin's work. In 1850 the Lion Barbican, no longer required by the Ordnance, was demolished.

But, by then, a new structure had appeared. It was the North Bastion, an artillery mount at the apex of the Outer Wall and it was the last defensive work to be constructed. It was erected in the 1840s at the time of the Chartist agitation. The earlier political and social discontent had brought about the Reform Act but this had not fully satisfied radical aspirations. The early Victorian era saw the struggles of the first trade unions symbolized by the Tolpuddle Martyrs. It also saw the agitation of the Chartists. In 1839 the Convention of the Industrious Classes was founded and a nationwide campaign launched to persuade parliament to approve a new political and constitutional charter. The six points of the charter were: annual parliaments; universal male suffrage (some Chartists wanted votes for women to be included but the majority decided that such an absurd demand would be to invite ridicule of the entire charter); equal electoral districts; the removal of the property qualification for members of parliament; secret ballot; and payment of members of parliament. The campaigners collected hundreds of thousands of signatures on their petition and presented it more than once at Westminster but such advanced ideas stood no chance of acceptance by the party political establishment with its vested interests in the *status quo*. It was then that the extreme wing of the movement began to talk in terms of *forcing* the charter on parliament. They held their own musters and trained their supporters in pike drill. The charter became a rallying cry for malcontents, unemployed, fanatics and desperadoes. There were sporadic outbreaks of violence. The Duke of Wellington was sufficiently alarmed to order dramatic demonstrations of artillery fire in potential trouble spots to drive home the inadvisability of rebellion. And at the Tower he had the North Bastion constructed so that Tower Hill, one of the obvious assembly points for any rebel army, could be more effectively dominated.

On a more peaceful note it was Albert, the Prince Consort, who was the prime mover behind the restoration of St John's Chapel. Before 1857 the simple splendours of this Romanesque house of God could only be guessed at. It had suffered three hundred years of neglect and, as well as some of the Records, held the accumulated lumber of generations. It was at the specific request of Victoria's husband that the Deputy-Lieutenant, Lord de Ros, had the chapel cleaned and fitted out once more as a place of worship with a simple dignity, pleasantly at contrast with the usual Victorian love of fussy detail. Lord de Ros was the last man to occupy the office of Deputy-Lieutenant. On his death in 1874 he was not replaced. The Major of the Tower, Colonel Sir Bryan Millman, was given a new designation: Major and Resident Governor of the Tower of London. This is still the official title of the senior officer in residence. Thus, after two hundred years, the division of functions between the senior prison officer and the senior military officer was abolished and the Tower once more came under the control of one man. The offices of Constable and Lieutenant, traditionally bestowed upon top-ranking military officers, were, of course, retained.

It was Lord de Ros who showed a serious concern for the restoration of the Tower's other place of worship. Over the centuries since Henry VIII's rebuilding the Chapel of St Peter ad Vincula had seen many changes. There were seventeenth-century box pews such as Samuel Pepys had sat in:

The Lieutenant of the Tower, Sir J. Robinson, would needs have me by coach home with him; where the officers of his regiment dined with him. I did go and dine with him, his ordinary table being very good, and his lady a very high-carriaged, but comely-big woman. I was mightily pleased with her. After dinner to chapel in the Tower with the Lieutenant, with the keys carried before us, and the warders and gentleman porter going before us; and I sat with the Lieutenant in his pew in great state. None it seems of the prisoners in the Tower that are there now, though they may, will come to prayers there.[1]

There was a gallery introduced in the time of George II. There was a massive Restoration reredos obscuring most of the east window. The walls had been whitewashed to obscure 'superstitious' paintings. The roof timbers of Spanish chestnut had been plastered over. An Elizabethan south porch had been added. The original west door had been bricked up. And a large triple-decker pulpit obscured part of the sanctuary. Earlier in the century the great historian, Lord Macaulay, had affirmed with characteristic bluntness, 'I cannot refrain from expressing my disgust at the barbarous stupidity which has transformed this most interesting little church into the likeness of a meetinghouse in a manufacturing town'.[2] The Deputy-Lieutenant set about recovering some of the chapel's ancient glories. Henry VIII's ceiling timbers were once more exposed. The porch was removed and the older entrance re-opened. The principal consultant for all this work was the indefatigable Salvin, now quite an old man. Admirable though de Ros's achievements were, it was felt that a much more drastic overhaul was required. Apart from anything else, the paving had become cracked and uneven due, no doubt, to the many, often hasty burials that had occurred there. It is Macaulay, in a celebrated passage, who reminds us of some of those dishonoured dead.

In truth there is no sadder spot on the earth than that little cemetery. Death is there associated, not, as in Westminster Abbey and Saint Paul's, with genius and virtue, with public veneration and imperishable renown; not, as in our humblest churches and churchyards, with everything that is most endearing in social and domestic charities; but with whatever is darkness in human nature and in human destiny, with the savage triumph of implacable enemies, with the inconstancy, the ingratitude, the cowardice of friends, with all the miseries of alien greatness and of blighted fame. Thither have been carried, through successive ages, by the rude hands of gaolers, without one mourner following, the bleeding relics of men who had been the captains of armies, the leaders of parties, the oracles of senates, and the ornaments of courts. Thither was borne, before the window where Jane Grey was praying, the mangled corpse of Guildford Dudley. Edward Seymour, Duke of Somerset, and Protector of the realm, reposes there by the brother whom he murdered. There has mouldered away the headless trunk of John Fisher, Bishop of Rochester and Cardinal of Saint Vitalis, a man worthy to have lived in a better age, and to have died in a better cause. There are laid John Dudley, Duke of Northumberland, Lord High Admiral, and Thomas Cromwell, Earl of Essex, Lord High Treasurer. There, too, is another Essex, on whom nature and fortune had lavished all their bounties in vain, and whom valour, grace, genius, royal favour, popular applause, conducted to an early an ignominious doom. Not far off sleep two chiefs of the great house of Howard, Thomas, fourth Duke of Norfolk, and Philip, eleventh Earl of Arundel. Here and there, among the thick graves of unquiet and aspiring statesmen, lie more delicate sufferers: Margaret of Salisbury, the last of the proud name of Plantagenet, and those two fair Queens who perished by the jealous rage of Henry.[3]

In 1876 it was decided to restore the chapel to what the Victorians conceived to be its original Tudor state. The cumberstone box pews, pulpit and reredos vanished, to be replaced by less obtrusive furnishings and the number of memorial plaques was reduced. But the real problem was the floor, or more accurately what lay beneath it.

On removing the stones of the pavement it was found . . . that the resting places of those who had been buried within the walls of the chapel during the troublous times of the sixteenth and seventeenth centuries, had been repeatedly and it was feared almost universally desecrated.

When the Tower ceased to be a residence of the sovereign or a state prison, the chapel of St Peter appears to have gradually come to be regarded much in the light of a mere ordinary parish church, in which the interment not only of those who had lived in the Tower, but even of residents in the neighbourhood, was freely permitted.

It is true that the bodies of those who had perished on the scaffold, or died as prisoners within the walls of the Tower, were buried (no doubt intentionally) 'in great obscurity', but even if some memorial stone had recorded their burial place, it is doubtful whether that would have protected their remains, for in the instance of the three Scotch lords (Lovat, Balmerino and Kilmarnock) although their grave was specially marked by a stone, which is still preserved, it was found that their bones had been much disturbed, so much so indeed as to be beyond all possible means of identification. It is even feared that in some instances coffins had been designedly broken up and their contents scattered in order to make room for some fresh occupant of the ground.

Many of the more recent interments were barely two feet below the surface, and in no instances were any graves found lower than five or six feet.[4]

The Tower's gruesome past may be said to have caught up with it.

If the floor was to be properly re-laid and the required heating system installed the remains would have to be cleared. Queen Victoria's permission was sought for this excavation. Her Majesty gave her approval but only on the condition that the disturbed bones were treated with the utmost respect and every attempt made to re-inter each parcel of remains as complete and undisturbed as possible. So began a macabre jigsaw puzzle as the scattered remnants of long-decayed cadavers were scrabbled together and laid in boxes to await re-committal. When the chancel was excavated, among the bones of the many notable persons buried in this favoured spot those of Anne Boleyn (whose neck was, indeed, discovered to be 'little', as she had commented before she went to the scaffold), Seymour and Dudley were readily identified but of that other poor queen, Catherine Howard, there was no trace and it was assumed that they had already disintegrated, perhaps as a result of quicklime being used at the inter-ment. With the exception of the more notable bodies, most of the remainder were placed in the crypt to the north of the chapel. The building was re-opened for worship in June 1877.

By that time the Tower had been stripped of yet another of its ancient functions. Generations of Keepers of the Records had strug-gled valiantly to maintain in order a steadily mounting collection of ancient documents. The upper floor of the Wakefield Tower had to be supported by a post in the chamber below to enable it to take the weight of the chests, and presses full of papers and parchments. Among the more industrious of the Keepers was Samuel Lysons who held office from 1804 to his death in 1819. He catalogued and preserved, according to John Bayley, 'a vast collection of royal letters, state papers, and parliamentary and other documents of the highest value and importance.' He obtained more space in the White Tower for the Records and began a calendar of Chancery proceedings. In addition he produced a number of detailed books enshrining the results of his own research on historical and archaeological matters and found time to encourage such other scholars as Bayley. The Tower of London was only one repository of state documents. Many more were housed at Westminster while others had found their way into private collections. In the nineteenth century very considerable concern was displayed by both scholars and statesmen not only for the better organization and cataloguing of these muniments but also for their accessibility to researchers and the public in general.

The years of peace saw the visitors and the old routine return. The bed of the moat was once again grassed over and the old allotments disappeared. A further restoration of St Peter's Chapel gave the inside of the building a simpler, lighter look. Victorian varnish was removed from the ceiling timbers, the pitch pine pews were replaced by chairs of a more open design, a dignified memorial to Sir Thomas More was built and other fittings of a modern vogue were installed.

The most momentous change that has come over the Tower in recent decades is the enormous growth in the number of visitors it receives. Tourists from all over the world have passed through its gates and listened to the entertaining commentaries of the Yeomen Warders as they outlined the more dramatic events of the building's history, each putting his own individual gloss on the narrative of facts, gruesome and heroic. By the last years of the millennium the annual count of visitors has passed three million, making the Conqueror's fortress by far the most popular tourist attraction in Britain. The building's income well surpasses the cost of its upkeep and provides the Historic Royal Palaces Agency with funds to expend on other properties in their care.

It may well be in the fullness of time that of all the functions this remarkable complex has performed that of heritage museum may turn out to be its most successful. In this age of theme parks and sophisticated multi-media presentations the question of how best to tell the Tower's story to visitors is constantly being addressed. Permanent and temporary exhibitions have been designed for various locations within the walls. Models, dioramas, televised displays and animations are among the techniques used to present information entertainingly without falling into the trap of vulgarity. And, of course, other visitor needs must be met – cafés, toilets, souvenir shops – without encroaching on the time-hallowed buildings or their atmosphere. The logistics of making the most of such a sensitive site are daunting.

Probably the most notable attraction – certainly in terms of visitor numbers – is the Crown Jewels gallery purpose-built for both spectacle and security in the old Waterloo Barracks. The removal of the regalia enabled a long overdue restoration of the Wakefield Tower to be carried out in the 1970s. This building, after its chameleon centuries, has now returned almost exactly to the appearance it had when it was first built, c.1230. The nearby St Thomas's Tower has also been the subject of careful renovation based on the latest research into the possible layout of the medieval Royal Lodgings. Visitors can now obtain, with the aid of costumed guides and well-mounted exhibits, some idea of how the King's apartments may have appeared in the time of Edward I. After several decades the Royal Armouries' extensive exhibition of arms and armour has been removed from the White Tower, following the decision of the agency to locate their headquarters in Leeds. By 2000 it will have been replaced by selective displays more relevant to the building's history which will give the tower a more open internal aspect and allow visitors to understand more readily the building's architecture. The most enthralling prospect for the early years of the second millennium is that of re-flooding the moat. Were that project to go ahead it would be possible to see again Edward III's formidable bastion as it appeared to would-be assailants in the fourteenth century.

Mention of the moat project brings us to the continual archaeological research being carried out at the Tower. It might be supposed that the generations of scholars who have probed every nook and cranny of these ancient buildings have left little still to be discovered. Not so. The Tower has many well-guarded secrets for experts equipped with ever-improving technology to prise from it. The flood scheme, for example, is associated with a long-term archaeological project undertaken by the Oxford Archaeological Unit on behalf of the Historic Royal Palaces Agency. The objectives are to discover exactly what is lurking beneath the turf of the moat and whether significant structural remains could be preserved intact if the moat were to be refilled with water. The discoveries made during the early stages of exploration were sensational. On the conjectured site of Henry III's impressive western gateway (the one chroniclers gleefully described as collapsing in 1240) the archaeologists found a masonry structure faced in expensive Purbeck marble. The foundation had tilted so badly that an attempt had been made to shore it up with beech piles. By using dendrochronology it was possible to date these trees precisely. The verdict? 1240. Other intriguing discoveries were a wickerwork Tudor fish trap and the remains of a tide-driven flour mill. Such mills were known to have existed in medieval times. Now the proof was found. It seems that these structures never lasted very long. Thanks to the notorious unreliability of the tides they soon became silted up.

When the large display cases full of arms and armour were removed from the White Tower in the mid-nineties archaeologists could obtain access to parts of the building which had been inaccessible for years. Among the intriguing discoveries they made was some lead guttering dating from the earliest days of the keep beneath the galleries running around the top of the walls of what are known as the King's Hall and the King's Chamber. This suggested – to some experts, at least – that what had always been regarded as a clerestory looking down into the building was, originally, an external passage-way outside a roof pitched lower than the one in place today and that it was there for external defence. This and related revelations have opened up a debate about the original purpose of William the Conqueror's castle. Was it ever seriously intended as a royal residence? There is no evidence of the building providing the degree of comfort a king would expect. Were its high external walls, rising above the original roof level, designed to make the structure appear larger and more formidable than, in fact, it was? Can it ever had held a garrison sufficiently large to repel a serious assault? Can this building still be considered the prototype Norman castle, an effective military edifice with offensive and defensive capabilities? May it not, rather, have been a piece of aggressive showmanship, a permanent symbol of royal power, used by kings only on ceremonial or emergency occasions?

The fact that such issues can be raised and the very origins of the Tower of London can be open to reinterpretation serves to remind us that history is not a closed book. It is a story that must be re-read and re-evaluated in every age. We must not allow ourselves to be duped by the Tower's massiveness and venerability into believing that the last word has been said about it. Any account of this structure which has dominated the eastern approach to London for the greater part of a millennium is open to challenge and question. That is certainly true of this book.

Some readers may well be dissatisfied with my account. They may reject some points of interpretation or take me to task for neglecting some worthy hero or accuse me of dealing scantily with some significant event. It is no mere sheltering behind rhetoric if I respond 'How does one write the history of a legend!' For the Tower of London is not the stones and mortar of which it is constructed nor the men and women whose destinies have been bound up with the castle. It is a part and an important part of our national life and culture. It is a vital ingredient of what we and most of our overseas friends think of as 'England'.

Nor is the Tower unique only in terms of national history. No country can boast an older royal palace. Moscow's Kremlin and the Palazzo of the Venetian doges were built at the time of King Henry III. The oldest corner of the Vatican is the work of the Borgias and when England fought its civil war Versailles was still a swamp. As a citadel and gaol the 'bloody prison, fatal and ominous to noble peers'[6] is ante-dated among surviving buildings only by the Castel Sant' Angelo in Rome. The Bastille has gone. Florence's Bargello belongs to the fourteenth century and Spandau, the great castle of the Hohenzollerns, was not fortified until the time of the first Elizabeth.

The treasures of the Escorial near Madrid and the Seraglio in Istanbul are impressive but can scarcely rival the splendours of the Crown Jewels. Stronghold, palace, prison and treasure-house – the Tower of London has been all of these and much else besides. It has, therefore, seen more of magnificence and misery, heroism and hatred, despair and defiance than probably any other single spot on earth. As we enter a new millennium it provides a very tangible link with the one that is passing. But it moves with us into the future, ready, as ever, to adapt itself and serve the centuries ahead in whatever ways the nation may require.

APPENDIX 1

A CHRONICLER MORALISES ABOUT THE COLLAPSE OF HENRY III'S GATEWAY
1253

Matthew Paris, *Chronica Majora*, Corpus Christi, Cambridge, MS16, 143, recto.

Round about that time, a certain wise and godly priest had a vision by night, in which an Archbishop, dressed in all his finery, and brandishing a cross in his hand, appeared at the wall which the King had recently built around the Tower of London. His face shining with anger, he struck the wall hard with the cross in his right hand and cried out, 'Tell me for what purpose you are now being re-built'. Suddenly, the walls came tumbling down, though newly-built, as if they had been struck by an earthquake. At this, the vision of another priest appeared behind the Archbishop. When he saw this, our priest asked it, 'Who is this archbishop?' The vision replied 'This is the Blessed Martyr Thomas, a Londoner by birth, who has seen all these things now being done to harm the people of his city: he has therefore destroyed them irreparably'. Our priest cried 'But how costly and wonderfully-made were those walls!' The vision answered him 'the poor hungry workmen deserve to be paid and fed, that is fair, but these works were made not for the defence of the kingdom, but to harm innocent citizens and if the blessed Thomas had not destroyed them, the holy confessor Aedmund, his successor, would have taken up the task even more violently.' Our priest awoke suddenly from his sleep, rose from his bed and although still in the silent hours of the middle of the night, told all those in his house what he had seen. In the morning, the rumour of this went round the whole city of London, that the walls around the Tower, on which the King had spent more than 12,000 marks, had fallen down irreparably: it was as if they had been forewarned of this by some evil omen, since exactly a year before, namely on the evening of the feast of St George, the same walls had collapsed together with the Towers built onto them. The citizens kept quiet about this, but were not a bit sorry! The walls had been like a thorn in their eye: they had heard an old wives' tale that the buildings had been constructed to their harm, so that if anyone should dare to stand up for the rights of the city, he could be thrown into prison by the justices. Many cells could be seen in the new buildings for the imprisonment of a large number, in such a way that none of them could speak with another.

APPENDIX 2

A DECLARATION OF THE STATE OF THE TOWER OF LONDON, 1598

Bodleian Library Western MSS Eng Hist. e. 195

A declaration of the state of the Tower of London at such time as it please your Majesty to command me (your Highness's most humble, loyal and devoted servant) unto the service of the same, under the guard whereof there is contained, as followeth

First, your Majesty's royal stores of ammunition for war, with the dangerous charge of your Highness's magazine of powder.
Secondly, your Majesty's rich treasure, of jewels, plate and furnitures.
Thirdly, your Highness's records.
Fourthly, the prisoners for causes of State.

The place itself, under the guard whereof these your royal stores, with treasures contained under the charge and conduct of the Captain and Lieutenant whose office and duty (by precedent of former times), seemeth to consist of these parts, viz Military, Justiciary, Politique.

The Military part consisteth in judicial discerning the state of the place, how it standeth, seated, guarded and munited for defence and in what sort weakened by decays, disorders or deserts and what may be added for the better safety of the same:
To govern and command the guard and such others as by your Majesty shall be appointed in their assistance for the better strengthening of your service in this place, under and martial and civil rule of discipline and obedience.
And finally to manage and dispose all things appertaining unto the safety and defence of this your Highness's royal castle in such sort as may best stand with the security thereof.

The Justiciary part is civilly to govern and retain in good correspondence of obedience and peace as well the officers and warders appointed for the guard of the place as also all other persons residing within the liberties of this government.

To restrain and punish all insolencies, violencies and disorders of which are now in this latter contentious and disobedient age exceedingly multiplied. Small offence suffered in this place may suddenly prove great dangers and therefore necessary to be quenched and suppressed in the smoke before they come to the fury of flame.

The reforming power and justiciary authority of the Lieutenant in such cases is by discontinuance grown doubtful, which may in some sort prove inconvenient.

The Politique part is to discern and apprehend the sufficiency, dilligency, duty and loyal obedience of all officers and other persons appertaining to the place, or residing within this charge or the liberties thereof.
To hold good correspondence in all your Highness's service with all the said officers and other persons and also with the confining liberties of the City of London.
And finally to discover the nature, disposition, policy, dependency and practice of all such as shall be (for causes of offence against your Highness's person or state) detained under bands of restraint.

These, most Gracious Sovereign (being necessary and dependent duties to be expected from him unto whom your Highness shall commit the charge of so high a trust, being in these practising and conspiring times of more importance than ever), do enforce me out of the true discovery of mine own imperfections, most humbly to confess that this place requireth a person of far better parts and judgment than standeth with my ability to perform. Notwithstanding to supply some part of my wants, I will add a loyal duty and diligent endeavour without any dependency, end, or other respects, but only upon your sacred person and to do your Majesty all faithful and loyal service.

Differences necessary to be decided

Imprimis. The City of London did and doth pretend title unto your Majesty's soil of Tower Hill and East Smithfield even unto the ditch of the Tower and also unto divers houses at the Postern gate and at the Bulwark, the possession whereof hath always been in your Majesty.

To admit of this their challenge were dangerous and inconvenient unto the safety of the place by colour whereof the citizens of London should have power to make their muster even at the Tower ditch, and also their disordered multitude of artificers, journeymen and prentices by whose insolencies in former times offence unto the peace of the State heth been often offered, might at their pleasure assemble upon the counterscarp of the ditch, from whence they may pass with little impeachment to the walls of the Tower, the ditch being at this present in main parts decayed and passable, and the wall in the same place easy to be mounted.

All manner of assemblies near the counterscarp of any castle or citadel are by policy and martial discipline utterly restrained, and therefore of purpose before all such Royal defences a spacious Place of View is ever left plain and unbuilded, to the entend the captain and guard that have charge of the same might better discern any approach or attempt intended, and from the which place (in dangerous times) all concourse and trooping of people are to be inhibited.

If your Highness should suffer this pretended intrusion and encroachment upon the ancient Liberties of your Majesty's Castle Royal, then followeth this inconvenience, that if your Majesty in your princely providence and wisdom, for the better defence and safety of this place, (your Majesty's magazines of ammunitions and treasures herein remaining, being of high and inestimable consequence), shall determine to make any royal or perfect fortification, the sole and only advantage for that purpose shall be by colour and pretext of the City's right withdrawn and detracted.

For deciding of this ancient and inconvenient controversy touching the Tower Liberties and privileges, your Majesty hath granted a commission to the judges unto whom I have delivered apparent proofs for your Highness's title, upon whose report your Majesty's princely pleasure touching this question (of your Highness's right and prerogative royal) being signified, will be a means of union and good correspondence to be held (in all your Highness's services) betwixt the City and those unto whose trust your Highness shall commit the charge of this place.

There is also of late some difference between the Lieutenant and the Mr Porter touching the jurisdiction and ordering of the wharf, in which the Gentleman Porter intrudeth upon the authority of the Lieutenant, confounding hereby the jurisdiction of place and duty of office.
The wharf being a special part of the fortification of the Tower, the order and jurisdiction thereof (as in all defensive places of like nature) doth belong unto the commander of the place, no other officer being therein interested further, then to execute such a direction as for your

246

Majesty's service shall be commanded, the which is also proved by your Majesty's Records.

The houses upon the East end of the wharf and under London wall are challenged by the Master of the Armoury. And the houses upon the West end of the Wharf at the Bulwark, the postern and the water-gate by the Gentleman Porter as appertaining to their office, which have been in former times (by your Majesty's most noble progenitors) demised unto the warders, officers and artificers belonging unto the Tower, but of late inhabited by strangers many of them being very poor and disordered persons, by means whereof contentions and quarrels are daily moved. Of these houses there are four score builded since the time of your Majesty's most happy reign, and many of them in places inconvenient.

These houses, being worth £200 *per annum* are generally conceived to be in your Majesty's disposition, and neither granted nor belonging unto any officer or other person; it were therefore a great advancement unto your service and to the peaceable government and safety of this place to have the same houses inhabited by your Majesty's immediate tenants, without any terms granted but at your Highness's pleasure, who might be enjoined to strengthen the watch and to perform all other necessary duties. And yet notwithstanding, your Majesty might of your bounty, allow unto the Master of the Armoury and the Gentleman porter out of the farms of the said houses, as great a benefit as they do at this present receive.

Defects needful to be supplied

Item. There are allowed for the guard of this your Majesty's royal castle but 30 warders, whereof there are but four keep the whole night watch (without relieving) five nights in the week, and five the other two nights, being nothing sufficient nor proportionable, considering the largeness of the place, which containeth by the counterscarp of the ditch 693 paces, under the guard whereof there is also contained your Majesty's store of munition and powder, treasure of Jewels and plate and also the prisoners of great charge, all which (being dispersed in divers places) cannot be safely guarded with so weak a watch.

These 30 warders your Majesty doth allow by 8 pence apiece *per diem*, in respect of which small wages, regarding the deerness of these times wherein the price of all things and all men's labours are increased, they are grown to exceeding poverty, and those most poor that best attend your Majesty's service.

Your Highness's Yeomen of the Great Chamber have twice tasted of your princely bounty by advancing their wages; these poor men's travails, exceeding all other your Highness's servants, do merit commiseration, the which out of compassion, I humbly remember to your Majesty's good pleasure.

There be among the warders divers unfit for the place, some of them utterly neglecting their duties in service, others given to drunkness, disorders and quarrels, others for debility of body being unable to perform their duties, others double-officed and cannot attend in two places, the means whereof the guard in this place is much weakened.

In this your Majesty's pleasure is most humbly desired.

Your Majesty by bill assigned hath granted divers warders rooms in reversion and divers other are to be presented unto your Highness's name of the parties being unfit for the place. The manner of your Majesty's grant by those bills is for term of life, by means whereof such as are to be found negligent, unable or unfaithful in your service cannot be by course of law discharged.

It may therefore please your Majesty to grant more rooms *ad bene placitum* and not for life, which will be an occasion to keep the warders in better regard of their duties and more diligent in your Highness's service.

Your Majesty hath in pay divers officers and artificers belonging unto the Ordnance and also 140 gunners and 20 labourers, all which ought to watch and ward in the Tower.

Proved by Establishment 25th July 1st Year of the reign of Henry VIII.

The 20th October 3rd Year of the reign of Henry VIII. Sir Thomas Seymour, Knight, then being Master of the Ordnance, Sir Thomas Arundel and Sir Robert Terwitt, commissioners of the said Ordnance, composition was by them made that the officers, artificers and gunners should pay certain money in discharge of the said service.

Proved by the order signed by the said Thomas Seymour.

All inhabitants whatsoever dwelling within the Tower or the Liberties of the same may by equal proportion observe their times in watching, in respect they are privileged from all service in other places.

There are also by ancient precedent (the which have been continued since your Majesty's most happy reign) 17 hamlets belonging unto the Tower viz St Katharine's, East Smithfield, Stepney, Ratcliffe, Limehouse, Blackwall, Mile End, Bethnal Green, Stoke Newington, Hackney, Branley, Finsbury, Whitechapel, Hoggsden, Shoreditch, Norton Foregate and Stratford on the Bow. All these have upon occasion of command given their attendance both to watch and guard this your Majesty's royal castle in respect whereof they have ever been freed from muster out of their own Liberties, and from certain other extraordinary charges.

These privileges have been infringed by the [*illegible*], whereby the hamlets hold themselves freed from their ancient service by the which they were by custom bound, without any pay or charge unto your Majesty to repair unto the guard and defence of your Majesty's Tower whensoever they should be commanded.

Your Majesty's store of munition etc being by your princely providence more royally increased than ever, the place itself weakened by decays and defects, do consequently require a stronger guard than in former times. In respect whereof I have in all loyalty presented unto your Highness's princely consideration these ancient orders and service-duties before-specified, most humbly beseeching that for your better service your Majesty will be pleased to command the recontinuance of these neglected duties prescribed by former establishments.

Disorders to be reformed

Item. It hath been suffered that all prisoners having the liberty of the Tower might have continual access of all manner of persons unto them without number or any notice taken of their names or occasions of repair, a thing most dangerous in respect of the small guard allowed for the keeping of a place of such consequence, and not possible, allowing so great a concourse of people, to restrain the traitorous prisoners from intelligence and practice.

It hath also been permitted that all persons coming unto a prisoner having the liberty of the Tower, might continue with him in his chamber, elsewhere in meal times and in times of divine service, the gates of the Tower being shut and the guard thereof retired, the which may give occasion of great inconveniences.

Also prisoners having the liberty of the Tower have been allowed to keep their wives and whole families there resident, all which in meal

249

times and in times of divine service have had liberty within the Tower at their pleasure.

The danger whereof is humbly referred to your Highness's consideration.

The warders, minters and other inhabitants have usually lodged their friends and other strangers within the Tower without any allowance of the Lieutenant or notice thereof given unto him.

There hath also been suffered a common brewhouse and backhouse to be kept within the Mint and also a common hackney stable to let horses to hire, who have had their continual passage, with their carriage and horses in and out of the great gates, which being very disgraceful and inconvenient, I have restrained.

By means of the new erected tenements within the liberties of the Tower, the inhabitants are so increased as there is not within the Tower any place sufficient for their burial, the which limes of insertion will be most dangerous and in other respects very inconvenient.

It may therefore stand with your Majesty's pleasure that some place in East Smithfield, being within the liberties of the Tower, may be appointed for that purpose.

Decays necessary to be repaired

Item. The inhabitants upon the wharf, in the Bulwark and at the Postern, have intruded with their buildings upon the Tower ditch and have builded noisome houses in the same by means whereof the ditch is much impaired and the water corrupted.

Also that your Majesty's lodgings and many other buildings within the Tower are in decay and may be in time repaired with small charge being well-surveyed and providently bestowed.

The Tower gates and prisoners' lodgings are in decay.

The ancient sluices and vaults that were wont to be maintained to take in water out of the Thames (for the strengthening of the Tower ditch), are now utterly decayed.

The Tower ditch, being the special strength of the Tower, is in great decay and in many places landed up to the Tower wall, of the which if some repair be not had, the charge to your Majesty will be excessive.

It appeareth by your Majesty's records in the Tower that the same was repaired by the fines imposed on the usurers of London; by the record, the said usurers were at one time fined at 50 marks apiece. Some help may also be added from the inhabitants within the liberty in respect that the said ditch is by their default in part decayed. The like help may also be added from the Tower Hamlets by way of men-works, the which I conceive they will willingly perform if your Highness pleasure be to have them restored to their ancient dependency and privileges. And for the remain, which notwithstanding will amount to a great charge, your Majesty may be pleased to grant unto the party that shall undertake the work some commission or other suit which be convenient for the performance thereof without any charge to be expanded out of your Majesty's coffers.

In these respects, most gracious sovereign, I have presumed out of a loyal motive and zeal to your service to present unto your most excellent Majesty this declaration of the state of your Highness's Tower and Castle Royal, most humbly beseeching that out of your princely discerning judgement, your Highness will be pleased by way of establishment to determine your royal pleasure touching the premises.

Your Majesty's most loyal devoted servant

John Peyton

September 1598

SELECT BIBLIOGRAPHY

The first major study of the history of the Tower of London was J. Bayley's, *The History and Antiquities of the Tower of London*, 2 vols (1821–5). This is still the principal published source though, inevitably, it has been superseded in several points of detail and interpretation. R. Sutherland Gower, *The Tower of London* (2 vols, 1901–2) is valuable, particularly on the main historical events associated with the building. Other useful general studies are: J. Britton and E. W. Brayley, *Memoirs of the Tower of London* (1830), W. G. Bell, *The Tower of London* (1921), G. Younghusband, *The Tower of London from Within* (1918), and R. J. Minney, *The Tower of London* (1970). On the architectural history of the fortress there is nothing to compare with A. J. Taylor and H. M. Colvin (eds.) *A History of the King's Works* (1963–75). J. Charlton (ed.) *The Tower of London: Its History and Institutions* (1978) is not, as its title may suggest, a narrative history but it does present the very latest scholarly thinking on many aspects of the Tower's buildings and historical functions. The following are some of the more important special studies dealing with aspects of the subject:

Doyne C. Bell, *Notices of the Historic Persons Buried in the Chapel of St Peter ad Vincula, in the Tower of London* (1877)
E. T. Bennet, *The Tower Menagerie* (1829)
J. G. Broodbank, *History of the Port of London* (2 vols, 1921)
P. B. Clayton and B. R. Leftwich, *The Pageant of Tower Hill* (1933)
J. Craig, *The Mint* (1953)
Charles ffoulkes, *The Inventory of the Armouries* (1916)

There are, in addition, the excellent series of guides and booklets published by Her Majesty's Stationery Office and available at the Tower and HMSO shops.

I am grateful to Sir Arthur Bryant for permission to quote from *The Age of Chivalry*, Collins, 1963; to Oxford University Press for permission to quote from S. Anglo, *Spectacle, Pageantry and Early Tudor Policy*, 1969 and *The Diary of John Evelyn*, ed. E.S. de Beer, 1959; and to Bell and Hyman Ltd and University of California Press for permission to quote from S. Pepys, *Diary*, eds. R. Latham and W. Matthews, 1970.

NOTES

Chapter 1
1. D. C. Douglas, *William the Conqueror*, 1964, p. 217.
2. J. Stow, *Survey of London*, ed. C. L. Kingsford, 1908, Vol. I, p. 45.
3. *Anglo-Saxon Chronicle*, ed. G. N. Garmonsway, 1953, p. 182.
4. Orderic Vitalis, *Historia Ecclesiastica*, Vol. IV, pp. 108–10.
5. *Anglo-Saxon Chronicle*, pp. 264–5.
6. W. Fitzstephen, *Life of Becket*, eds. D. C. Douglas and G. W. Greenaway, English Historical Documents 1042–1189, II, p. 103.
7. William of Newburgh, *Gesta Stephani*, p. 104.
8. Rot. Claus., 26 H.III, p. 2, m. 9.
9. William of Newborough, *Historia Rerum Anglicarum*, ed. R. Howlett, 1884–9, IV, c, 14.
10. Roger of Wendover, *Chronicle*, p. 278.

Chapter 2
1. Rot. lib. 25 Hen. III, m. 20.
2. Cal. Close Rolls, 1296–1302, 261.
3. Cal. Close Rolls, 1302–1307, 539.

Chapter 3
1. Concilia, II, 393. J. B. Williamson, *The History of the Temple*, 1924, p. 63.
2. Cal. Close Rolls, 1317–1318, 308. P. T. B. Clayton and B. R. Leftwich, *The Pageant of Tower Hill*, 1933, pp. 58–9.
3. A. Bryant, *The Age of Chivalry*, 1963, p. 239.
4. Rot. Claus. 10 Edw. III. m. 26.
5. Cal. Close Rolls, 1369–1374, 365.
6. *Archaeologia*, XVIII, pp. 275, ff.
7. Cal. Close Rolls, 1333–1337, 2.
8. Seymour's *Chronicle*, I, p. 91.

Chapter 4
1. J. Foxe, *Actes and Monuments*, ed. J. Pratt, 1877, III, p. 542.
2. Dominic Mancini, *The Ursurpation of Richard III*, ed. C.A.J. Armstrong, 1969, p. 112.
3. For a full summary of the evidence about the murder of the princes see P. M. Kendall, *Richard III*, 1955, pp. 393–418. On the sources themselves see A. Hanham, *Richard III and his Early Historians 1485–1535*, 1975.

Chapter 5
1. cf. C. G. Cruikshank, *Elizabeth's Army*, 1946, pp. 121–3.
2. E. Hall, *Chronicle*, 1548, p. 139.
3. W. Maitland, *History of London*, 1756, Vol. I, p. 238.
4. J. Stow, *Survey of London*, ed. C. L. Kingsford, Vol. I, p. 59.
5. Stow, op. cit., Vol. I, p. 49.
6. *Letters and Papers of the Reign of Henry VIII*, Vol. V, p. 323.
7. British Library Egerton MS. 985, fol. 41v.
8. S. Anglo, *Spectacle, Pageantry and Early Tudor Policy*, 1969, p. 16.

9. Ibid., p. 49.
10. *Opus Epistolarum Des Erasmi Roterodami*, eds. P. S. and H. M. Allen, 1906, Vol. I, p. 214.
11. Lord Herbert, *History of Henry VIII*, 1719, Vol. I, p. 6.
12. *Letters and Papers of the Reign of Henry VIII*, Vol. III, p. 1.
13. A. G. Dickens, *Thomas Cromwell and the English Reformation*, 1959, p. 173.
14. Ibid., p. 185.
15. E Hall, *Chronicle*, p. 798.
16. Matthew Tanner, *Societas Europaea*, p. 18.
17. R. W. Chambers, *Thomas More*, 1945, p. 324.
18. R. Sutherland Gower, *The Tower of London*, 1901–2, Vol. I, p. 134.
19. G. R. Elton, *Policy and Police: The Enforcement of the Reformation in the Age of Thomas Cromwell*, 1972, p. 411.
20. cf. G. R. Elton, op. cit., pp. 400 ff.
21. H. Ellis, *Original Letters*, 1st series, II, pp. 64–5.
22. *Letters and Papers of the Reign of Henry VIII*, XI, p. 714.
23. Ibid., XII (i), p. 946.
24. Ibid., p. 1175 (3).
25. Ibid., p. 976.
26. R. Moryson, *An Invective Against Treason*, 1539.
27. M. H. and R. Dodds, *The Pilgrimage of Grace and the Exeter Conspiracy*, 1971, Vol. II, pp. 324–5.
28. E. Hall, *Chronicle*, 1539.
29. H. Ellis, *Original Letters Illustrative of English History*, series II, ii, p.143.
30. J. Bale, *Select Works*, ed. H. Christmas, 1849, p. 220.

Chapter 6.
1. J. Stow, *Survey of London*, ed. C. L. Kingsford, Vol. II, pp. 72–3, 262.
2. Quoted in R. Sutherland Gower, *The Tower of London*, 1901-2, pp. 58, 66.
3. J. Stow, op. cit., I, p. 126.
4. C. Wriothesley, *Chronicle*, Camden Society, new series XI, i, p. 179.
5. J. Strype, *Ecclesiastical Memorials*, 1820–40, Vol. II, p. 20.
6. J. Cornwall, *Revolt of the Peasantry 1549*, 1977, p. 231.
7. S. Gardiner, *Answer to Bucer* in P. Janelle, *Obedience in Church and State*, 1930, p. 205.
8. J. G. Nichols, ed. *Literary Remains of King Edward VI*, 1857, Vol. II, p. 233.
9. *Acts of the Privy Council*, III, p. 407.
10. Cal. S. P. Span. X, p. 392.
11. R. Grafton, *A Chronicle at Large*, ed. H. Ellis, 1827, Vol. II, p. 520.
12. Edward VI, *Chronicle*, ed. W. K. Jordan, p. 109.
13. Ibid., p. 526.
14. H. Machyn, *Diary*, ed. J. G. Nicholls, 1848, pp. 13–14.
15. British Library, Stowe MS. 1066.
16. C. Wriothesley, *Chronicle*, Vol. II, pp. 90–1.
17. British Library, Harleian MS. 194.
18. *The Chronicle of Queen Jane and of two years of Queen Mary*, Camden Society, XIVIII, pp. 49–50.
19. British Library, Harleian MS. 425.
20. Quoted in J. E. Neale, *Queen Elizabeth*, 1934, pp. 46–7
21. Ibid., p. 47.
22. Machyn, op. cit., p. 80.
23. Machyn, op. cit., p. 109.
24. Quoted in J. E. Neale, op. cit., p. 65.
25. *The Queen's Majesty's passage through the City of London* (Elizabethan Club edition), sig.E. iiii[r-v].

26. Quoted in R. S. Gower, op. cit., I, p. 208.
27. Quoted in R. S. Gower, op. cit., II, Appendix 1, p. 151.
28. *The Elizabethan Journals*, ed. G. B. Harrison, 1938, Vol. III, p. 132.
29. J. Stow, op. cit., I, p. 59.
30. Bodleian Library Western MSS Eng. Hist.e.195. I am greatly idebted to Anna Keay and Jeremy Ashbee for drawing my attention to this manuscript.
31. Ibid.

Chapter 7.
1. J. Nichols, *The Progresses, processions and magnificent festivities of King James I . . .* , 1828, Vol. I, pp. 60–9.
2. J. Stow, *Annales*, p. 935.
3. J. Aubrey, *Brief Lives*, ed. A. Clark, 1898, p. 287.
4. British Library Hatfield MS., 113.54.
5. British Library Hatfield MS. XVII, p. 364.
6. Quoted in W. D. M. Raeburn, 'The Officers of the Tower and the Yeoman Warders', in *The Tower of London: Its History and Institutions*, ed. J. Charlton, 1978.
7. Salisbury Papers, XVII, 387, 402.
8. Ibid., XVII, 558.
9. British Library Harleian MS., 7002.
10. R. Winwood, *Memorials of Affairs of State . . .* , ed. E. Sawyer, 1725, Vol. III, p. 481. This is from a letter to Elwes from the Earl of Northampton, great-uncle of Frances and head of the Howard family.
11. Sir Walter Raleigh, *History of the World*, preface.
12. D. C. Bell, *Notice of the Historic Persons buried in the Chapel of St Peter and Vincula*, 1877, pp. 250–1.
13. Ibid., p. 252.
14. Ibid., p. 252.
15. Ibid., p. 253.
16. Quoted in R. S. Gower, *The Tower of London*, 1901–2, Vol. II, p. 36.
17. J. Evelyn, *Diary*, ed. E. S. de Beer, 1959, p. 17.
18. *Cromwell's Letters and Speeches*, ed. T. Carlyle, 1845, Vol. III, p. 282.
19. J. Evelyn, op. cit., p. 280.
20. J. Evelyn, op. cit., p. 406.
21. J. Nicholas, op. cit., II, p. 62.

Chapter 8
1. S. Pepys, *Diary*, eds. R. Latham and W. Matthews, 1970, Vol. III, p. 39.
2. J. Evelyn, *Diary*, ed. E. S. de Beer, 1959, p. 419.
3. *Dictionary of National Biography*.
4. S. Pepys, op. cit., III, pp. 89 ff.
5. Ibid.
6. Ibid.
7. Ibid.
8. Ibid.
9. J. Evelyn, op cit., p. 498.
10. S. Pepys, op. cit., III, p. 142.
11. *Roxburghe Ballads* (Ballad Society edition), VI.
12. J. Evelyn, op. cit., p. 553.
13. Ibid.
14. J. Reresby, *Memoirs*, ed. J. J. Cartwright, 1875, p. 107.
15. J. Lingard, *History of England*, 1830, Vol. IX, p. 258.
16. J. Evelyn, op. cit., p. 761.
17. Ibid., p. 747.

18. Ibid., p. 815.
19. D. C. Bell, *Notice of the Historic Persons buried in the Chapel of St Peter ad Vincula*, 1877, pp. 276–7.
20. Quoted in R. S. Gower, *The Tower of London*, 1901–2, Vol. II, p. 89.
21. *A True and Full Account of the Death of George, Lord Jeffreys*, published by James Fraser, 1689. It seems likely that Jeffreys, died of cancer.
22. Quoted in R. S. Gower, op. cit., p. 94.
23. S. Pepys, op. cit., III, p. 73.
24. *Dictionary of National Biography*.
25. H. Walpole, *Memoirs*, ed. E. Warburton, 1851, p. 297.
26. Quoted in J. H. Plumb, *Sir Robert Walpole: The Making of a Statesman*, 1956, p. 221.
27. *Gentleman's Magazine*, August, 1746.
28. R. Chandler, *The History and Proceedings of the House of Commons from the Restoration to the Present Time*, 1742–4, Vol. IV, pp. 246–7.

Chapter 9
1. cf. C. Hibbert, *King Mob*, 1959, p. 145.
2. G. Cruickshank, in *The Omnibus*, cf. R. S. Gower, *The Tower of London* 1901–2, Vol. II, p. 144.

Chapter 10
1. S. Pepys, *Diary*, eds. R. Latham and W. Matthews, 1970, Vol. III, p. 39.
2. T. B. Macaulay, *History of England*, ed. C. H. Frith, 1914, Vol. II, p. 620.
3. Ibid.
4. D. C. Bell, *Notice of the Historic Persons buried in the Chapel of St Peter ad Vincula*, 1877, pp. 16–17.
5. cf. *State Papers Published Under the Authority of His Majesty's Commission*, 1831, I.v.
6. Shakespeare, *Richard III*.

INDEX

257